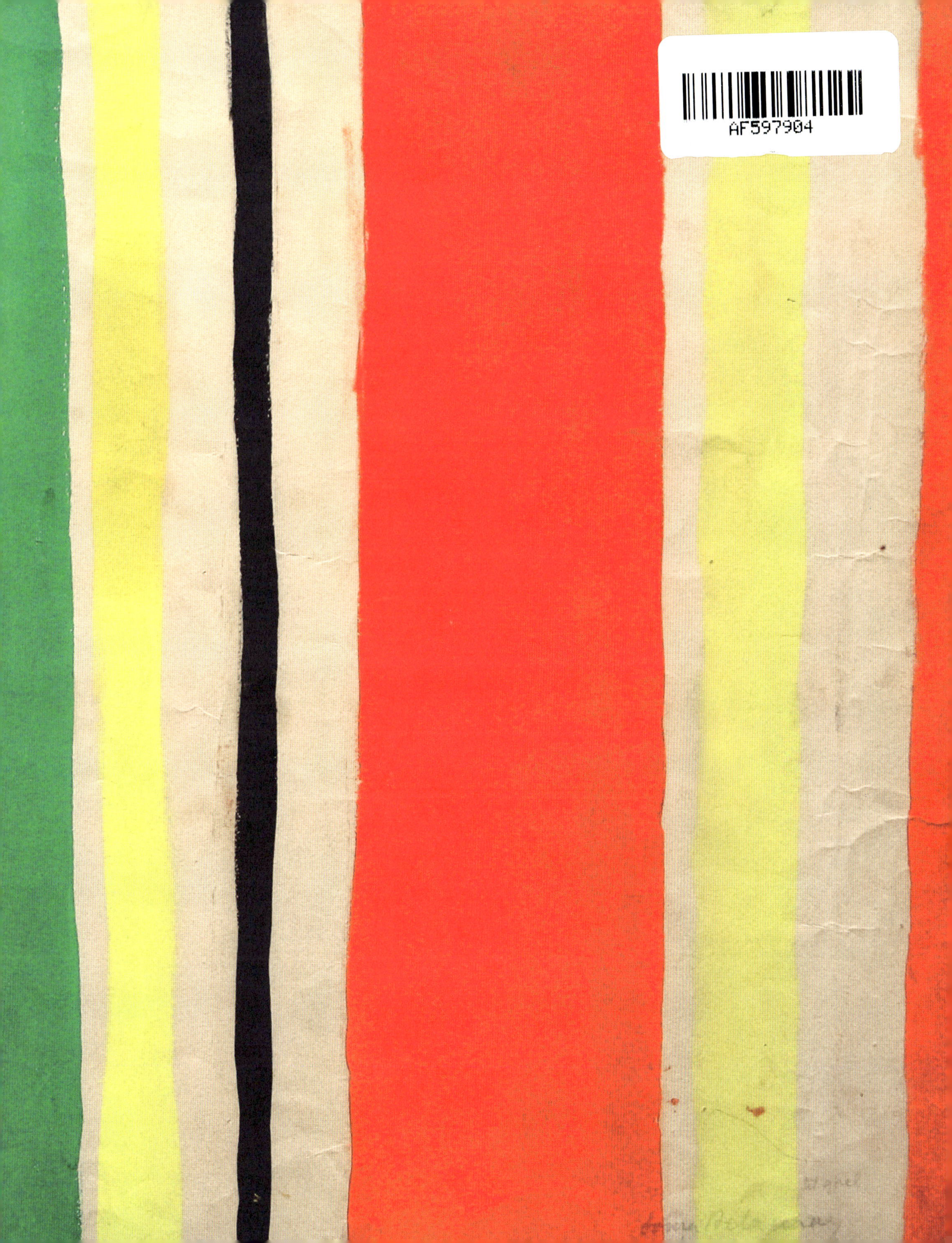

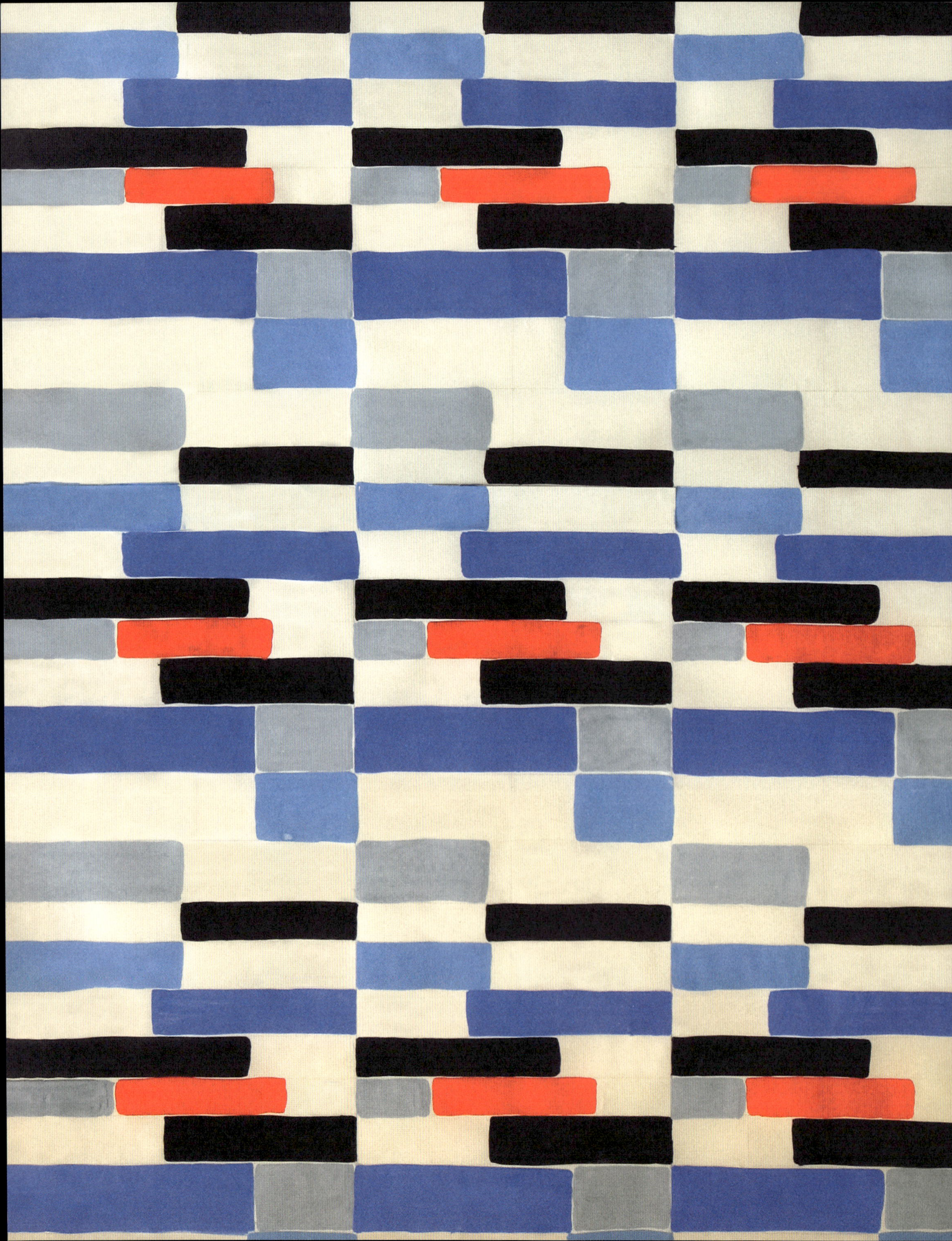

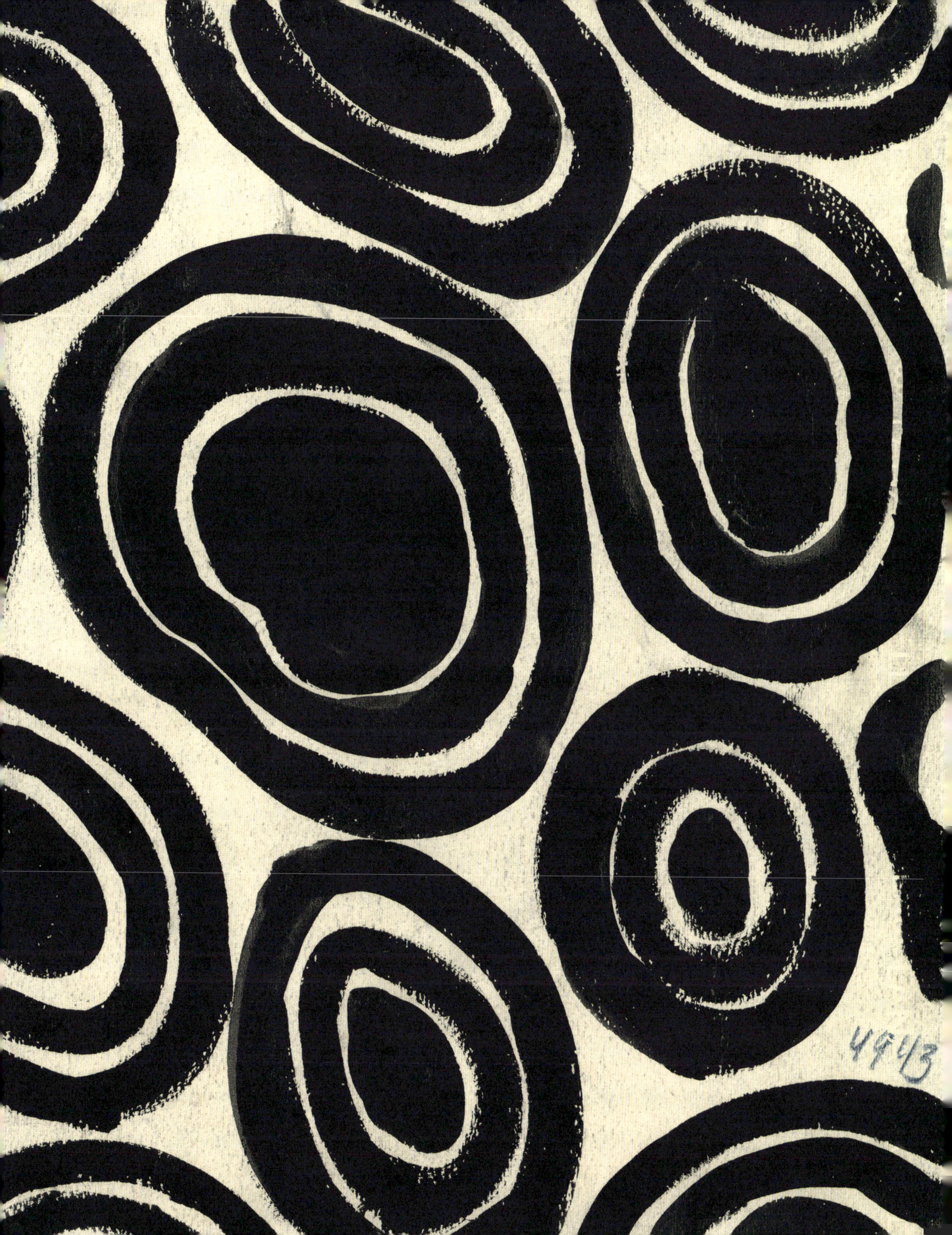
4943

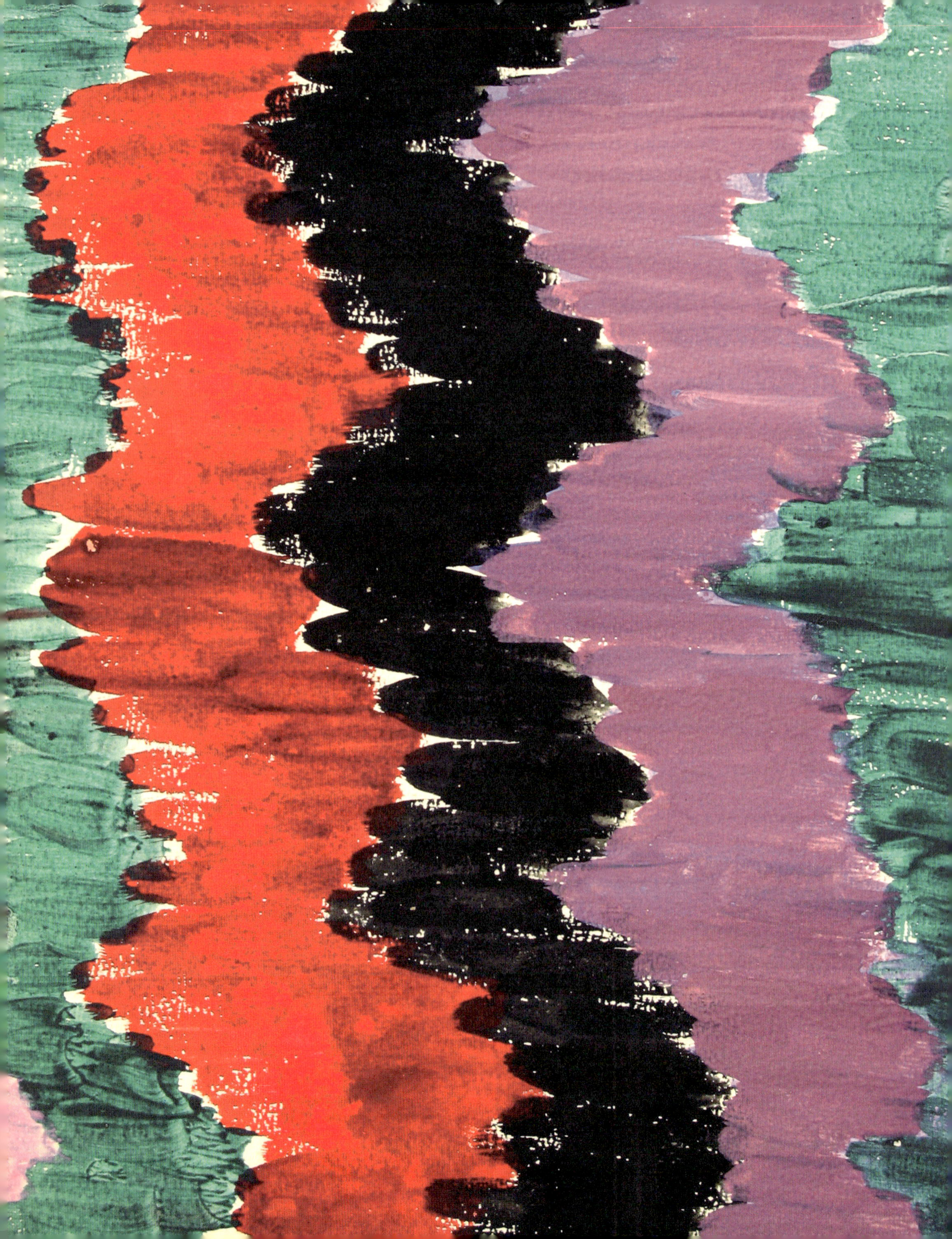

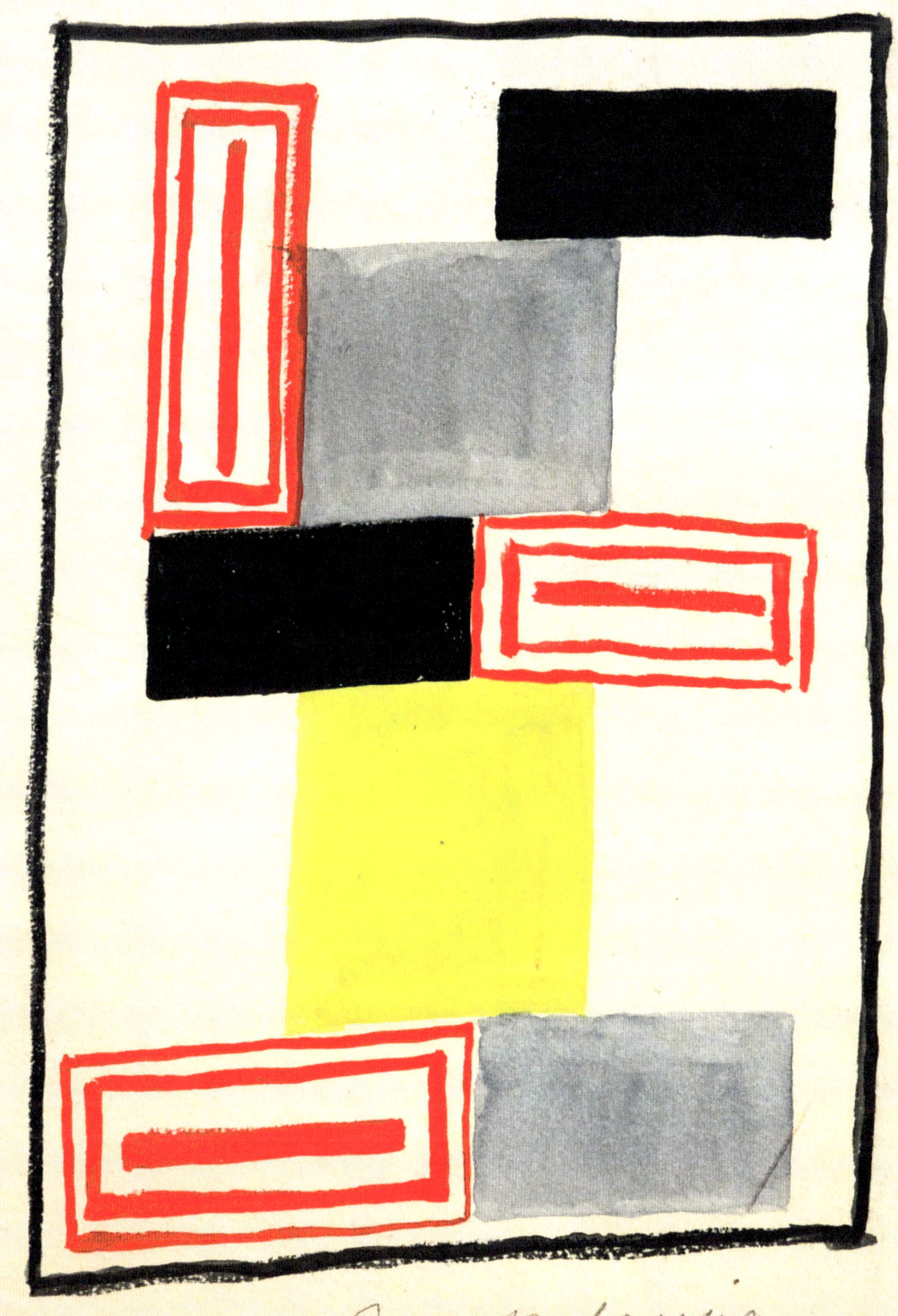
Sonia Delaunay
Paris 53.

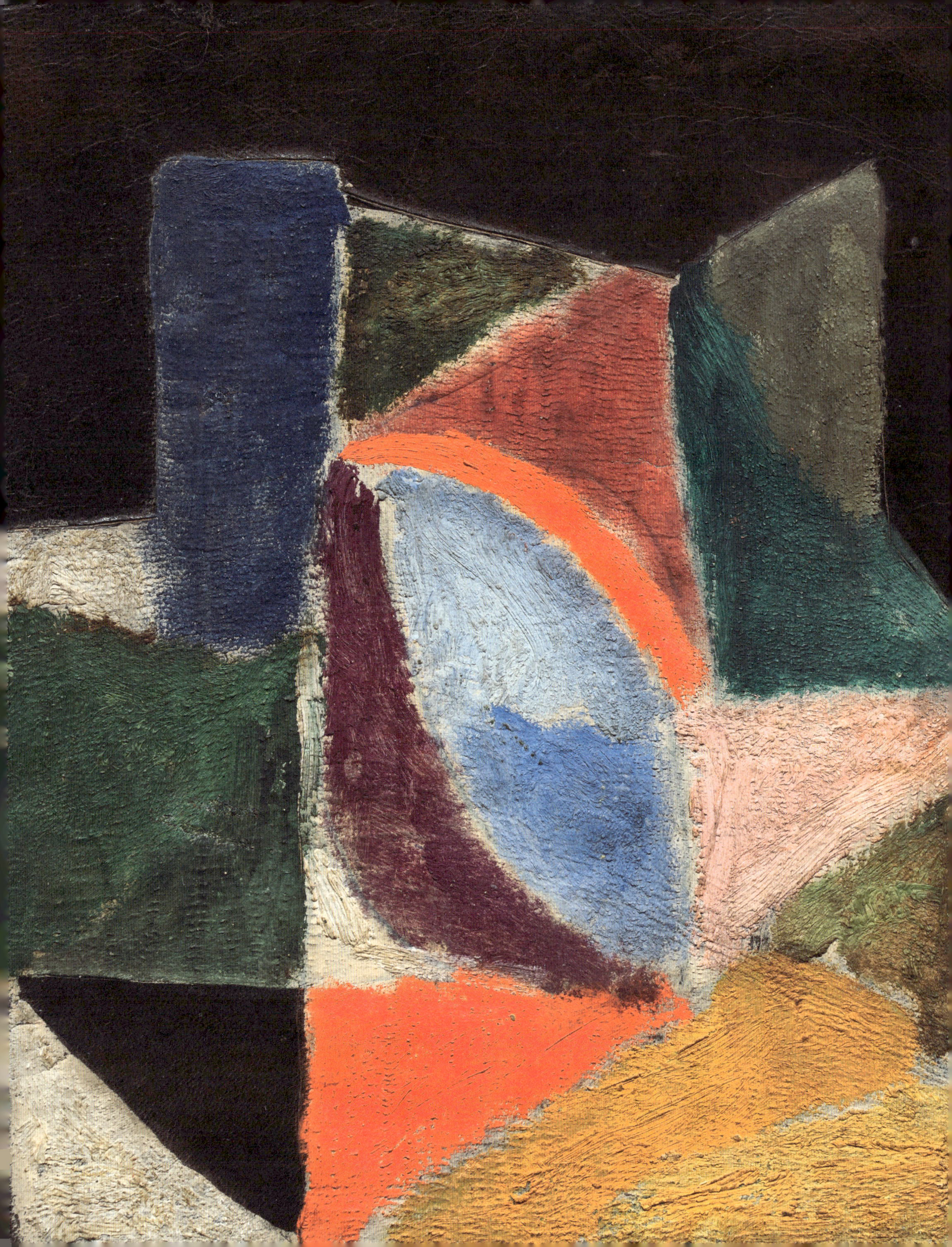

SONIA DELAUNAY

LOUISIANA MUSEUM OF MODERN ART

THANK YOU

For their crucial financial support in our being able to accomplish the exhibition at all, our thanks go first and foremost to the Aage og Johanne Louis-Hansens Fond.

We owe a special thank you to Matteo de Leeuw-de Monti for his unfaltering dedication and kind support towards the project, and for his generous sharing of knowledge and help throughout the curatorial process.

We thank Anne Montfort-Tanguy for great collegial support and for sharing her knowledge and her own research, which has been critical to bringing the exhibition to fruition.

Cécile Godefroy also receives our thanks for her valuable support and, as with the two mentioned above, for her written contribution to this catalogue. We also thank Griselda Pollock for the article she contributed.

Thanks also to Fabrice Hergott and Per Jonas Storsve for their commitment to the project from the beginning.

From our own ranks, thank you to the entire Louisiana team and to exhibition architect Jens Kamp, as well as Maja Sofie Rasmussen, who has helped with exhibition texts.

Thank you to everyone from institutions and private collections who has helped the project along the way, and who in some cases made an extraordinary effort. We are grateful for the support the project has received from many of the most important institutions for Sonia Delaunay's work. Many thanks to all the lenders who have made valuable works available for the exhibition:

Ateliers Pinton
Bibliothèque nationale de France
CAM – Fundação Calouste Gulbenkian, Lisbon
Centre national des arts plastiques (France)
Centre Pompidou, MNAM–CCI
Galerie Le Minotaure
Kunsthalle Bielefeld
Kunstmuseum Den Haag
Paris Musées / Musée d'Art Moderne de Paris
Musée d'arts de Nantes
Musée des Arts Décoratifs, Paris
Musée Matra, Espace Automobiles
Museo Nacional Centro de Arte Reina Sofia, Madrid
Museo Nacional Thyssen Bornemisza, Madrid
Museum of Avant-Garde Mastery of Europe (MAGMA of Europe)
Museum of Modern Art, New York
Skissernas Museum – Museum of Artistic Process and Public Art, Sweden
Statens Museum for Kunst / SMK – National Gallery of Art
TATE
Victoria and Albert Museum
Würth Collection, Germany
And lenders who wish to remain anonymous.

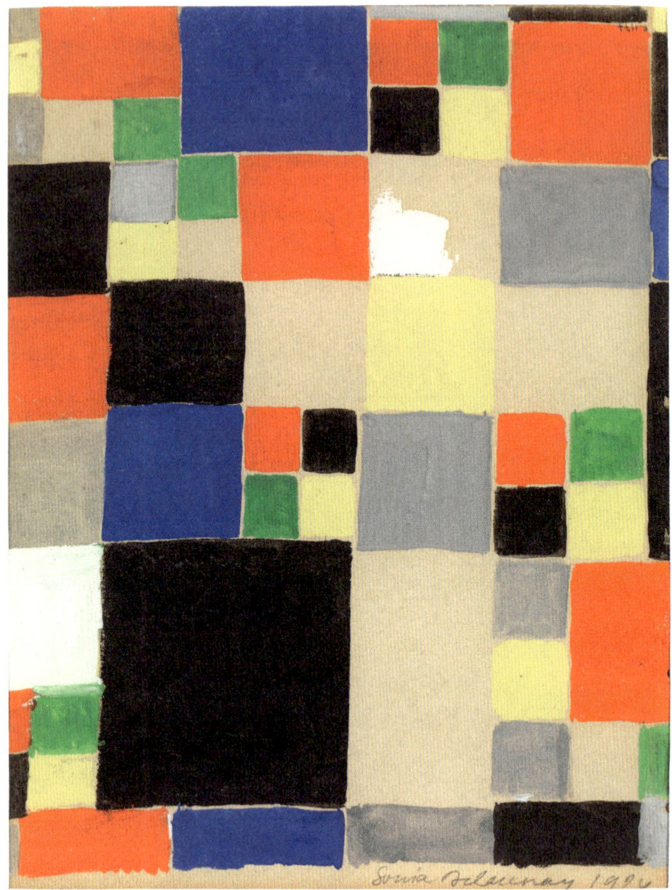

Study for fabric design, 1924

FOREWORD

Russian-French Sonia Delaunay (1885-1979) worked across the visual arts and design and is one of the original figures of the 20th-century avant-garde. She was among the first generation of artists to cultivate a non-figurative mode of expression in the 1910s, when, like wildfire, abstract art spread in a blaze of directions across the western art world. Alongside her husband, the painter Robert Delaunay, Sonia Delaunay developed an abstract idiom rooted in colour contrasts – a basic formula that she expanded on across mediums, including in her extensive fashion and textile design work. By coupling abstract art with couture, Delaunay helped shape the modern woman of the 1920s, *the new woman*, of which she was an embodiment. In an open and independent oscillating across boundaries, she took part in experimental Dada collaborations, started several small enterprises, and entered into commercial agreements for her textile designs.

Sonia Delaunay was a well-known figure on the French and European art scene in her day, and her vast network numbered many of the period's now more famous artists, such as Pablo Picasso, Marc Chagall, Wassily Kandinsky, Piet Mondrian, the couple Jean Arp and Sophie Taeuber-Arp, Tristan Tzara, and others – many of whom had migrated, like herself, to Paris, modern art's international melting pot. Her wide-ranging practice across mediums has long condemned her to be somewhat cut off from modernism's canon, which has had a particular focus on the development of abstract *painting* and on the differences between the isms – while Delaunay has a foot in many camps. While she may not yet, therefore, be among the most familiar names in the history of avant-garde art, she has long been a classic point of reference in textile design and fashion history. In qualitative terms – and in contrast to traditional art history – she herself made no distinction between her work in the various genres.

The Louisiana Museum of Modern Art's exhibition programme blends both well-known and less familiar takes on 20th-century art. As such, in recent years it has been possible to encounter the Swedish painter Hilma af Klint, who was a pioneer of non-figurative art from a spiritual vantage point. And while spirituality made a substantial mark on 20th-century art, Sonia Delaunay's project stems to a greater degree from a fascination with modern life. At the museum it has recently been possible to become acquainted with another figure, the American painter Marsden Hartley. We know from his diaries that he visited the Delaunays in Paris in 1912. The German expressionist Gabriele Münter, also recently presented at the Louisiana, must have met Sonia Delaunay in the coterie of artists around Der Blaue Reiter – and so the stories we know already can begin to be interwoven with many new ones.

At the Louisiana it has often been possible to view the three Sonia Delaunay works on paper that the museum holds in its collection – vibrant gouaches, one of which is a textile design. In 2012, several of her works were included in the exhibition *Women of the Avant-Garde 1920-1940*, and since that time the Louisiana has had an express desire to present her modern project on a larger scale. The exhibition is the largest presentation of her work hitherto in Scandinavia, where the artist was last presented solo in an exhibition at Skissernas Museum in Lund, Sweden, in 2007. Following a number of major exhibitions throughout the 2010s which have acknowledged the breadth of Sonia Delaunay's practice, the Louisiana's interest is precisely in accentuating this breadth as the core of her artistic project and position. The exhibition includes painting, works on paper, clothing, textile designs, book collaborations – and a sports car – as a clear illustration that Sonia Delaunay, with her then-revolutionary, modern expression, was engaged in transforming numerous areas of life. Whether in the major fashion houses or at IKEA, the impact of her work is easy to spot.

In the midst of a pandemic, it has been challenging to plan and realise an international exhibition such as this. On the other hand, it is our belief that this is precisely what we could do with right now: an exhibition of an artist who criss-crosses boundaries, opening up a space greater than that in which we ourselves currently travel. Welcome to the world – Sonia Delaunay's world – welcome to the Louisiana.

Tine Colstrup
Curator

Poul Erik Tøjner
Director

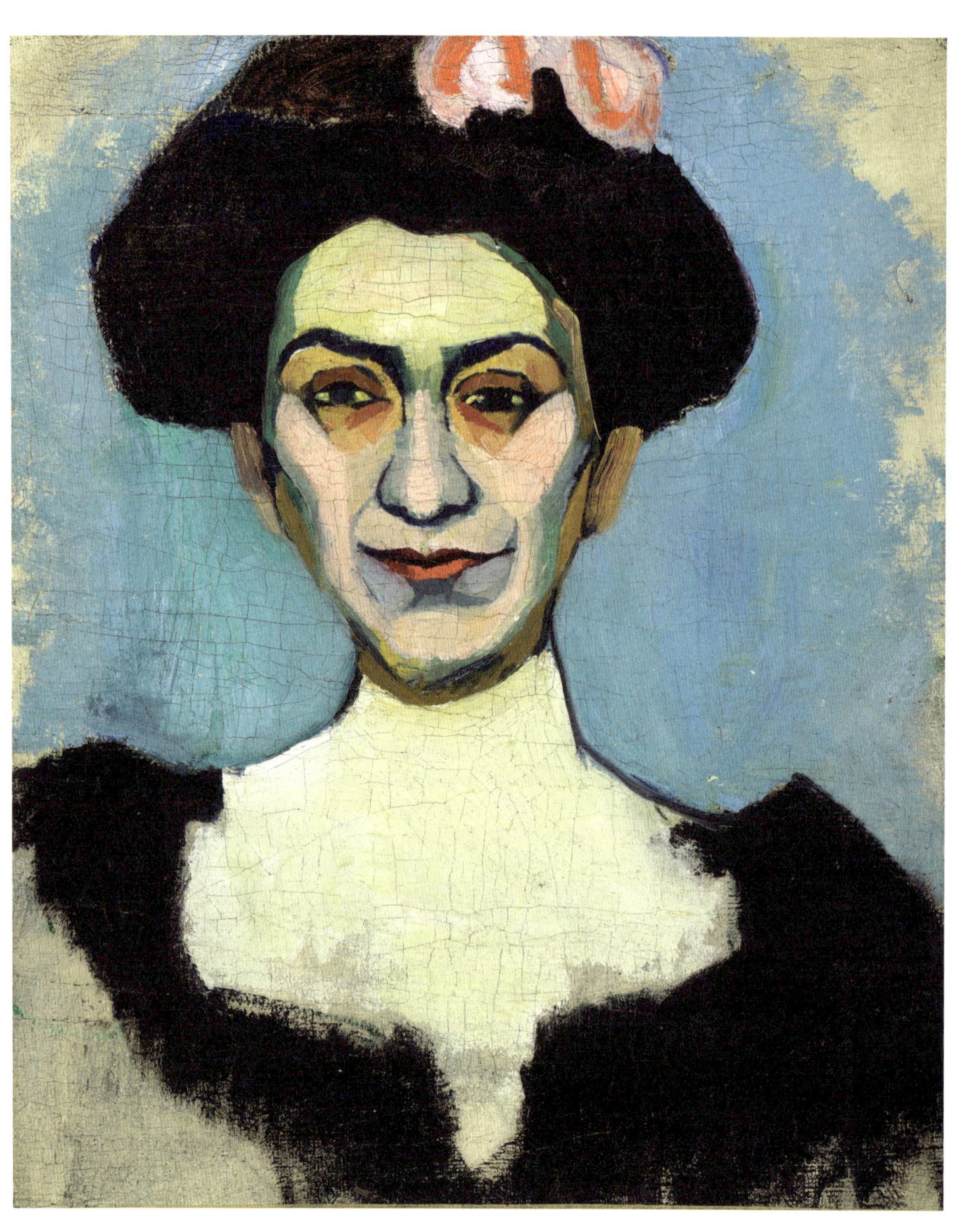

Portrait de Mme Minskaya (L. N. Vilkina), 1907. Portrait of Mme Minskaya (L. N. Vilkina)
Right page: *Philomène*, 1907

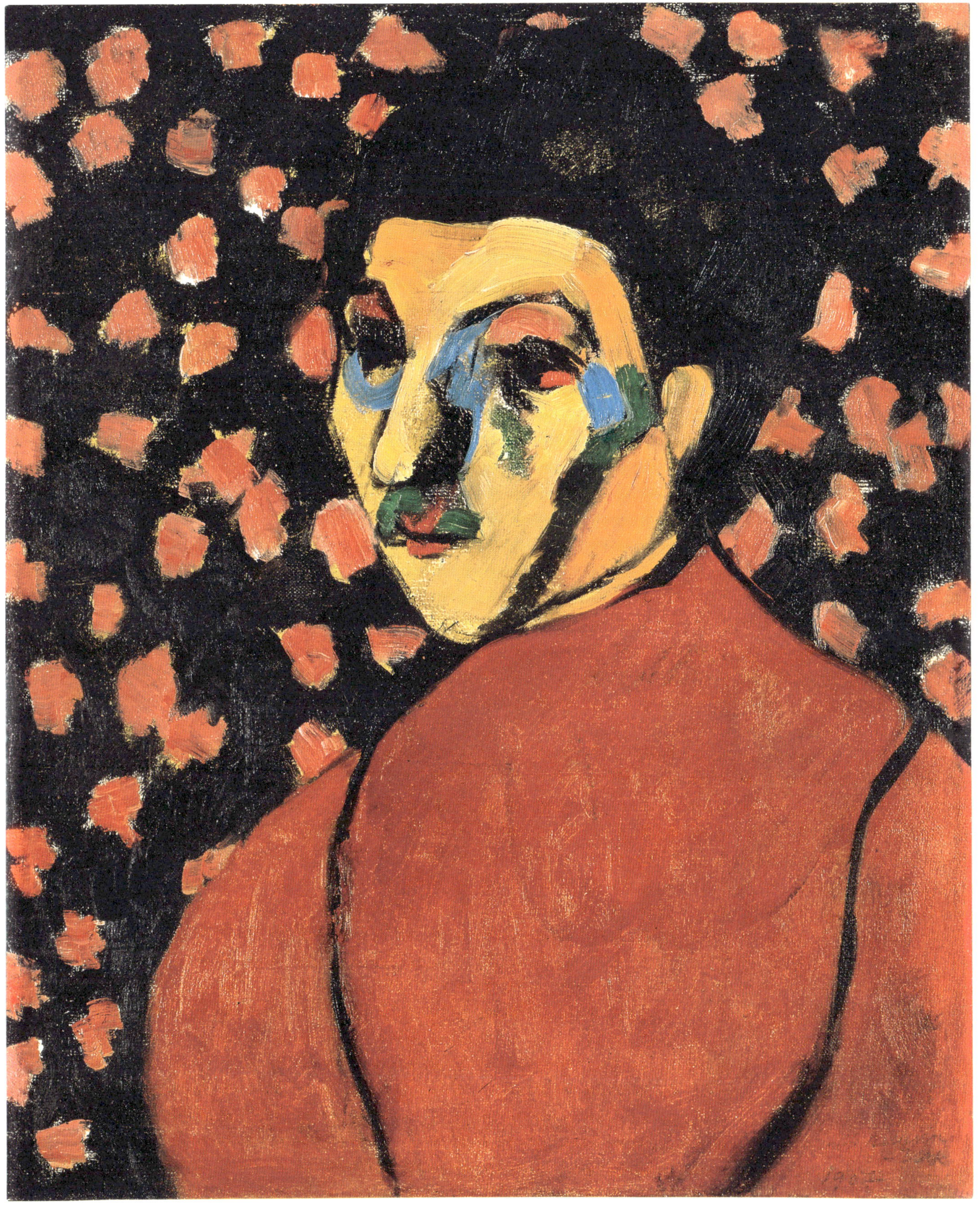

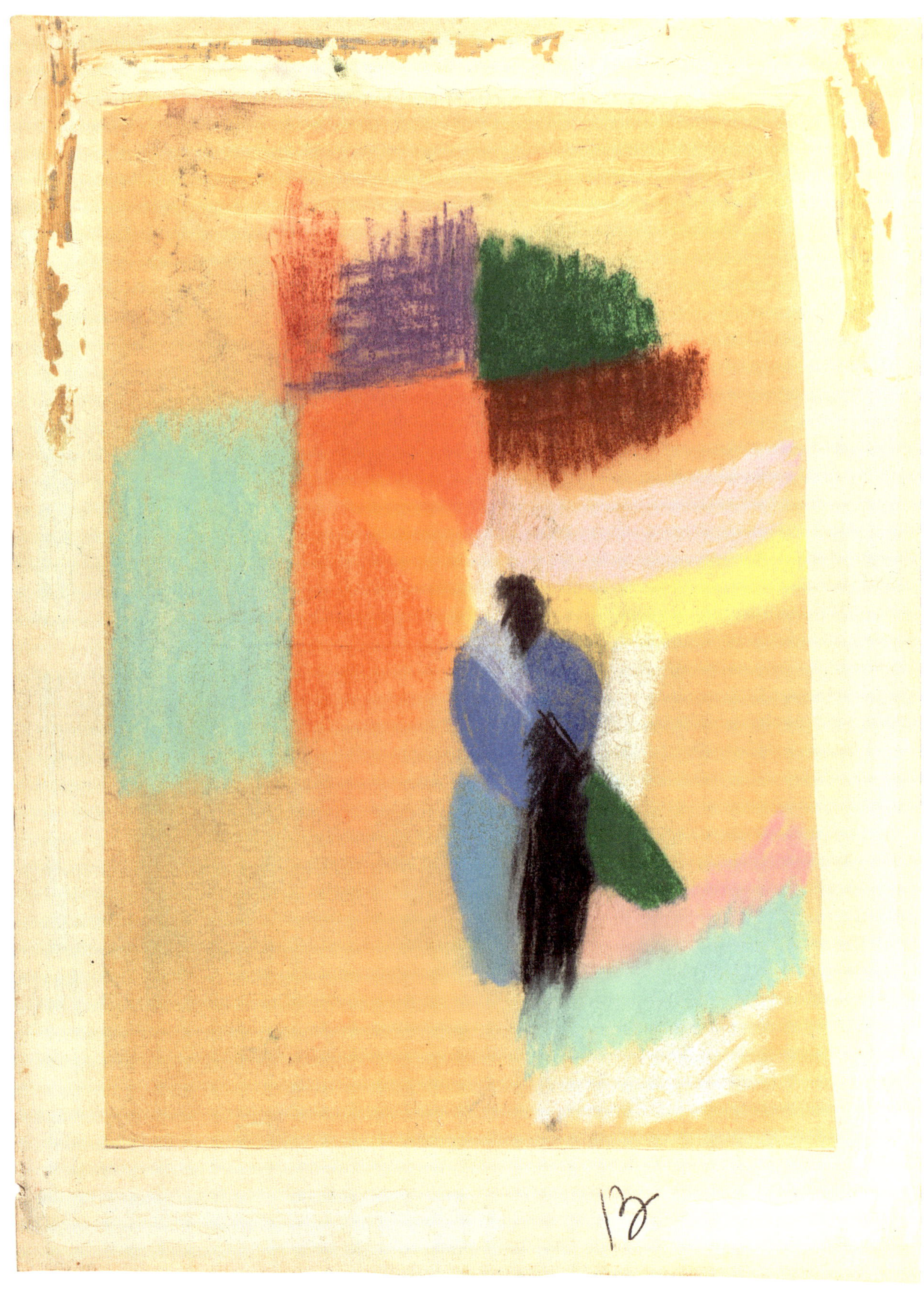

Les prismes électriques, 1913. The Electric Prisms

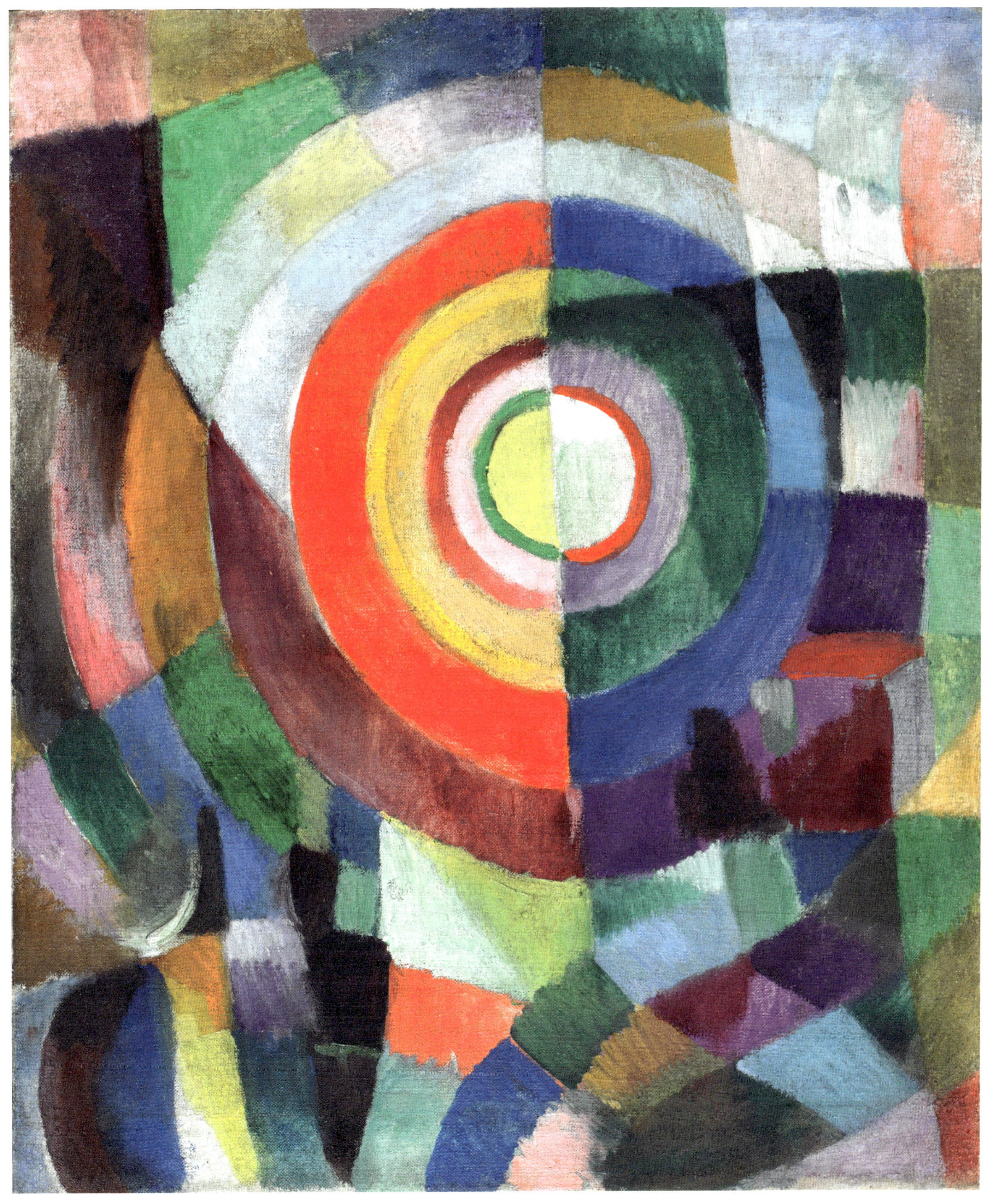

Prismes électriques, no 41, 1913-1914. Electric Prisms, No. 41

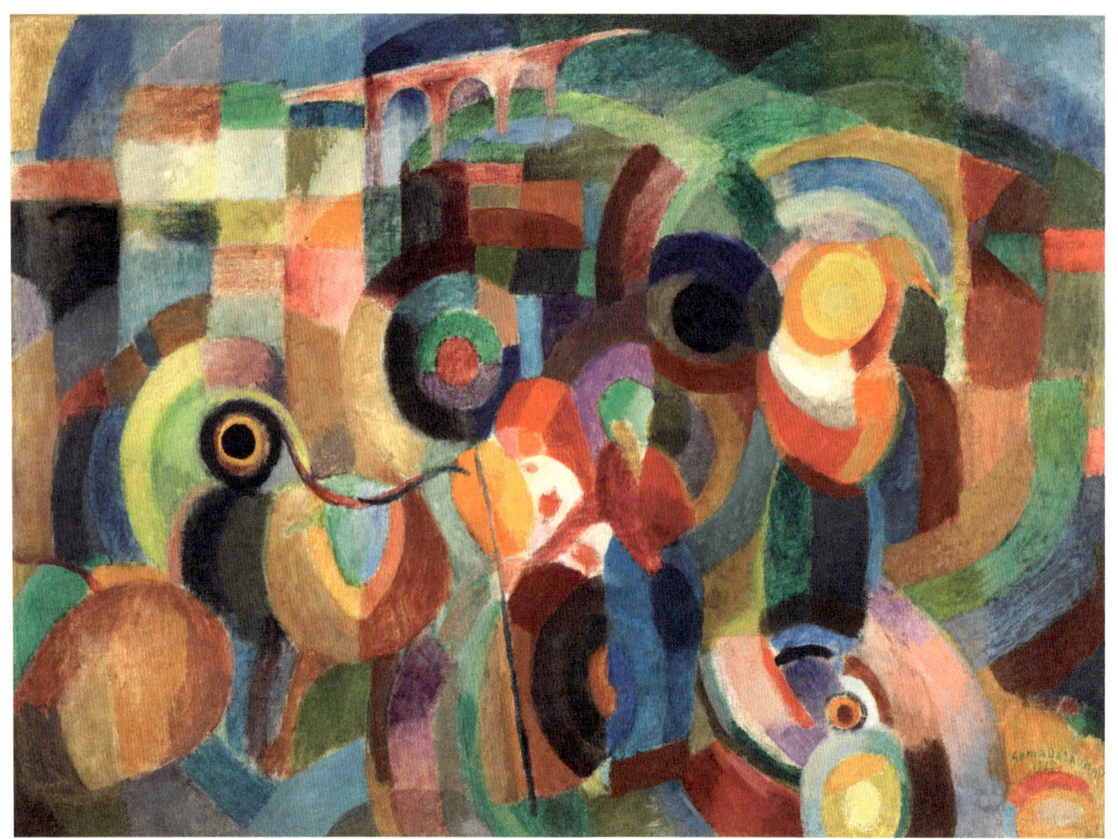

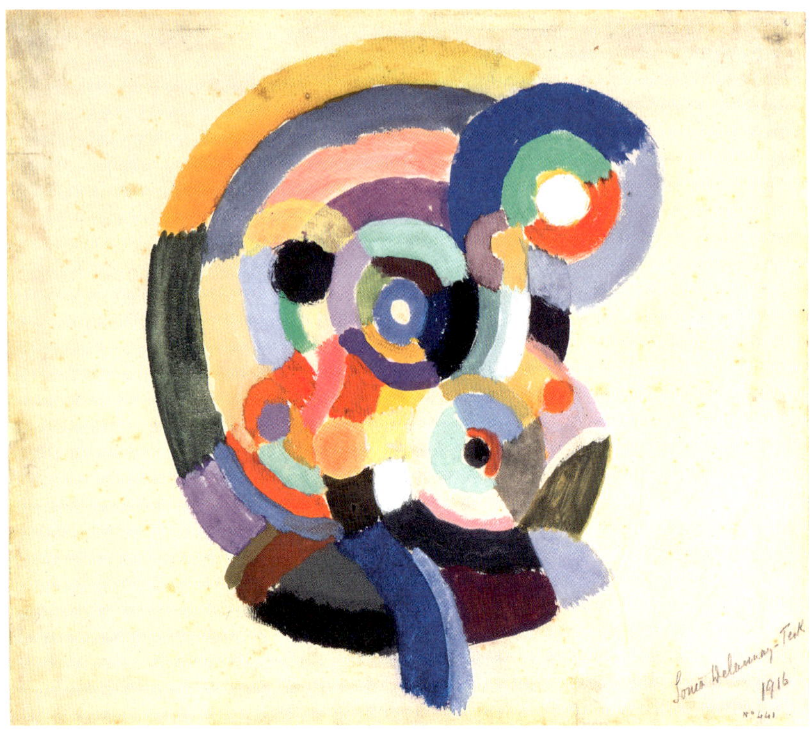

Top: *Marché au Minho*, 1915. Market in Minho
Bottom: *Chanteur Flamenco* (dit *Petit Flamenco*), 1916. Flamenco Singer (known as Little Flamenco)
Right page: *Chanteurs Flamenco* (dit *Grand Flamenco*), 1915-1916. Flamenco Singers (known as Large Flamenco)

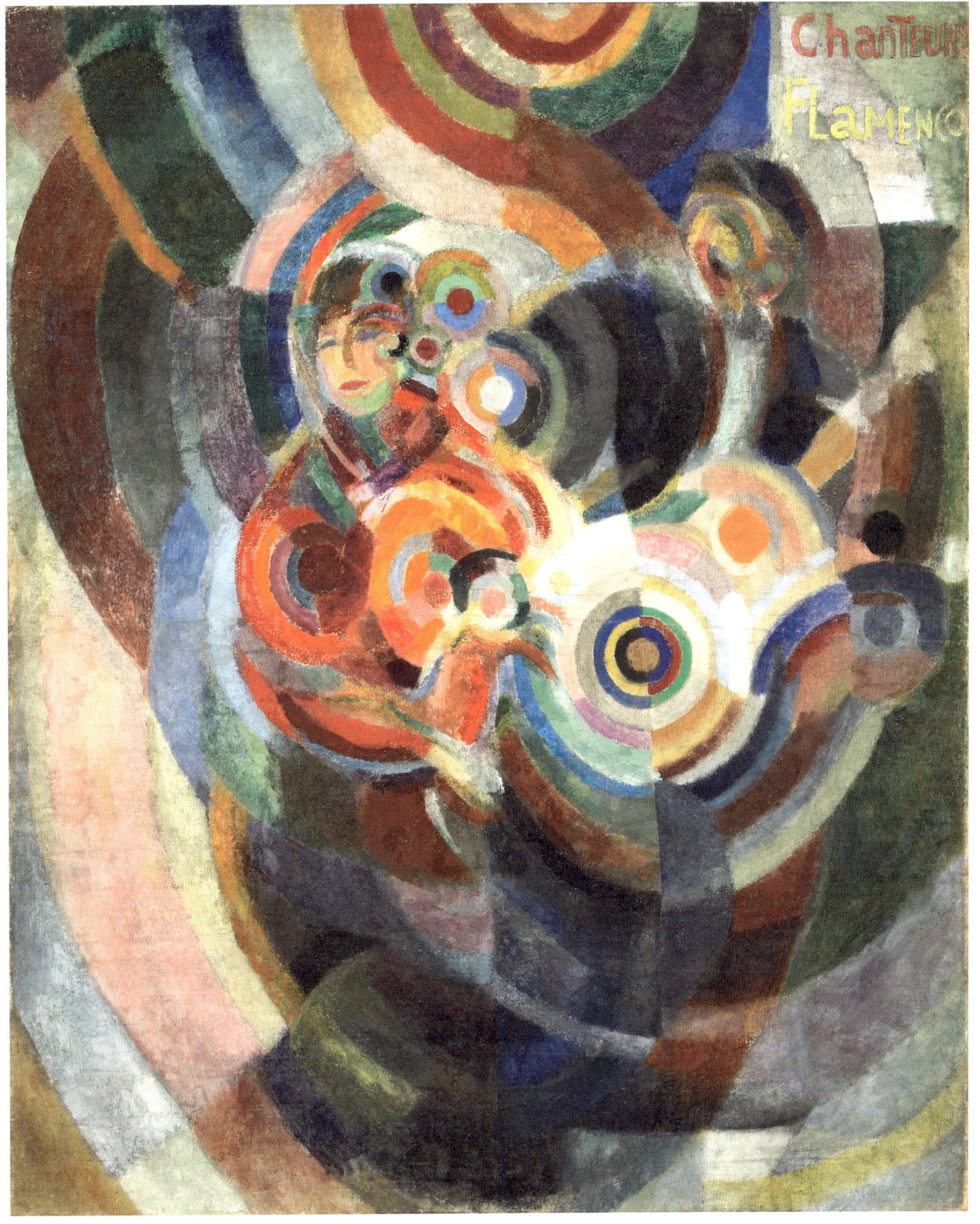
ChanTeurs
FLaMENCO

BECAUSE WOMEN WORE IT – SONIA DELAUNAY'S SIMULTANEOUS PROJECT

Tine Colstrup

The Russian-French artist Sonia Delaunay (1885-1979) worked across media, art forms and cultural spheres, merging art and design and pushing abstract art far beyond the frame of painting. Encompassing multiple projects at once, her art unfolded over 60 years, from the 1910s to the 1970s. Colour – in particular, dynamic colour interaction – is at the heart of her work. In painting and other disciplines, Sonia Delaunay cultivated nonfigurative compositions in which colours did not have to colour anything, as in figurative pictures, but work instead by their own power through dynamic, evocative contrasts. Colours affect each other when seen side by side. With cultivation of such simultaneous colour contrasts as the jumping-off point, the term *simultaneity* became the ultimate key to her work. The concept embraces the vibrant dynamism of the modern world and an artistic position simultaneously engaged in multiple areas.

As an artist, Sonia Delaunay herself is thoroughly simultaneous, moving freely in and out of isms and roles. Embodying the prolific experimentation and interaction between artists and genres that characterized the European art scene in the years before Second World War, her work is a shining example of how the abstract-geometric vocabulary from the very beginning evolved across different media and materials, while drawing on numerous sources of inspiration. Sonia Delaunay's inspirations include traditional Russian crafts, the modern metropolis and the experimental breakthroughs in art, literature, music, performing arts, advertising and fashion that were happening all around her, and that she had a hand in herself. The following will look at highlights of Sonia Delaunay's simultaneous art practice.

Manifesto in a Dress

Sonia Delaunay made a statement in 1913 when she entered the Bal Bullier dance hall in Paris wearing a collage-like dress resembling a colourful Cubist painting (page 15 and 16). In one swift motion, avant-garde art strode out of the narrow frame of painting and went on the town, dancing the modern foxtrot and tango and mixing with modern, dynamic life. While abstract art was still taking its baby steps in a variety of styles and constellations across the European art scene, Sonia Delaunay simply wore it. Her performance sent waves through the avant-garde milieu. The following year, the poet Blaise Cendrars wrote a poem to the dress, and in the *Mercure de France* magazine, the influential French poet and critic Guillaume Apollinaire urged his readers to go the Bal Bullier on Thursdays, when Sonia and Robert Delaunay were there, and experience their reformation of clothing for themselves. Sonia Delaunay made clothes for her husband, as well. Apollinaire, a friend of the couple, described Robert Delaunay's gaudy outfit, which might consist of a red coat with a blue collar, a green jacket, red socks, a sky-blue vest and a red tie. Sonia Delaunay's creations looked like nothing else, Apollinaire implies. The couple – and eventually several of their friends – jointly spread her colourful break with sartorial convention as part of her overall artistic project, which from the beginning pushed the abstract vocabulary far beyond the frame of painting, integrating it into modern life.

Merging Light and Motion

New notes were struck, including in Sonia Delaunay's paintings of evenings at the Bal Bullier (page 16). Choosing this subject, she inscribed herself into a tradition established by the generation of artists before her, depicting modern society and nightlife at bars and dance halls. "The Bal Bullier was for me what the Moulin de la Galette had been to Degas, Renoir and Lautrec," she later wrote in her autobiography.[1] Unlike those artists – Picasso's pictures of night cafés and dance halls can be included, as well – Sonia Delaunay created an abstract version of the subject. There are no interiors, wine glasses or fancy or scantily clad dancers to be seen. Hers was no portrait of decadent Parisian nightlife. Instead, she made an abstract, simultaneous portrait of energy and atmosphere, tango music and gaudy garments under the electric lights of the dance hall. Contrasting planes of colour, rhythmically arranged, entwine in dynamic syncopation on the picture plane. "Blending light and motion and scrambling the planes," as she put it.[2]

Sonia Delaunay's work with light, colour and motion in her painting *Bal Bullier* is clearly related to Robert Delaunay's first series of purely nonfigurative works from the year before (the so-called *Windows*). He had been preoccupied with perception and the colour theory of "simultaneous contrasts" devised by Michel Eugène Chevreul in 1839. The French scientist described how colours mutually affect each other when they are placed side by side.[3] From the beginning, flat compositions of strong colours had been central in Sonia Delaunay's painting. Under the banner of Simultanism, she and her husband worked closely together, exploring the same painterly subject matter to such a degree that their paintings from certain periods can be hard to tell apart.[4]

Circular forms appear in abundance in both their works, as seen in Sonia Delaunay's big painting *Chanteurs Flamenco*

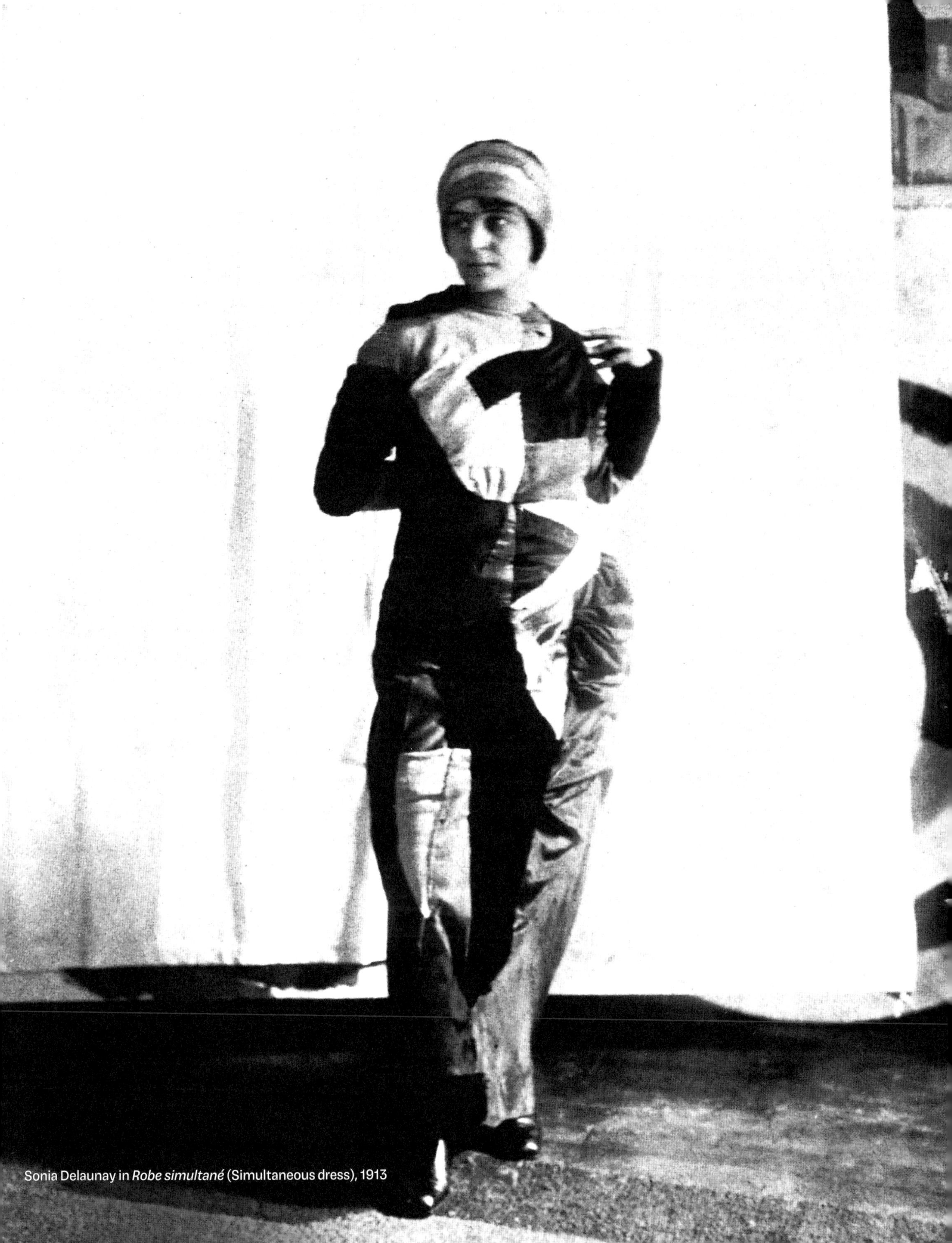

Sonia Delaunay in *Robe simultané* (Simultaneous dress), 1913

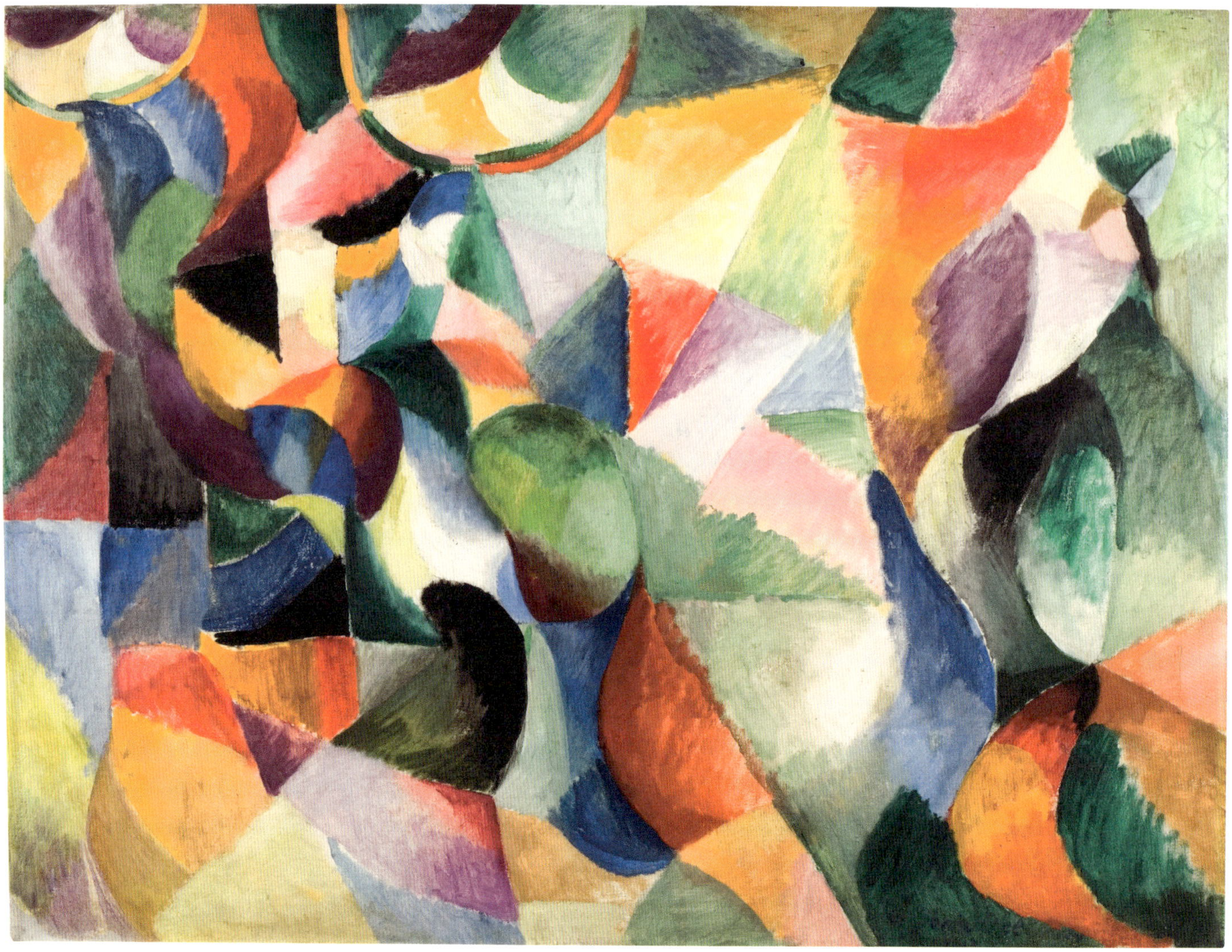

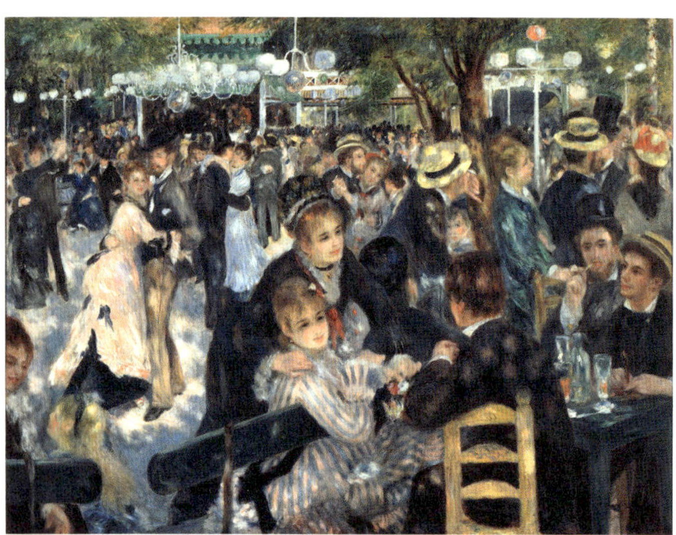

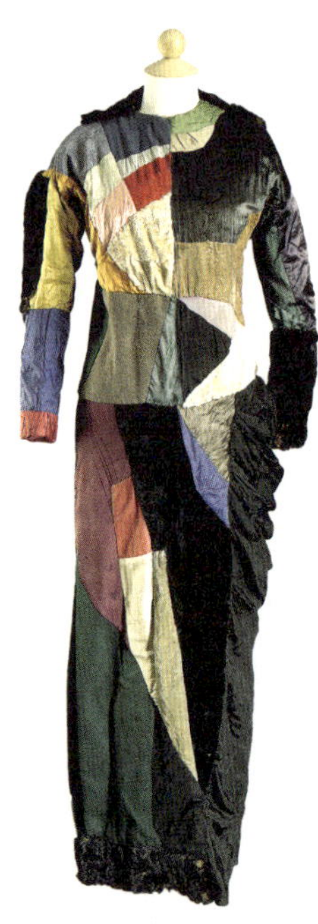

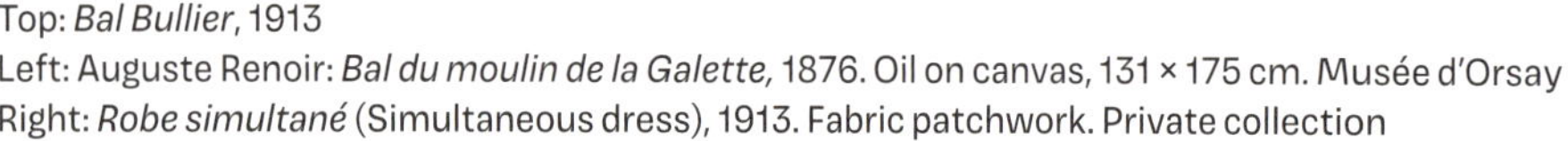

Top: *Bal Bullier*, 1913
Left: Auguste Renoir: *Bal du moulin de la Galette,* 1876. Oil on canvas, 131 × 175 cm. Musée d'Orsay
Right: *Robe simultané* (Simultaneous dress), 1913. Fabric patchwork. Private collection

(Flamenco Singers, 1915-1916, page 13) when the couple were staying in Spain and Portugal during First World War. Expanding on her interpretation of tango music, rhythm and motion in her paintings of the Bal Bullier, she now captured the energy of flamenco. The figures of two flamenco singers are suggested, but they dissolve in the all-over painterly representation of sound and impressions in circular shapes and colour contrasts. Crisp circles of bright colour burst from a guitar and snap from castanets or clapping hands, the rhythm radiating in concentric circles towards – and beyond – the edges of the painting.

The Modern Woman

The 1913 simultaneous dress kicked off the wide-ranging engagement in design, garments and textiles that has long since made Sonia Delaunay a classic point of reference in fashion and fabric design.[5]

In 1918, when the Delaunay family was living in Spain, she opened her first design company, in Madrid. Her shop, Casa Sonia, sold clothes and home furnishings of her design, including decorated pillows, ceramics and storage boxes. All her designs continued the simultaneous clothes and home furnishings she had been making for herself and her closest friends all along. A new step in her simultaneous project, the company also provided her family with some much needed income.

Textile and fashion design became Sonia Delaunay's primary activity in the 1920s. After she and her family returned to Paris, she founded an actual design company with a staff and opened a new boutique in extension of her studio – all in the couple's apartment (page 38). She continually decorated the apartment with her own designs of wall textile, furniture, carpets and the like, combined with her own and Robert's paintings, and poems and other marks left on walls and doors by the family's many artist friends. Her home was a simultaneous statement unto itself.

With bold colours and big geometric patterns, Sonia Delaunay made her name in the mid-1920s as an innovative avant-garde designer merging art and fashion. Making no qualitative distinction between the two spheres, she cultivated the act of productive fusion, garments and fabrics conveying her colourful compositions out of the studio, including as images in the media.

Sonia Delaunay painted the compositions for her fabric designs mainly in gouache (page 44-48). As those clearly show, she approached her work in design from a painterly point of view and as an integrated part of her artistic project: "My ideas for women's dresses were at the same time studies in colour."[6] In many cases, the gouache studies are abstract compositions in their own right and she was adamant that the finished fabrics keep the handmade quality of the painted studies. The patterns should never be too perfect but preserve the painterly spontaneity, both in the fabrics she made in her own studio and in the many designs she made for external manufacturers (including Metz & Co of Holland – see Matteo de Leeuw-de Monti's essay in this catalogue).

Viewing Sonia Delaunay's work in textile design and fashion, one overall quality stands out: its flatness. In her fashion design, she continued the elimination of the space of perspective and the plastic modelling of figures and objects that was a signature of her painting – and of modern painting in general, where flatness was key.

Flatly superimposed on bodies in her drawn or painted studies for outfits, abstract compositions of colours and patterns characterize her production of dresses, coats and fabrics in general. Anyone wearing one of her brightly coloured geometric designs was bound to cause a stir. But as modern people with their finger on the pulse of the avant-garde, not as curvy female bodies. The body had disappeared already in Sonia Delaunay's first simultaneous dress which, instead of following and emphasizing the curves of the body, effectively camouflaged them in geometric patchwork.[7] In her colourful designs, Sonia Delaunay stoked the headlong evolution of women's fashion after First World War, when European women finally discarded their tight corsets and began dressing in looser fitting clothes suitable for an active, modern lifestyle. In her designs, she aimed to bring colour and abstract art into everyday life, but her work equally remains a gender political statement.[8]

The female body likewise disappears in the photographs that Sonia Delaunay carefully staged of herself or others modelling her designs (staged photography plays a major role in Sonia Delaunay's artistic project, as described in depth by Cécile Godefroy and Anne Montfort in this catalogue). The images on page 19 and 29 show the artist posing in front of one of her own paintings and works by Robert Delaunay, respectively. As these setups clearly indicate, modernizing painting and modernizing fashion – and, in turn, women – were one and the same project. Placing bodies in patterned fabrics against the patterned backdrop of the paintings ties the space together optically. The photographs aim for the same scrambling of spatial planes as her paintings.

In 1907, Picasso caused a sensation with his Cubist painting *Les Demoiselles d'Avignon.* Consciously or unconsciously, Sonia Delaunay almost seems to be paraphrasing that work, while adding her own set of rules. While Picasso flattened his female figures and compressed the spatial planes, the female figures in Sonia Delaunay's frontal compositions are dressed, and look neither distorted nor confused. Staring calmly at us, they appear neither as art's traditional objects of the gaze nor as advertising's pandering models. Sonia Delaunay matter-of-factly casts confident, modern women in the lead. Their heads are practically the only visible part of their bodies, as the female curves are afforded a break behind brightly coloured patterns.

A Poetry of Colours as Tall as the Eiffel Tower

The simultaneous dress is one programmatic work that Sonia Delaunay made in 1913. Another is the experimental book she made with the writer Blaise Cendrars that today is considered a seminal work of the artist's book genre.

Promoted as "the first simultaneous book," *La Prose du Transsibérien et de la Petite Jehanne de France* (Prose on the Trans-Siberian Railway and of the Little Jehanne of France) is designed as a unity of words, graphics and colour. Instead of just reading a text, you are asked to sense the poem's dynamism and rhythm through purely visual stimuli. Cendrars' free verse describe a fictional ride on the Trans-Siberian Railroad across Russia that the young poet imagined having taken during the first Russian revolution in 1905, when he was 16. Alternating times and places, the poem mixes observations with associations, as the mood changes from light to gloomy over the course of the long flowing text. Like painted free verse or an abstract interpretation of the text, Sonia Delaunay's rhythmic, brightly coloured composition unfolds in a column of its own. The text column includes coloured sections as well, and the text is set in no fewer than 12 different typefaces, jointly chosen by Blaise Cendrars and Sonia Delaunay. Together, they also picked the unusual vertical format to create an unbroken sequence mimicking the form of the extended poem and train ride.

The book may not look like much when folded into its cover, which measures just 19 × 11 cm. But when the double-pleated leporello unfolds accordion-style, it is two metres long, or tall. For the combined edition of 150 copies the concept was to equal the height of the Eiffel Tower when unfolded. However, only about half of the 150 planned copies were realized. Hailed at the end of Cendrars' poem, the Eiffel Tower is also the only figurative element in Sonia Delaunay's composition. Since its construction in 1889, the tower has been the ultimate symbol of Paris and modernity. It frequently appears in the work of both Delaunays, not least in that of Robert. Creating a work where painting and poetry together aspired to the height of the Eiffel Tower is abundant testimony to Blaise Cendrars' and Sonia Delaunay's lofty ambitions for modern art.

Sonia Delaunay exhibited her newly finished book in Berlin at the *Erster Deutscher Herbstsalon* (The First German Autumn Salon). The exhibition was organized by the Galerie Der Sturm, which through the efforts of its founder, Herwarth Walden, and his wife, Nelly Roslund, had become crucial in the dissemination of modern art, especially Expressionism, Futurism, Dada and Neue Sachlichkeit. Aiming to present the latest trends in international art, the big exhibition had the participation of ninety artists, including some affiliated with the Russian-German Der Blaue Reiter group (among them Kandinsky, Marc, Klee and Münter), which also co-curated the show. In addition it featured Italian Futurists like Balla and Boccioni, and numerous other artists who are well known today, including Chagall, Ernst, Goncharova, Hartley, Léger, Mondrian and Picabia, alongside Robert and Sonia Delaunay. Seizing the opportunity to showcase the range of her simultaneous practice, Sonia Delaunay exhibited 26 works in all. Apart from the book she made with Cendrars, she showed an almost four-metre-long painting and three smaller paintings, a number of decorated utilitarian objects and, not least, a selection of the many book covers she had decorated with painting and collage. In this varied selection of works across multiple media, Sonia Delaunay, with all possible clarity, communicated that her simultaneous project was about reaching out into the world and modernizing *everything*.

Sonia Delaunay's collaboration with Cendrars would be her most direct merger of poetry and colour composition. It manifests the interest in experimental poetry that is a line running through all of her work. Writers were a big part of the Delaunays' vast network, and while Sonia Delaunay did not herself write poetry, she saw a close link between painterly and verbal abstraction, and, like others at the time, was fascinated by synaesthetic perception.[9]

In graphic publications, books and portfolios, her works and design studies are accompanied by poems and texts by avant-garde writers. She even 'portrayed' several of them, published in a 1962 portfolio of prints, *Poésie de mots, poésie de couleurs* (Word Poetry, Colour Poetry, page 83). The portfolio consists of abstract portraits and selected writings by Arthur Rimbaud, Tristan Tzara, Philippe Soupault, Blaise Cendrars, Joseph Delteil and Stéphane Mallarmé – that is, both contemporary writers that she knew and had collaborated with in various ways and their avant-garde predecessors. The portfolio also includes the following short statement by Sonia Delaunay, reaching back to her early work as an abstract "colour poet" in the simultaneous book she made with Cendrars and making it clear that she thought of her colour compositions/constructions as wordless poetry,[10]

Poetry of words/ poetry of colours/ the rhythm of verses/
is construction/ and relation of values/ poetry moves/
through all/ the creations of art

While Sonia Delaunay detached colour from narrative painting, the poets that captivated her detached language from linear narrative and detailed, naturalistic description, cultivating instead suggestive, evocative connections of words in rhythmic text-sound compositions. Her abstract compositions, in particular those of the late postwar period, do not declare what they are "about" – beyond the words "rhythm and colours," which often appear in the titles. In her many literary collaborations, however, she clearly emphasizes that, like the word artists, she is expressing experiences, moods, sensations and notions ranging from Symbolist gloom to Dadaist bursts of richly visual associations.

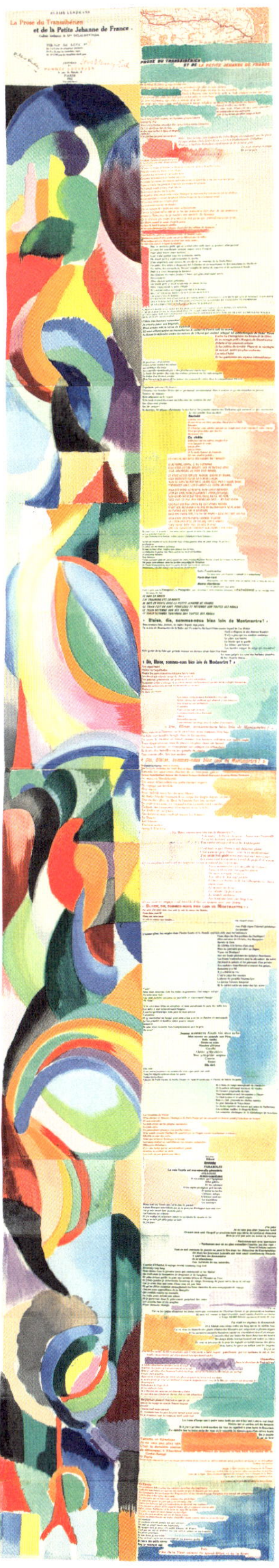

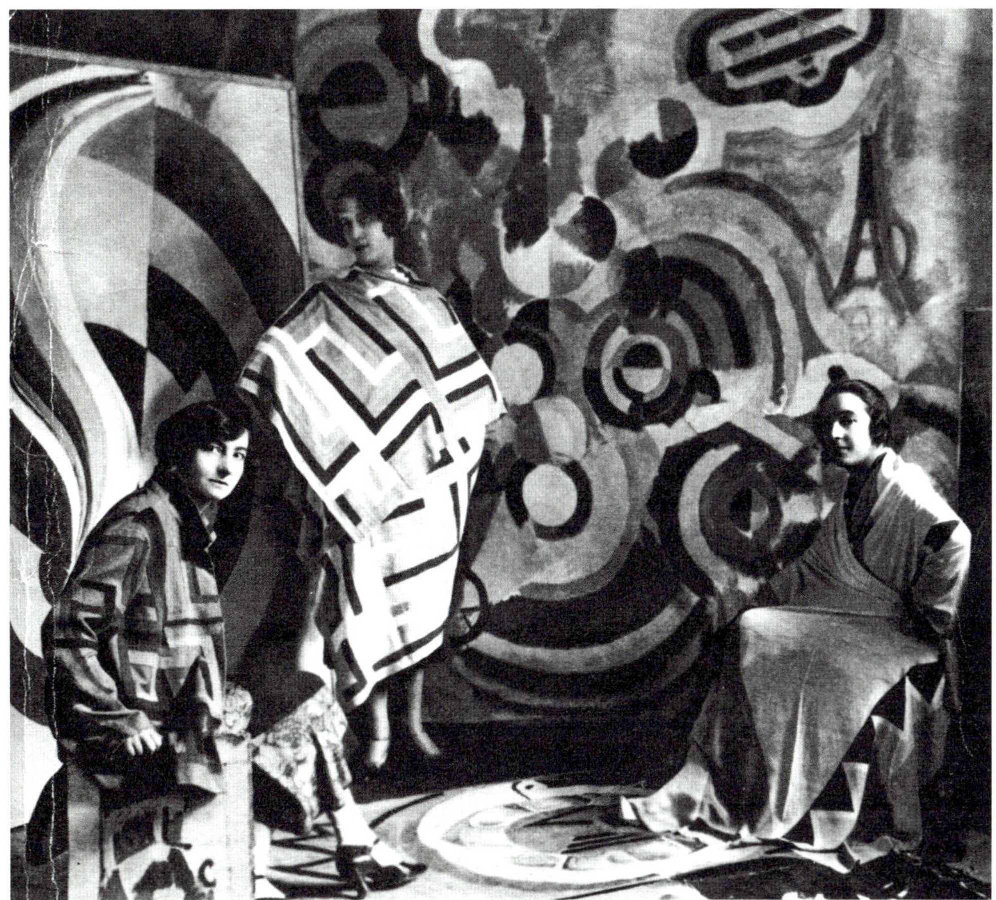

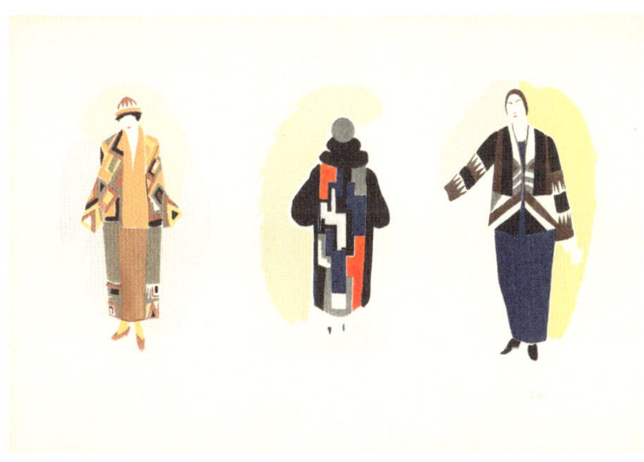

Top and right: Sonia Delaunay in collaboration with Blaise Cendrars: Advertising flyer and accordion-fold book *La Prose du Transsibérien et de la Petite Jehanne de France*, 1913. Prose on the Trans-Siberian Railway and of the Little Jehanne of France
Middle: Sonia Delaunay (right) with two friends in her designs in Robert Delaunay's studio, Paris, 1924
Bottom: Three fashion sketches in *Sonia Delaunay, ses peintures, ses objets, ses tissus simultanés, ses modes*, 1925

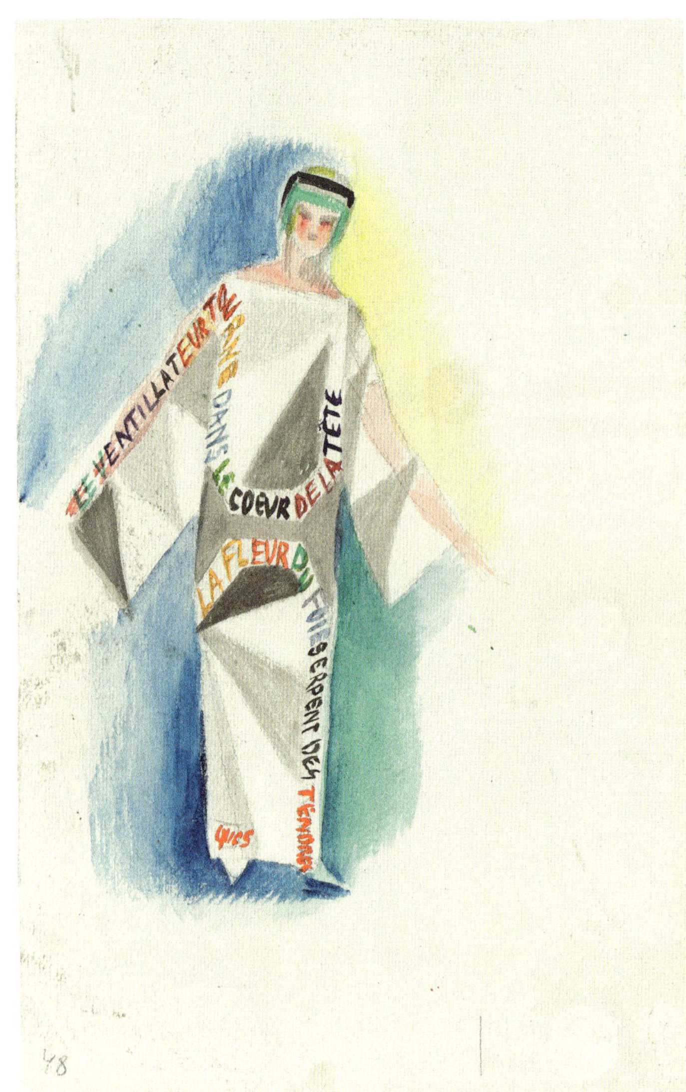

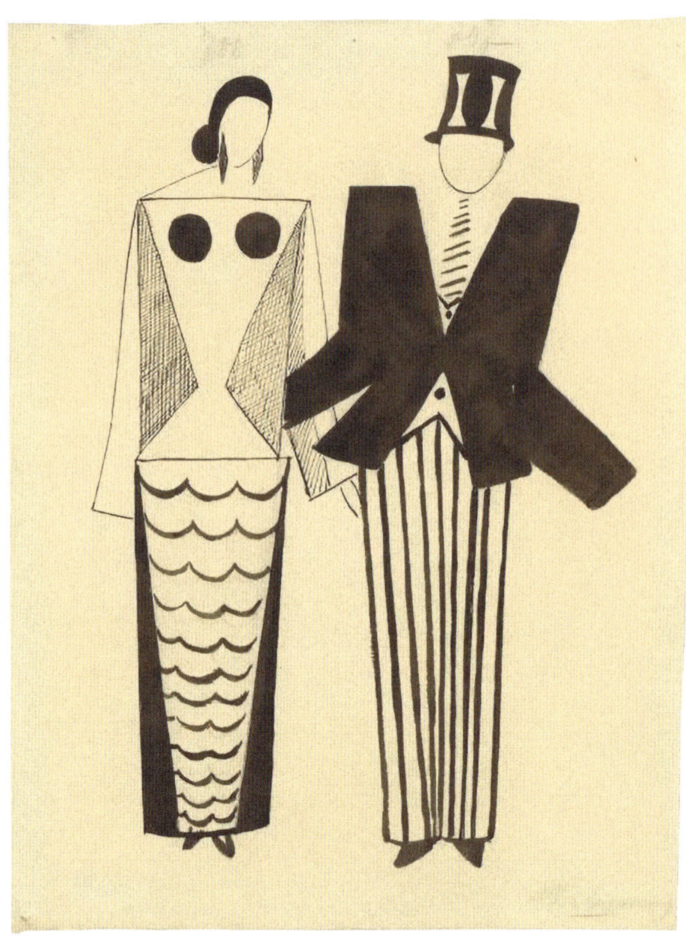

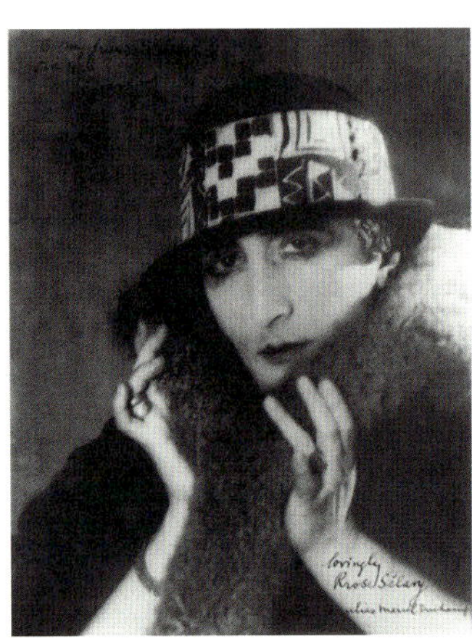

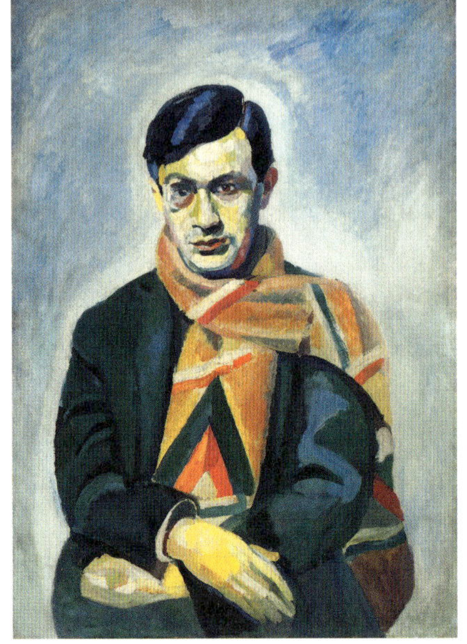

Top left: *Robe poème no. 1329*, 1923. Poem Dress No. 1329. The poem on the dress reads:
Le ventillateur tourney dans le cæur de la tête. La fleur du froid serpent de tendresse chimique
The extractor fan turns in the head's heart. Bloom of the cold snake of chemical tenderness
Top right: Miss Mouth and Mr. Eye. Costume design for the play *Le Cæur à Gaz*, 1923
Bottom left: Man Ray: Rrose Sélavy (Marcel Duchamp), c. 1921-1923
Bottom right: Robert Delaunay: *Portrait de Tristan Tzara*, 1923. Portrait of Tristan Tzara
Tzara wears a scarf designed by Sonia Delaunay

The Extractor Fan Turns in the Head's Heart

Returning to Paris in 1921, the Delaunays immediately formed a new network of artists from the Surrealist and Dadaist circles, especially through the central figure of Tristan Tzara, who became a close friend. They had both read Tzara's 1918 Dadaist manifesto the same year it was published, and the French-Romanian writer's norm-busting attitude and desire to merge art and life corresponded to several of Sonia Delaunay's own endeavours. Instead of sticking to one medium, one theory and one role for the artist, she consistently, sometimes pragmatically, cut across the lines. A lot of the same artistic temperament and programme can be seen in the freedom that Tzara hails in the final lines of his (anti)manifesto, "Freedom: Dada Dada Dada, a roaring of tense colours, and interlacing of opposites and of all contradictions, grotesques, inconsistencies: LIFE."[11]

In 1922-1923, Sonia Delaunay created a series of "poem-dresses" (page 20 and 27) featuring poems by Tzara and others. In the spirit of simultaneity, the dresses merged poetry and fashion through the poems emblazoned on them.[12] The following year, she designed the costumes for a production of Tzara's Dadaist parody of traditional theatre, *Le Cœur à Gaz* (The Gas Heart).[13]

The period saw an abundance of experimental theatre and dance, including collaborations between artists and stage directors. Sonia Delaunay designed costumes on several occasions. Her first effort was in 1918 for *Cléopâtre* (page 32) mounted by the Russian Ballets Russes company, which became popular for its experimental productions and interdisciplinary artistic collaborations, spearheaded by founder Sergej Diaghilev. Over the years, she also designed costumes for a number of smaller performances and projects. In 1926, she designed a great number of costumes – as well as sets, with Robert Delaunay – for the silent film *P'tit Parigot* (The Small Parisian One, page 32-33), directed by René Le Somptier.

During the period when the Delaunays' contact and collaboration with Tzara was at its peak, Robert painted a portrait of Tzara wearing a scarf of Sonia Delaunay's design. The painting testifies to the close partnership among the three of them and the poet was clearly more than happy to be portrayed wearing a Sonia Delaunay design as a modern attribute heralding a new age.[14]

Presumably, a design by Delaunay also appears on the hat band in the iconic portrait of Marcel Duchamp posing as his alter ego Rrose Sélavy (a pun on the French adage "Eros c'est la vie," literally "Eros is life").[15] Duchamp was intrigued by androgynousness. In the figure of Rrose Sélavy, he occupies a fluid gender position at a time when gender and sexuality were very much up for negotiation, though mainly it was women who were breaking with the stereotypes of their gender by cutting their hair short and dressing more androgynously. The portrait of Duchamp was taken by his friend, the American photographer Man Ray. A trendsetting member of the Dadaist circle, Man Ray was a frequent guest in the Delaunays' home and was close to Tzara, whose portrait he also took. Man Ray made several portraits of Rrose Sélavy. In this one, she is posing as a fashionable, confident modern woman, a typical *garçonne* of the times. In the picture, the bell hat and its patterned band are crucial markers of this new type of woman. Since no known study for it can be found in the archives, the band cannot conclusively be attributed to Sonia Delaunay. But several of the patterns that it combines bear a striking resemblance to fabric designs developed and signed by Sonia Delaunay in 1924.[16] Indeed, the style of lightly shimmering "imperfect" geometries is so Delaunay-esque that it could hardly be anyone else's. Considering her network and relationships, it is certainly highly likely that Duchamp and Man Ray picked a Sonia Delaunay design for this carefully staged photograph as a clear sign of a new style for an avant-garde hat lady.

Flat and Matte

In her late career, from Second World War on, Sonia Delaunay concentrated mainly on painting, though she also made numerous prints, organized and took part in exhibitions and featured in several more or less formal artists' associations.

Sonia Delaunay made a great number of paintings in gouache, which is one of her most frequently used media – from pochoir prints for the 1913 simultaneous poem to studies for fabric designs and numerous independent works. Gouache is watercolour that is opaque due to the combination of pigment, binder and filler, often chalk. It is quick-drying and has a completely matte finish. Indeed, a matte quality characterizes Sonia Delaunay's work in any media. Gouache colours are bright and luminous. But just as the colours rarely pander to one another in her compositions of adjoining coloured planes, they do not pander to the senses with sleek, glossy surfaces. Her pictures are always crisp, flat and matte.

Sonia Delaunay's late paintings are often on a large scale, their compositions more solidly constructed than in the prewar years, but there are still clear links back to her early work. In purely formal terms, it is remarkable how the late paintings have clear echoes of the composition, colours and combined textures of the simultaneous dress. The dress is stitched together from patches of available fabrics in different colours that reflect light in their own individual ways. In her two-dimensional works, including her late paintings, Sonia Delaunay seems to be converting the lustre of fabrics to painted planes of varying degrees of saturation, including hastily cross-hatched planes recalling light shimmering in the black velvet planes of the dress.

The aesthetic temperament of the late works is likewise clearly present in the early works, including in the rough finish of the dress. The dress is quite roughly stitched together, a typical trait of the artist. The seams are never perfect in Sonia Delaunay's work. Across paintings, prints and fabric designs, you sense a hand working quickly and resolutely – a natural fit for fast-drying gouache – and an artistic temperament that more than welcomes minor imperfections, because they keep the composition moving. The coloured planes are always roughly put together, often leaving a small space in between, where the white canvas or paper shines through. The elements of the picture may be geometric, but they are crooked and imprecisely joined. Exactly as they should be, of course. For it is there that the rhythm, the story and the energy of the picture emerge.

Wroom!

The Delaunays' early focus on creating optical illusions of movement in their abstract compositions makes them forerunners of the kinetic art, or Op Art, that emerged in the mid-1950s and culminated in the following decade. In turn, Sonia Delaunay attracted renewed attention as an Op artist. In 1967, she and four key figures of the movement were asked to decorate a car each for a charity project raising money for medical research by auctioning off the cars. Sonia Delaunay decorated a sports car by the French carmaker Matra (opposite page and page 78).[17] The geometric composition of coloured planes matches the two-dimensional works she was making at the time. As an optical finesse that only the car could realize since paintings do not ordinarily move, the coloured planes would blend together – like a work of kinetic art – when the car was speeding.

The car project dovetailed with the interest in modern life and the development of technology that she and Robert Delaunay had already cultivated in the 1910s in their impressions of the shimmer of electric street lights and in their large-scale projects for the railway and aviation pavilions at the 1937 World's Fair. Finally, of course, the sports car points directly back to the Citroën B12 that was decorated with one of her designs in 1925 (page 65). While that car has not survived, photographs of modern women behind the wheel, dressed to take charge at rapid speed, circulated in the period and are among Sonia Delaunay's most iconic statements. Executed by the 82-year-old artist in 1967, the sports car project stands as yet another sign of Sonia Delaunay's engagement in making artistic marks in the real world, sending colours into the streets, the city, real life.

Because Women Wore It

In 1970, French President Pompidou presented a Sonia Delaunay painting to American President Nixon as a state gift – the ultimate symbol that the Jewish-Russian migrant, who had made Paris her main base since 1906, was considered a significant *French* artist, whose work Pompidou was happy to present to the Americans. And perhaps as a reminder that many of the abstract trends of flat painting that were flourishing on the American art scene at the time and celebrated as American triumphs had originated in France – and in the work of Sonia Delaunay, a pioneer in the 1910s and now a *grande dame* of the nonfigurative vocabulary of coloured planes. Sonia Delaunay could thus be singled out for her abstract painting. But while it met every parameter of the "correct" abstract art that already dominated the writing of modernism,[18] it was just one among several paths that she took.

Working across the boundaries between "art" and "craft," as Sonia Delaunay had been doing since 1911, harmonized with many of the ideas coming out of the avant-garde movements at the time – ideas that she herself had helped spark and spread. Combining art forms to shatter outmoded norms and raise the quality of life, and the aesthetic value of one's surroundings in general, became an institutional programme at the Bauhaus art school, which opened in 1919 – building, in turn, on the work of the English Arts and Crafts movement that originated in the mid-19th century, the Art Nouveau of the fin de siècle, the Austrian Wiener Werkstätte, founded in 1903, and the concept of the *Gesamtkunstwerk* cultivated by those movements. When Bauhaus opened, Sonia Delaunay had long since found her own method. Through close friendships and collaborations with artists from the Bauhaus circle and the Dutch De Stijl movement – as well as Expressionism, Futurism, Constructivism, Dada, etc. – she was an integral part of a ramified network of avant-garde trends and interdisciplinary practices across Europe.

It is easy to forget the radical nature of a project like Sonia Delaunay's today, when abstract art, the simultaneous appearance of words and images, geometric fabric designs and modernist interior decorating have become par for the course. A pioneer of transforming the aesthetics of everyday life, Sonia Delaunay created an original role for the artist that embraced avant-gardist, entrepreneur and commercially minded businesswoman. In fact, she despised the commercialism and growing consumerism of her age, and she was relieved when she decided to close her fashion business after the economic crash in 1929. However, it is not least thanks to her work in design that she has had such a broad cultural impact. Today, most of us without even thinking about it, probably own at least one umbrella, toiletry bag, tea cosy, sofa cushion, dress or scarf with a pattern directly or indirectly echoing a Sonia Delaunay composition.

In a 1969 publication of her selected design sketches from the 1920s, featuring words by avant-garde poets, Sonia Delaunay concludes, "If painting has entered daily life, it is because women wore it."[19]

Tine Colstrup is a curator at Louisiana Museum of Modern Art. In addition to the Sonia Delaunay exhibition, she has curated exhibitions of Hilma af Klint, Paula Modersohn-Becker, Louise Bourgeois, Marina Abramović, Pipilotti Rist and Tetsumi Kudo.

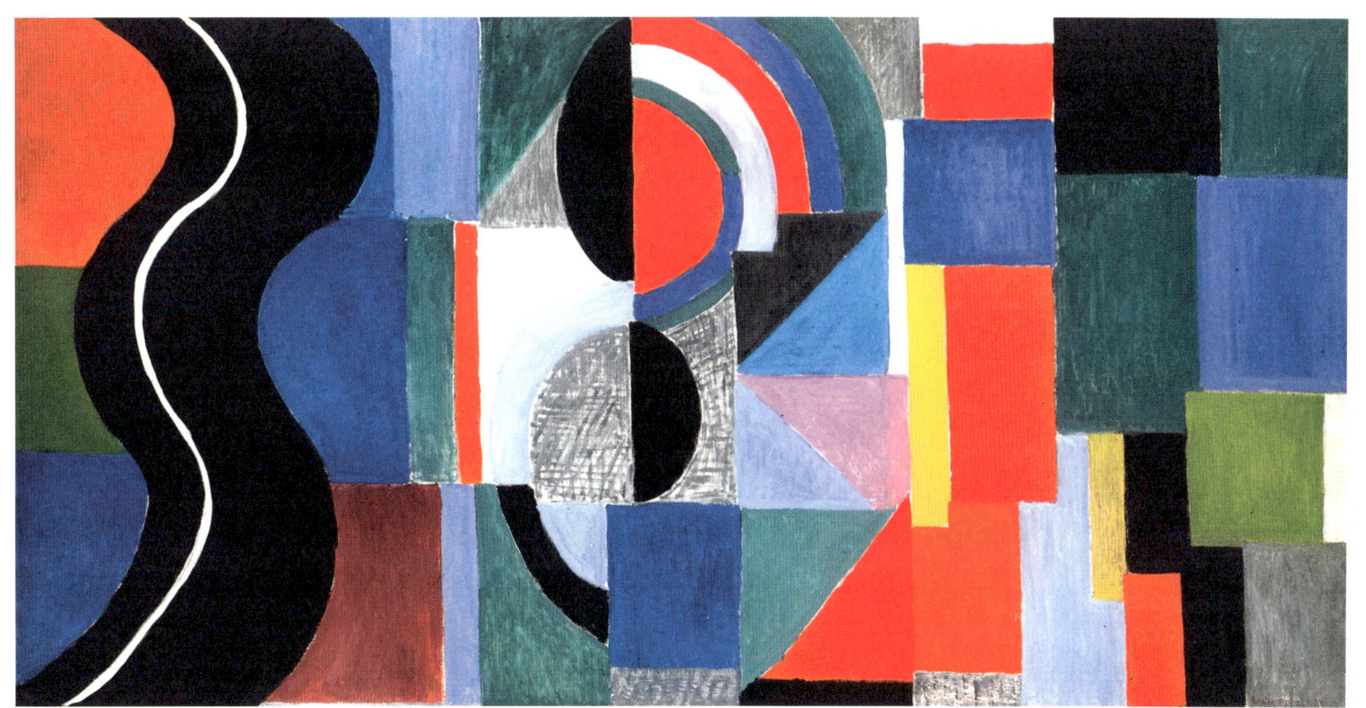

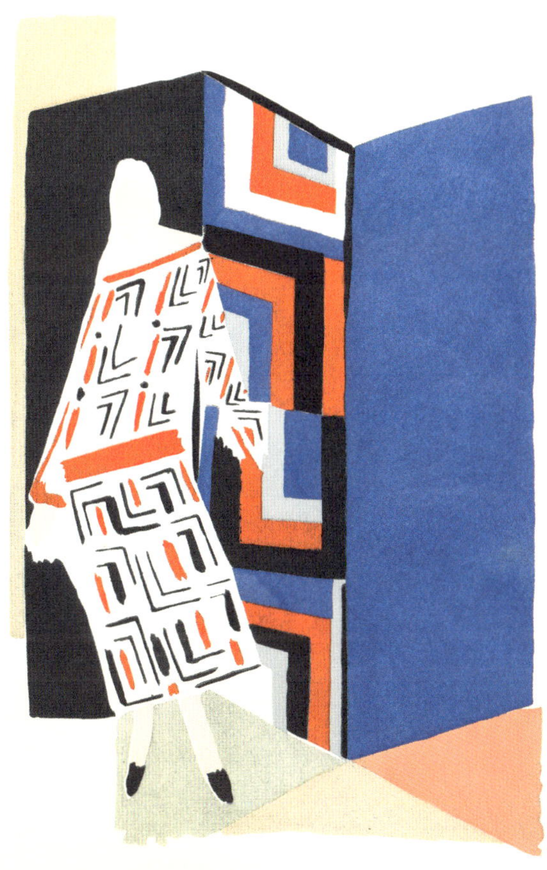

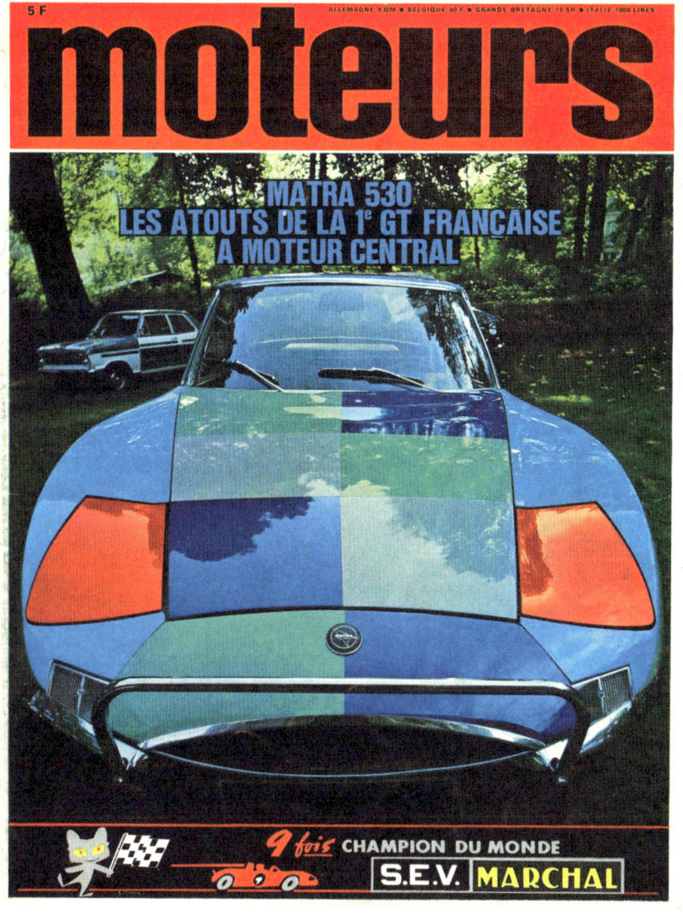

Top: *Rythme syncopé (*dit *Le serpent noir)*, 1967. Syncopated Rhythm (known as The Black Snake)
Bottom left: Fashion sketch from 1924 published in *27 tableaux vivants,* 1969
Bottom right: Sonia Delaunay's sports car design on the front cover of *Moteurs* January/February, 1968

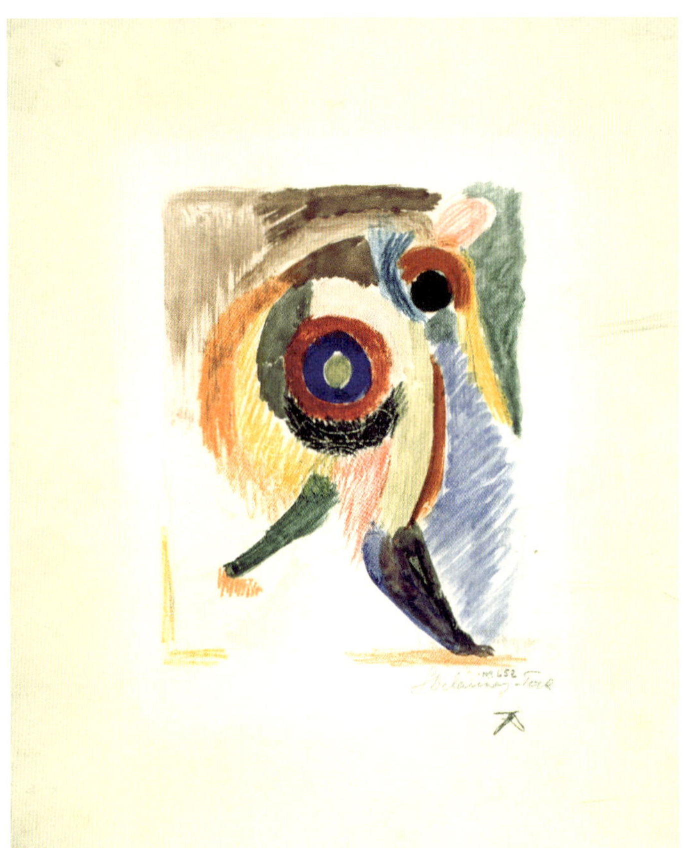

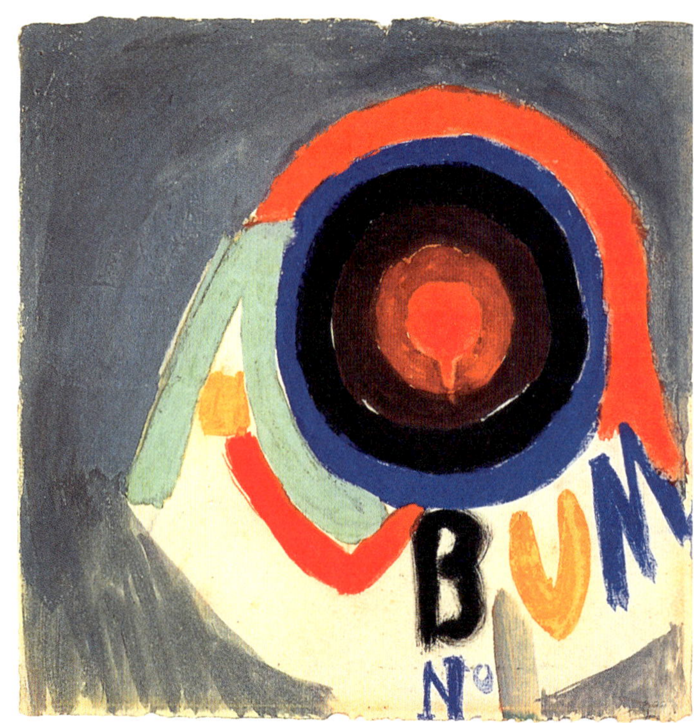

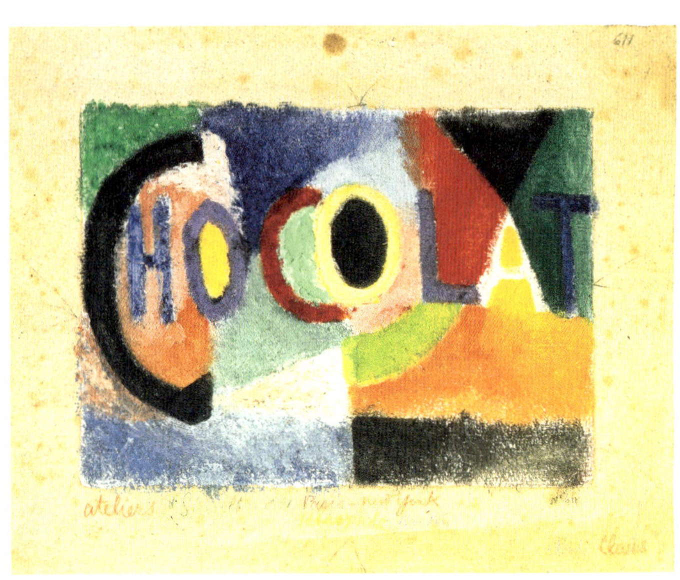

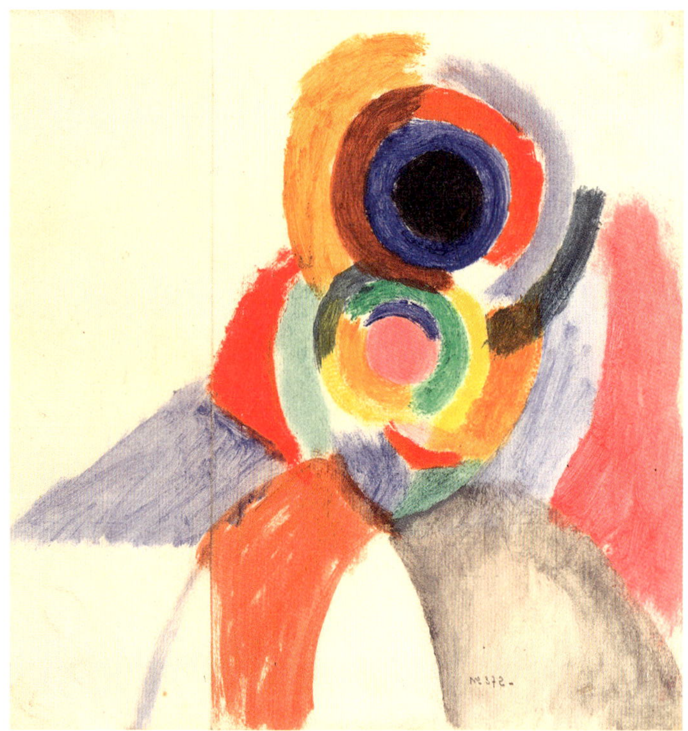

Top left: *Danseuse*, 1916. The Dancer
Top right: *Album No. 1*, 1916. Album No. 1
Bottom left: *Chocolat*, 1916. Chocolate
Bottom right: *Auto-Portrait*, 1916. Self-Portrait

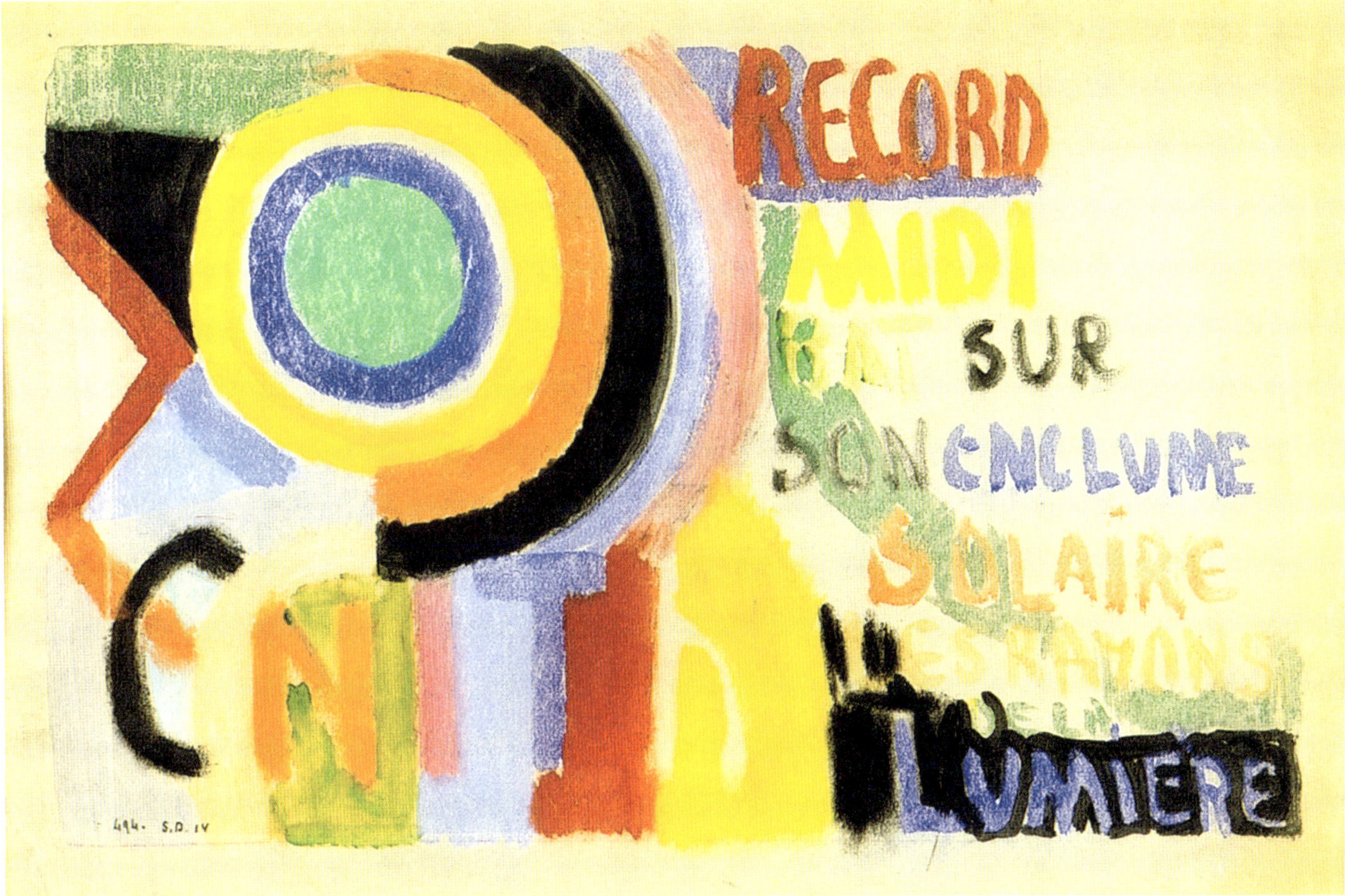

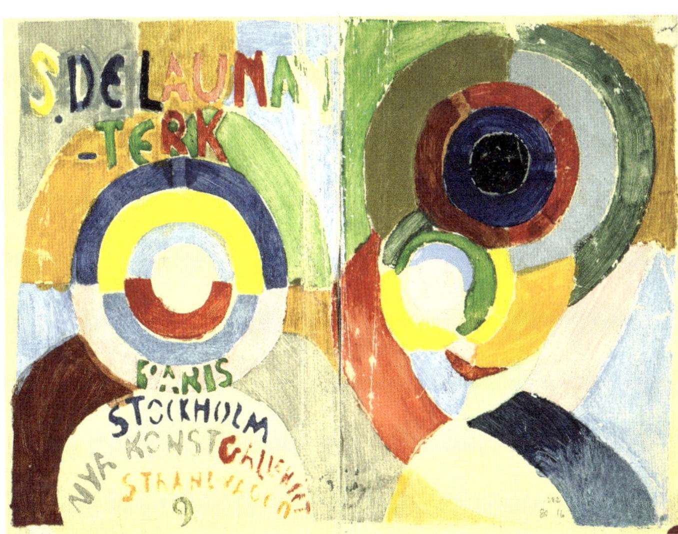

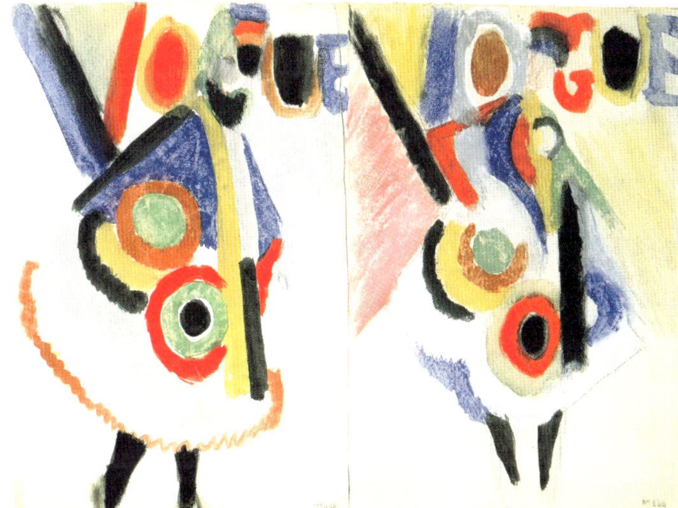

Top: *Zénith Étude*, 1914. Study for Zénith
Bottom left: Draft for catalogue book cover for the Stockholm exhibition, 1916
Bottom right: Cover designs for *Vogue*, 1916

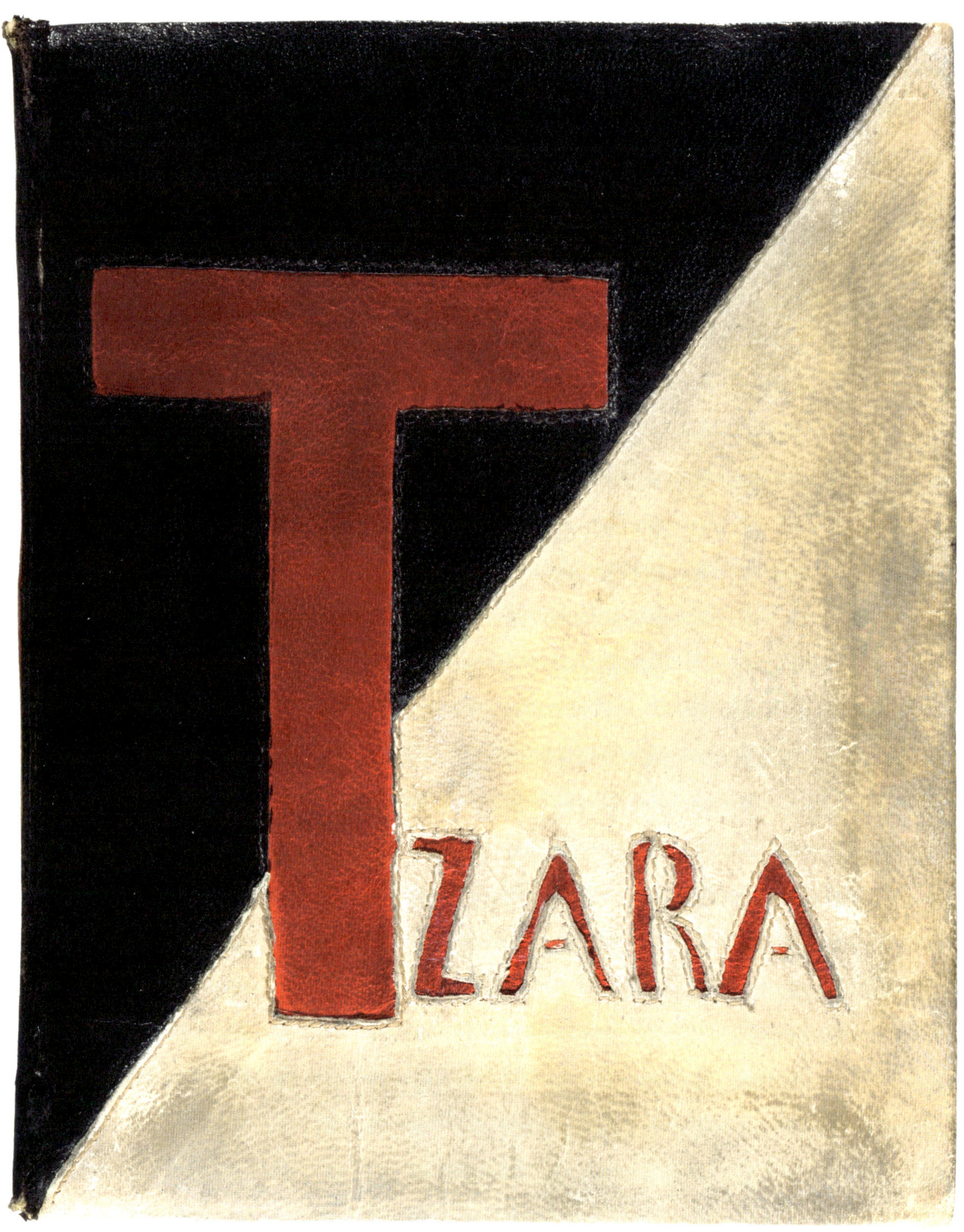

Bookbinding: Tristan Tzara: *De nos oiseaux,* Paris, Edition de la Sirène, 1923
Right page: Top left: *Robe poème no. 1328*, 1923. Poem Dress No. 1328
Top right: *Robe poème no. 688*, 1922. Poem Dress No. 688
Bottom left: Pajamas for Tristan Tzara, 1923
Bottom right: Yellow Dancer. Costume design for the play *Le Cœur à Gaz*, 1923

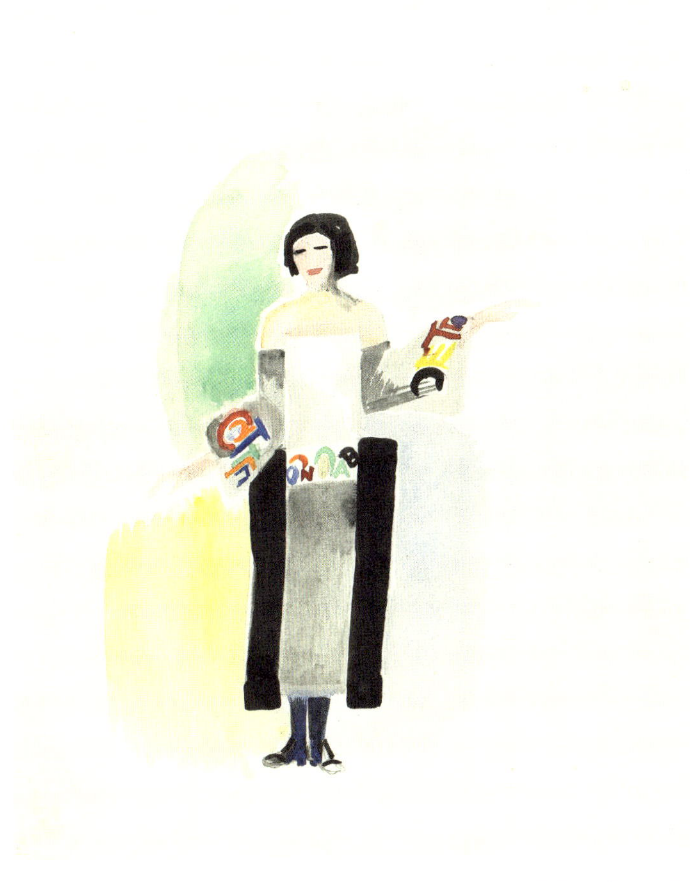

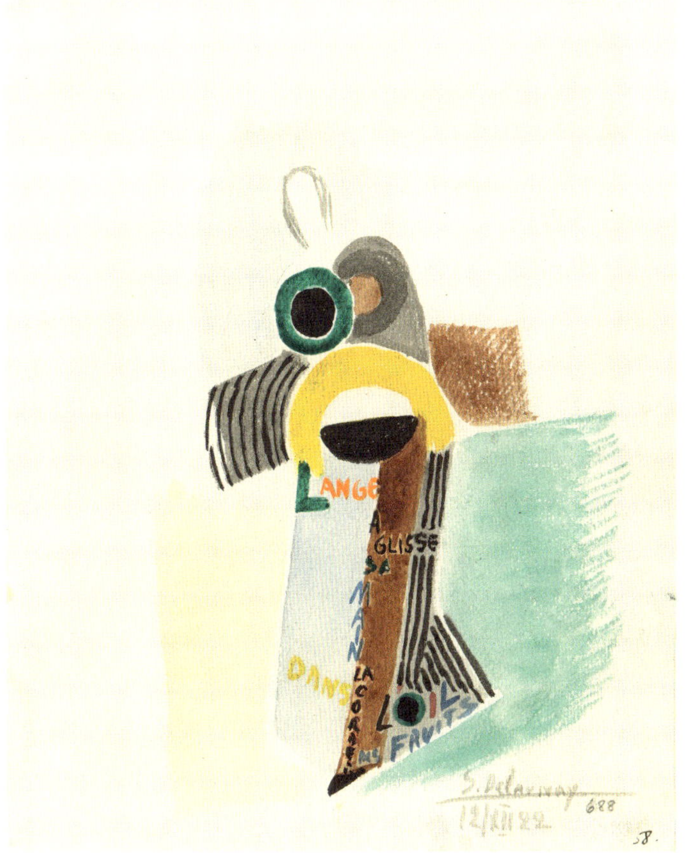
LANGE
A
GLISSE
SA
MAIN
DANS
LA
FRUITS
S. Delaunay
688

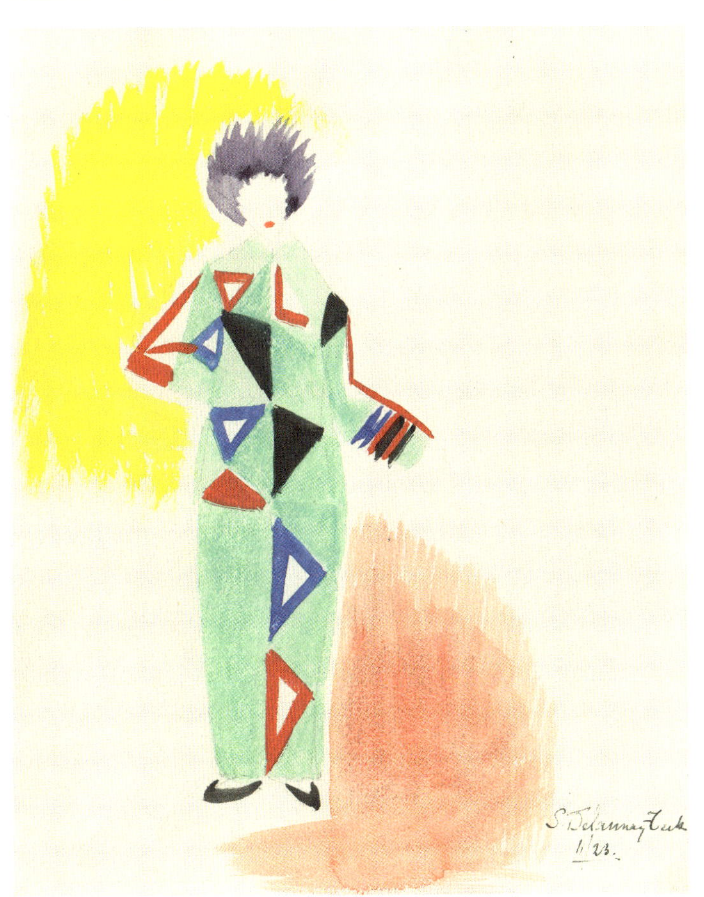

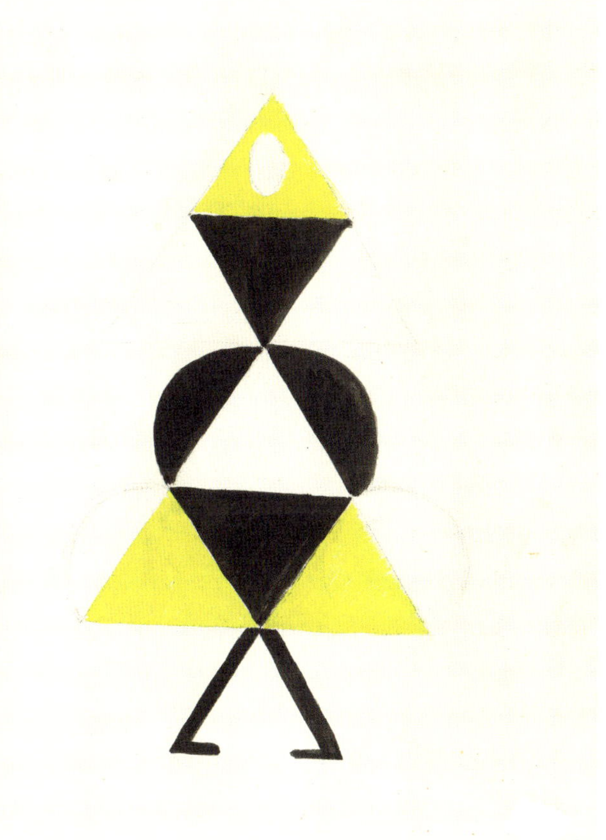

ART CRITICISM AND THE PROBLEM OF THE NON-MODERN STORY OF MODERN ART

Griselda Pollock

For four decades of the 20th century, abstraction was considered the destination of modern art. Abstraction was defined either by intellectual puritanism or by spiritual intensity. In its expressionist form, abstraction touched both the soul and the essence of the world's being. In the geometric inclination, it spoke to the intellect and to the structure of the world beyond mere appearance. Is it possible to accommodate to the elevated status of abstraction the idea that some of its key forms were reached by a woman before they were reached by men? How can art history thus recognise Sonia Delaunay, who has been permitted a respected place only on the sidelines of the history of modern and abstract art?

The fate of the modernist woman in art is a paradox. Modernist culture made it possible for ambitious, searching and creative women to enjoy new freedoms of movement, travel, living arrangements, and access to art education and exhibition. Modernist Paris became a centre for women, alongside men, from all over the world. Art history's account of art in the modern era has, in effect, failed to be modern. The discipline of art history retains pre-modern concepts of gender, resulting in a written history of art that is almost entirely masculine. Shockingly, the exclusion of women from the contemporary art historical record has been more systematic during the modern period than at any time in the history of art.

This contradiction – between the visibility of women making modern art side by side with men, and their effacement from the public record, or their marginal, supplementary status – still shapes any writing about artists who are women in the modern period. Thus an exhibition now dedicated to Sonia Delaunay has the appearance of 'recovery', rediscovery and reinstatement. It cannot, however, banish the ghost of doubt created by the disjunction between what may be claimed *now* about the importance of Sonia Delaunay to the historical moment of chromatic abstraction and the evidence of a relative silence over the preceding century.

Sonia Delaunay arrived in Paris in 1906 with a solid professional bourgeois upbringing, education and exposure to the cultural wealth of Europe, and as an artistically trained woman of independent means ready to resist the destiny that her background in the Russian Jewish bourgeoisie, into which she had been adopted, decreed for her sex, class and assimilating ethnicity. Since 1905, a critical moment, several of the marginal figures of the fragile Parisian avant-garde of the late nineteenth century would enter the imaginations of hungry young artists through a series of retrospective exhibitions at the Salon d'Automne: Manet (1905), Courbet and Gauguin (1906), Berthe Morisot and Cézanne (1907). Despite the egalitarianism of the first modernist movements in the later nineteenth century, we now tell the history of art as the history of the wild young men who showed at these exhibitions and as the history of the influence of the preceding generation, whose implications were waiting to be harvested. One line of descent passes through Cézanne to Cubism and abstraction. Another can be traced through the impact of Van Gogh and Gauguin on the Fauves. But clearly Gauguin's paintings, in colour structure and, I would contend, in his embrace of and reintroduction into the metropole of aesthetic as well as cultural otherness, seems to have been particularly stimulating for certain artists who were women. The pathway through Gauguin's colour led Sonia Terk, as she then was, to the revelations that a lifetime of painting would develop: the autonomy of colour, and the relationality of colour as logic for sustaining a pictorial entity. Something of this daring which precipitated the possibility of abstract or 'inobjectif' (non-objective) art, flew in the face of the existing combat between Fauves and emergent Cubists, but also between those seeking a non-structural reading of Cézanne holding to the Impressionist and Neo-Impressionist discovery of colour as light, or light as colour. Undertaking something so unprecedented, Sonia Terk found in the artist she would marry, Robert Delaunay, both sympathy and difference. Sympathy could sustain standing against the Cubist current; difference enabled two extremely creative artists to coexist without confusion or hierarchy. Yet socialized behaviors still led women to protect men from a rivalry with their wives that they, the men, could not handle, while the women could manage to sustain self-belief at the same time as protecting masculine egos. In addition, the political events that destroyed the economic foundation of the Delaunays' bourgeois class position in 1917, combined with the traditional Jewish customs in which women work to support scholarly men, made Sonia Delaunay-Terk adapt her creativity in line with what in fact was not unusual among Russian artists on either side of the Revolutionary opposition: engagement with textiles and art in daily life. Making things for daily use was not a turn to decorative art; it was the extension of the most advanced art to the living world

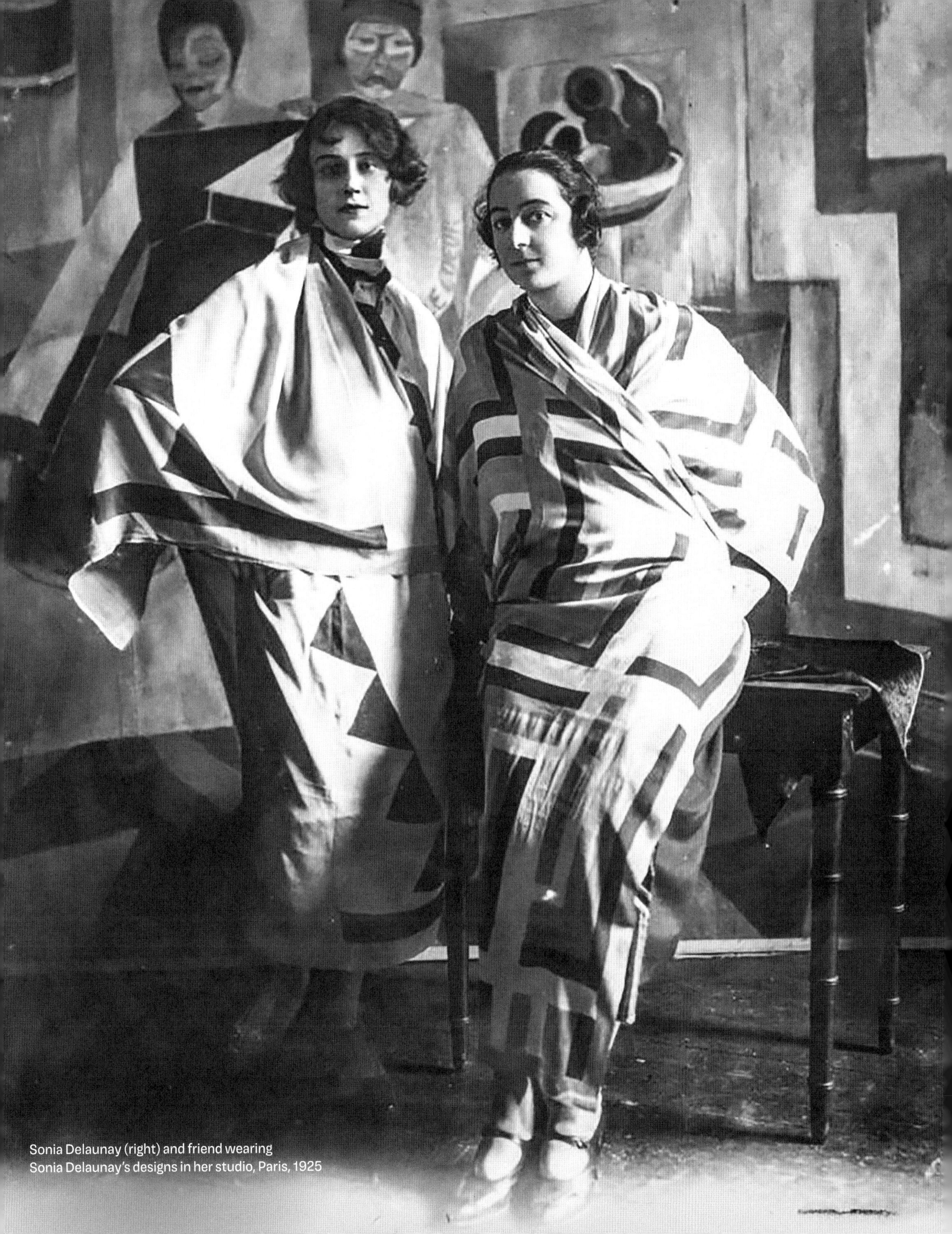

Sonia Delaunay (right) and friend wearing
Sonia Delaunay's designs in her studio, Paris, 1925

in line with a progressive modernist ethos shared among the many women from Russian lands congregating in Paris.

We need to understand the events of c. 1905 to 1917 in order to make sense of the moment, post 1945, when after the premature loss of her husband in 1941, and having survived the war years, Sonia Delaunay dedicated herself to painting in oil and gouache, exhibiting regularly, and receiving belated recognition through a series of appreciative articles and exhibition catalogue essays.

In this post-1945 literature we find typical phrases that placed the artist in relation to Robert Delaunay, such as "For she is also a painter," while stating in the same sentence that she "could sometimes even seem to be ahead of him."[20] The latter author went on to express regret at the time the artist 'wasted' on fashion designing, and to welcome the acclamation of her painting *Rythmes simultanés* (Simultaneous Rhythms) at the Salon des Réalités Nouvelles of 1948 as the most beautiful of the 700 abstract paintings on show.[21]

Another author writing in 1953 asserted the indissoluble bond between husband and wife artists in creating a totally new conception of painting, and he identifies their very different 'masters' (Cézanne versus Gauguin) and trajectories (light versus colour). He quoted, however, a statement from Robert Delaunay himself that exposes the orientalist attitude of Robert to his wife: "Like all artists and poets of the East, she has an atavistic understanding of colour."[22] This is quite shocking. Instead of seeing Sonia Delaunay's intelligent comprehension and transformation of Gauguinism and its residual figuration, Robert attributed Sonia's aesthetic orientation to Eastern origins: did he mean Jewish? Did he mean Ukrainian? Or both, in the eyes of an effete French aristocrat? He thus missed Sonia Delaunay's own participation in the urban Russian fascination with its own 'other': regional peasant material culture and aesthetics. This comment contrasts with the profound intellectual respect and intense sensibility with which Sonia Delaunay consistently spoke of her rapport with and support for Robert. Having introduced Robert Delaunay's orientalism with its side-effect of 'orientalising', essentialising and de-intellectualising Sonia Delaunay, Degand's essay then quotes Delaunay again who notes that Sonia Delaunay's evolution bypassed Cubism and attended more to Matisse, although in the preceding paragraph Degand has noted that the artist saw little but academicism in Matisse, having arrived at her own sense of colour before ever seeing his work.

Writing in 1956, Léon Degand sought to recuperate Sonia Delaunay's concurrent work in furniture, interior design, fabric design and fashion. Official narratives of modern art are flawed by their lack of *modernist* consciousness with regard to transgressing boundaries between forms of art as well as art and the everyday. This results in the systemic failure to recognise how widespread, how politically progressive were the many attempts by many modernists, men as well as women, to bridge the fields of esoteric artistic research and the aesthetic infiltration of daily life and material culture. The problem arises if a woman bridges abstract painting and making abstract designs. She falls prey to the stereotype that has divided the pure artist from the applied artisan, the intellectual from the decorative designer. Sonia Delaunay was only welcomed back into the category of high art once she had returned exclusively to painting that alone functions as the legitimate site of art *tout court*.

Herta Wescher's 1958 text on abstract painting exposes the challenge to art criticism and art history of a man and woman who demonstrate "mutual inspiration" and pursue "the parallelism of shared paths."[23] To maintain the hierarchy of gender, the text falls into another stereotype of art discourse. Line is masculine; colour is feminine. Robert Delaunay, also engaged in colour, must be described as 'virile' while Sonia Delaunay's poetry is considered 'retenue' (restrained). Instead of grasping the difference between artists, critics impose on them fixed ideas of sexual difference: robust versus withdrawn, tough versus gentle and so forth. This non-modern 'political unconscious' has disfigured the reception of Sonia Delaunay as a key artistic intelligence in the creation of modern art.

By the early 1960s, art critical writing became more forthright in its appreciation. R.V. Gindertaël, writing of the artist under the title "la poésie pure des couleurs" ("the pure poetry of colour"), represents a trend to associate women artists with the poetic, even though Sonia Delaunay's favoured image of her delicate and nervous husband was as a poet. Gindertaël quoted Sonia's insistence on Robert's primacy while concluding that it was clear that the idea of simultaneous contrast would not have emerged without her colour research and methods.[24] Again, the difficulty of theoretically holding together abstract art and decorative art emerges as a problem in the reputation of Sonia Delaunay.[25] In an essay written in 1960 for a joint exhibition of both Robert and Sonia Delaunay, Guy Weelen interwove a story focusing on Robert with asides on Sonia. Weelen identified as the latter's core objective the quest 'to break free from the shackles of the static outline of the object and its will to translate dynamism by the resources of colour alone'.[26] He noted that, when both artists exhibited in Germany in 1913, Paul Klee was influenced by Robert 's work while Sonia impacted on August Macke and Franz Marc. The issue of lineage, descent and influence constitutes a critical and legitimating aspect of the narrative of modern art. Rarely are women allowed to exercise influence. They are the influenced, learning from the masters but never functioning themselves as the 'master', and never influencing the course of art history or another artist.

By the later 1960s, following the donation of works by both artists to the Musée National d'Art Moderne in 1964, Bernard Dorival could positively affirm that Sonia Delaunay was one of the first abstract artists and that she was one of the rare and original artists to bring art into daily life. Nonetheless, it is for abstraction that the museum can now embrace her work. Yet by 1967, or in his later piece in 1971 on her recent paintings, it was too late to make this assertion. The museums of modern art had made their choices, built their collections, laid out their galleries, written their publications, with a story of art that left no space for almost any artist who was a woman. However many exhibitions were held after 1967 to frame Sonia Delaunay as an abstract painter and not just as a working wife who made designs, they came too late. The story of modern art had been established. Now all women would become mere additions.

In 1971, Sonia Delaunay was 86. She had made her breakthroughs in her 20s. This means she lived to overlap with the feminist critique of the exclusions of art history. In a series of interviews with women artists of the 20th century from the 1920s to her present, the American critic Cindy Nemser spoke with Sonia Delaunay. It is a fascinating and frustrating text to read.[27] Nemser is full of a feminist discourse of discrimination and difficulty. Sonia Delaunay is uncooperative. Like so many of the modernist women of her generation, she had embraced modern art precisely as a means to escape the over-feminisation of a woman's place and destiny. Being an artist, living among those escaping much of the formality of bourgeois expectations, and daring to change the very nature of art did not, for that generation, have anything to do with gender. They believed that the modern was the beginning of the new, the free, the uncharted. They would play their part in the modern as creative artists going beyond all existing bounds. When the elderly and belatedly recognised Sonia Delaunay encountered emerging feminist critique, she could not understand the tone, the attitude or especially the anger of younger women. With enormous dignity she explained that she had always done exactly what she wanted and what she felt was necessary. Her brief answers make for difficult reading. But they are part and parcel of what we need to learn from both parties to this interview.

Sonia Delaunay represents an artist enabled by her deep involvement with the modernist project in art. Her own practice flowered by working in comfortable and mutual stimulation with an artist whose ability she could also respect, and to support whose more fragile creativity she was more than capable of making their living in the world of exciting new fields of design and fashion. But what she could not anticipate was that the art historians and museum directors, and even the art critics who apparently respected her, would remain trapped in and even become the most adamant practitioners of a sexism that made the idea of women as intrinsic players in the making of modernism unthinkable.

Stressing that women make art as much because of as despite the difference society imposes on them, feminist art history has uncovered entire networks of women artists, and has reframed the hierarchies that cut high art off from material culture and daily life, studio from politics, creativity from lived lives.[28] We will never 'see' the singularity and particularity of Sonia Delaunay-Terk so long as we try to 'fit her in' to the official story constructed out of the ruinous partiality of a non-modern history of modern art and culture. The integrated presence of women as co-creators of the modern, in mixed networks and groups and in women-driven networks and groups, is the story waiting to be told in all its wonderful complexity.[29] In some small way the difficulties I have noted in these texts are symptomatic of the role of a hierarchical and gendered discourse to which art history and the museums cling. Sonia Delaunay lived a life of partnership generosity, necessity and sustained research into the field in which she must now be understood as historically an innovator, a creator, a first. But her value lies precisely in never having found that claim as important as doing her work faithfully over seventy years and still being a creative force in 1979, just as women awoke from the delusion official art history had created and began to demand to know the real story of art in the 20th century made by women and men together.

Griselda Pollock is a professor of Social and Critical Histories of Art at the University of Leeds, England. She is an accomplished art historian, who has specialized in feminist studies in the visual arts and critical studies of contemporary art. She is the author of more than 40 books.
Griselda Pollock's text was first published in the exhibition catalogue *Sonia Delaunay*, London, Tate Modern, 2015.

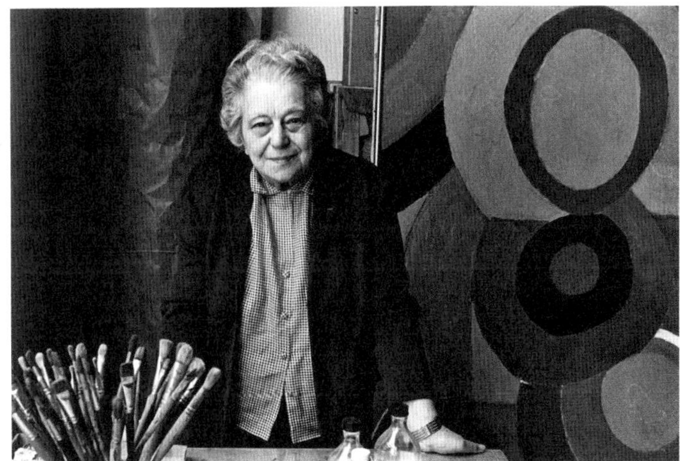

Sidney J. Waintrob: Sonia Delaunay in her studio, 1965
Silver-Gelatine print, 23 × 34 cm. Collection Albright-Knox Art Gallery, Buffalo, New York; Gift of the Waintrob Family, 1980

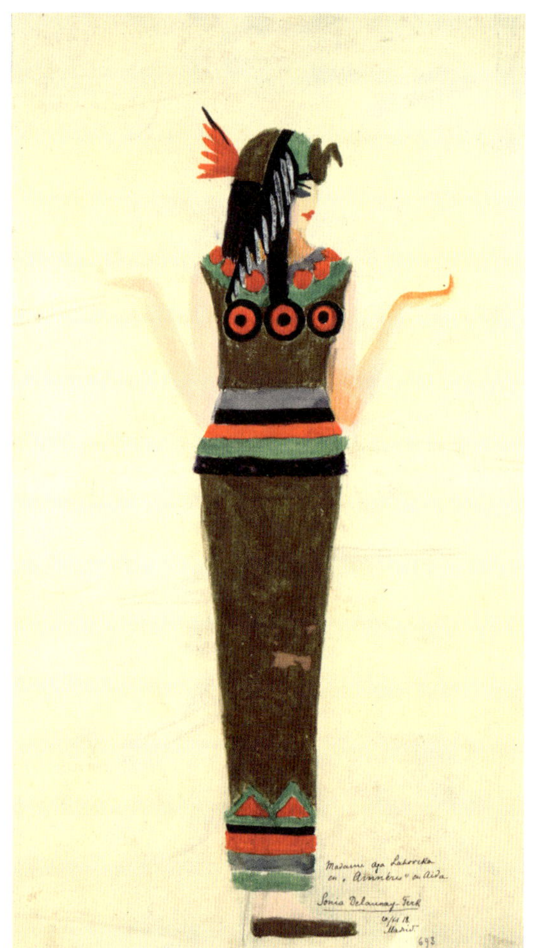

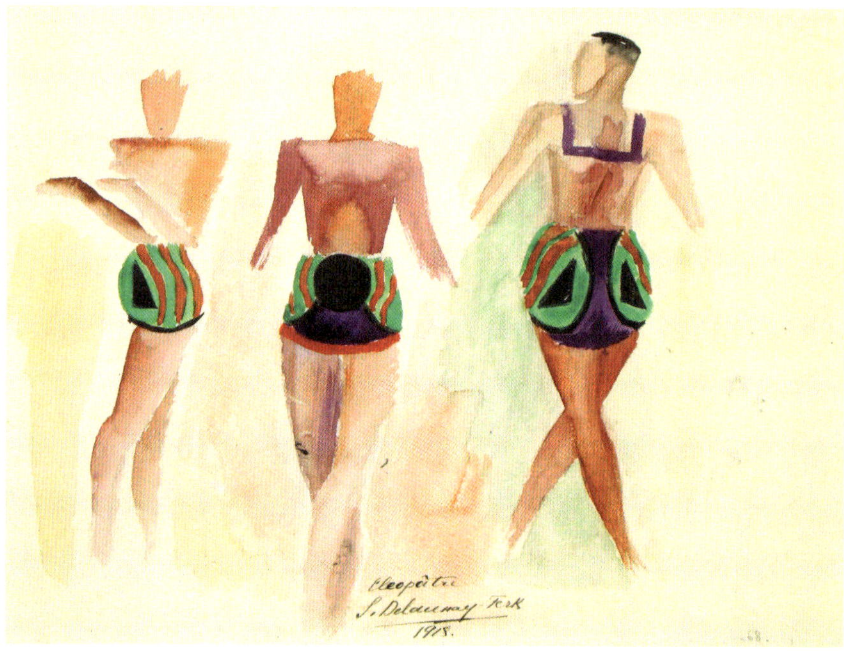

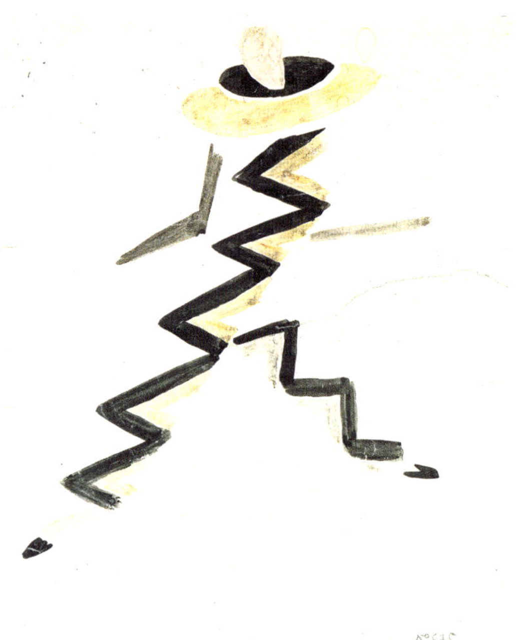

Top left: Costume design for Cleopatra for the ballet *Cléopâtre*, 1918
Top right: Costume design for (Léonid) Massine for the ballet *Cléopâtre*, 1918
Bottom: Pierrot Éclair, 1926. Flash Pierrot for the film *Le P'tit Parigot* (The Small Parisian One), 1926
Right page: Lizica Codreano wearing Pierrot Éclair costume designed by Sonia Delaunay, 1926

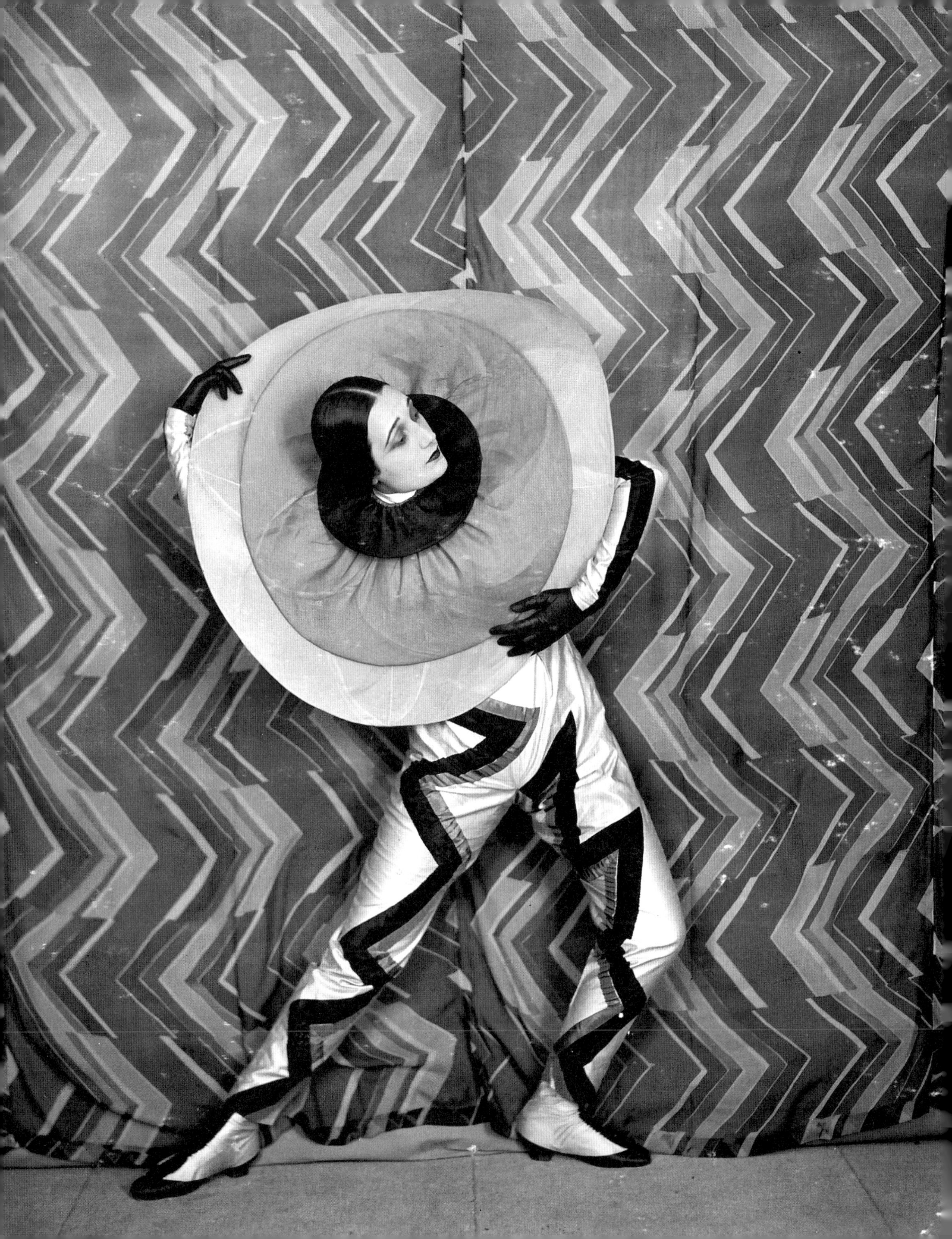

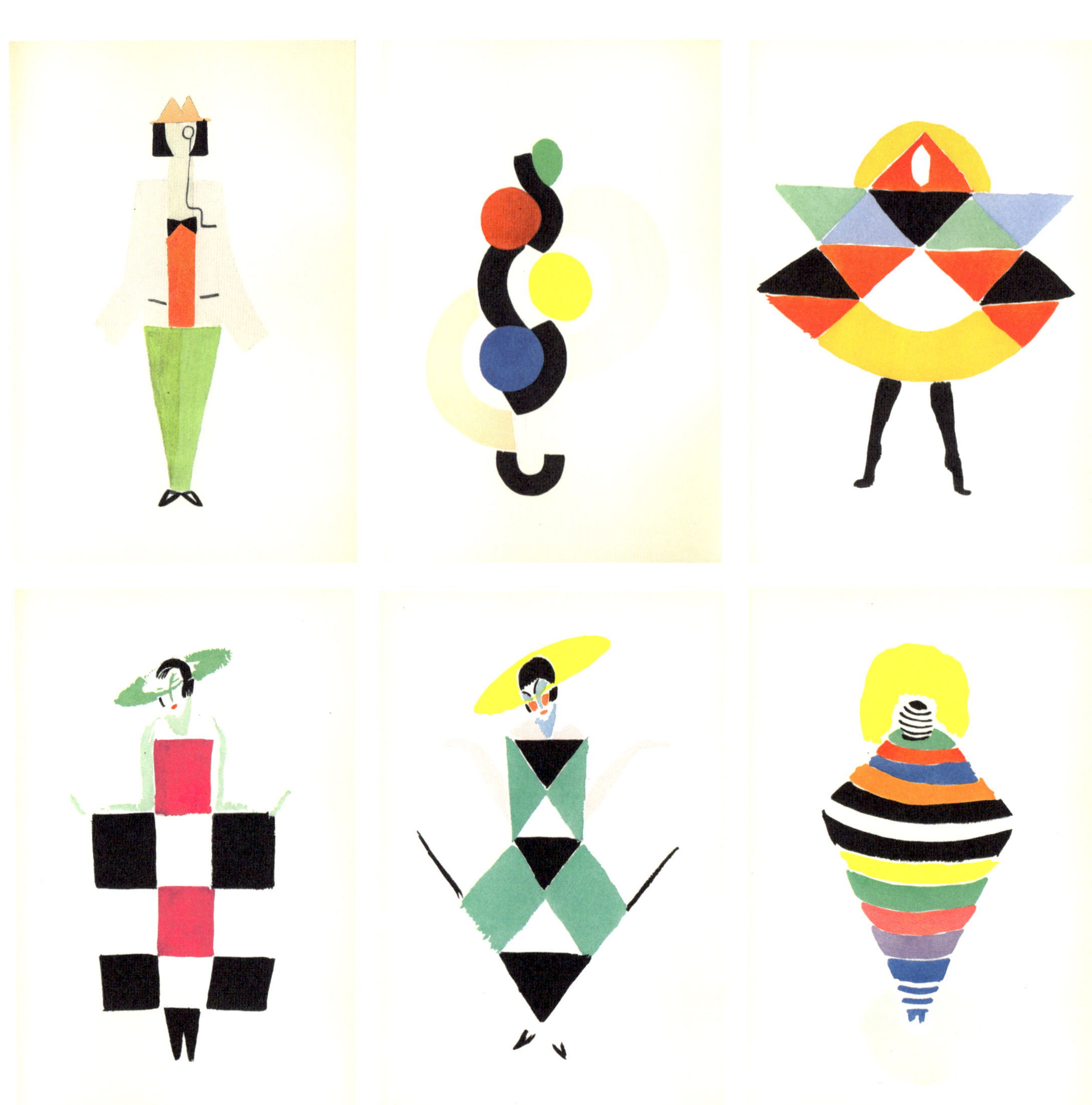

Fashion and costume designs from 1922-1928 in *27 tableaux vivants*, 1969

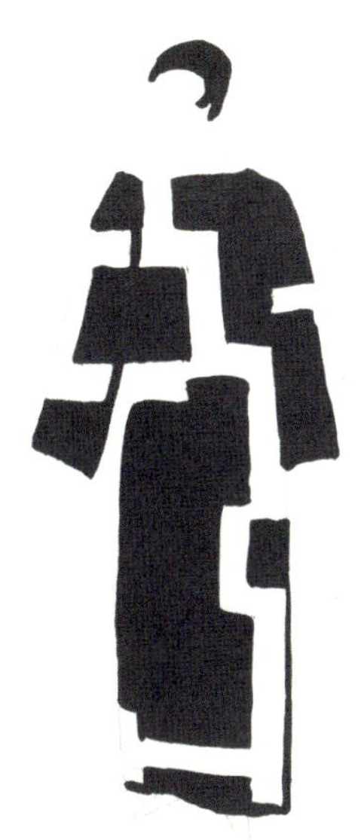
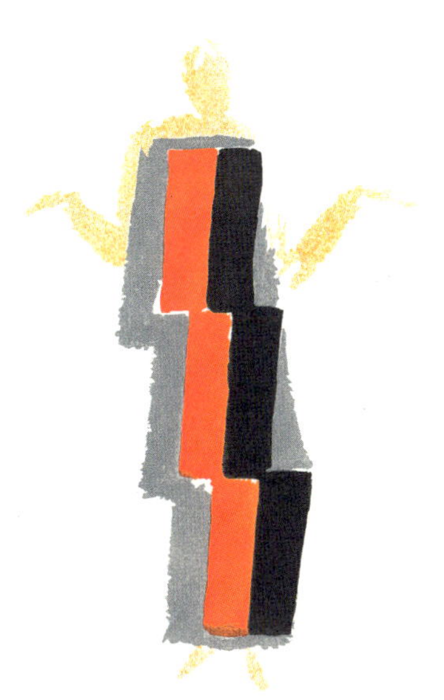
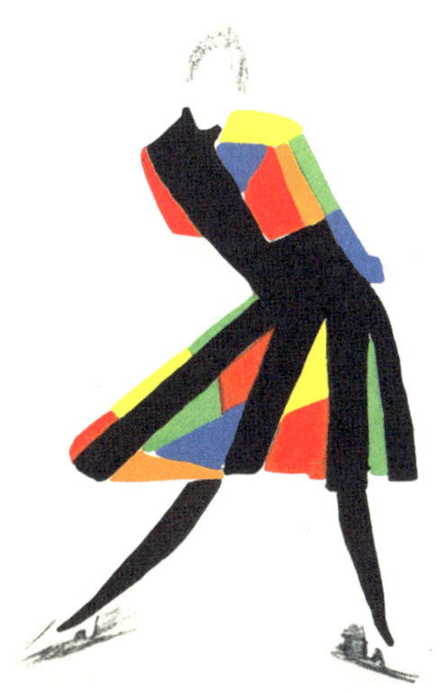
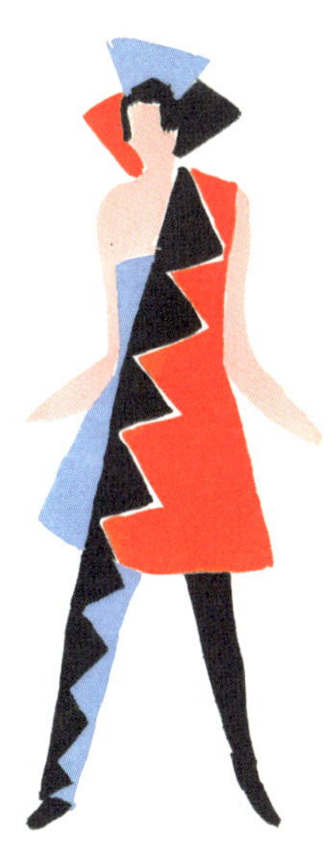
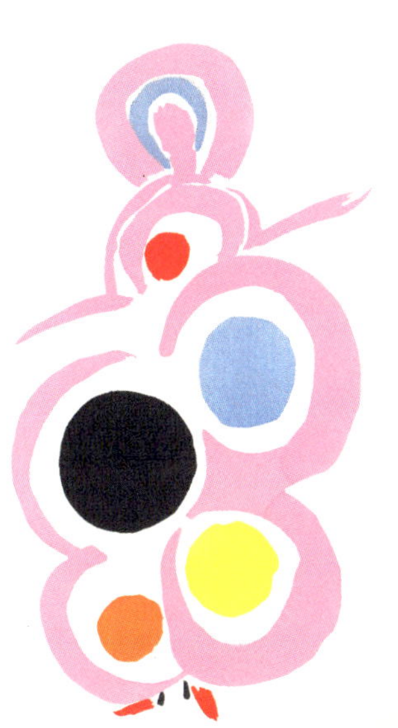
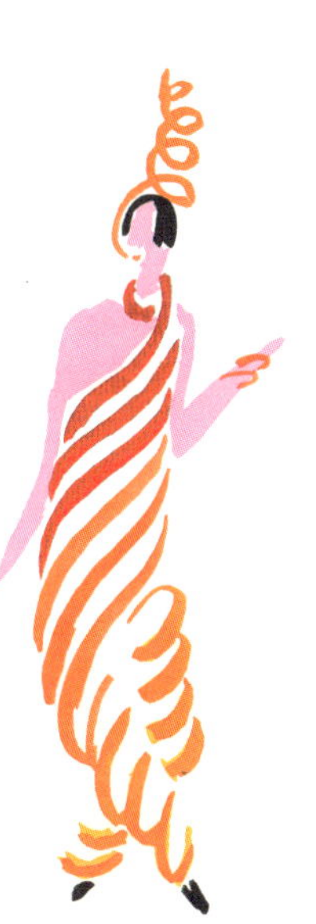

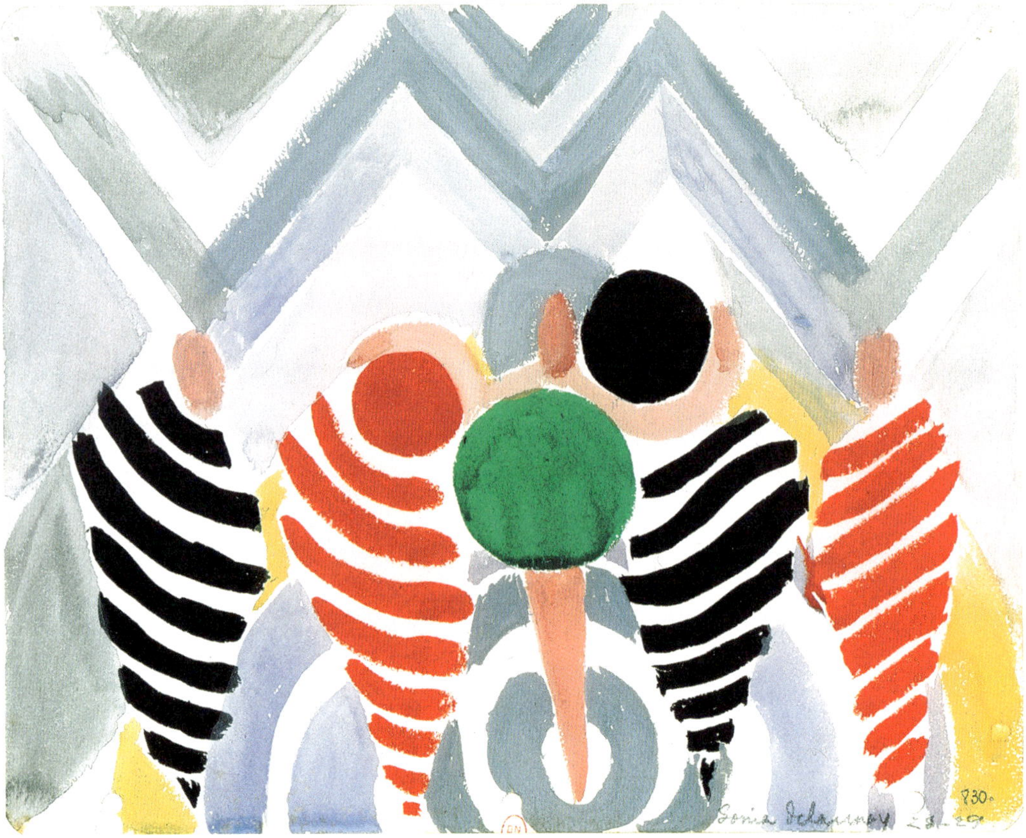

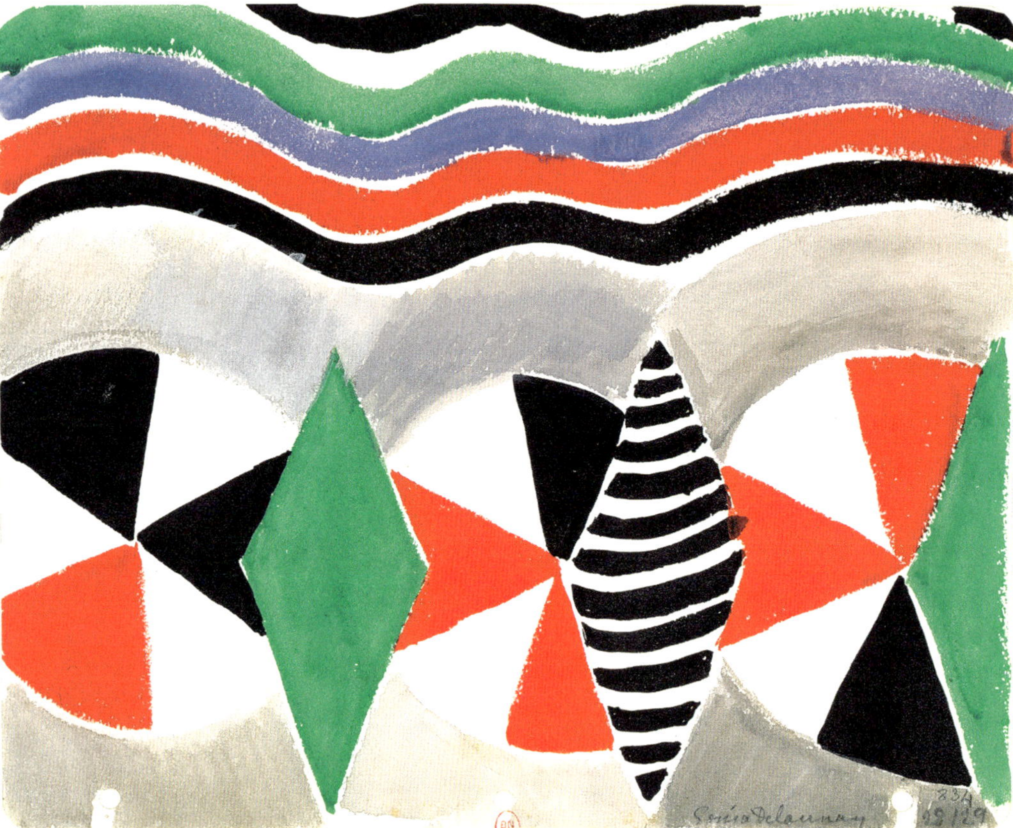

Top: Set design for the ballet *The Four Seasons*. Spirals on a background of herringbones and circles, 1928-1929
Bottom: Set design for the ballet *The Four Seasons*. Red, black, white parasols. Sea with waves, 1928-1929

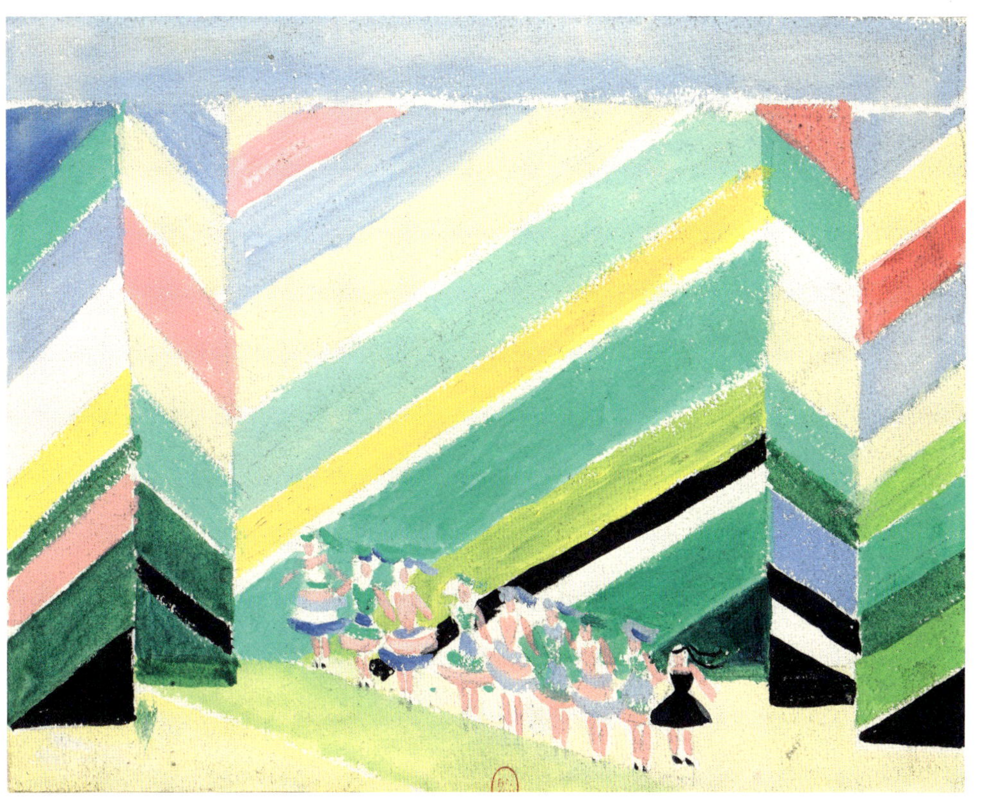

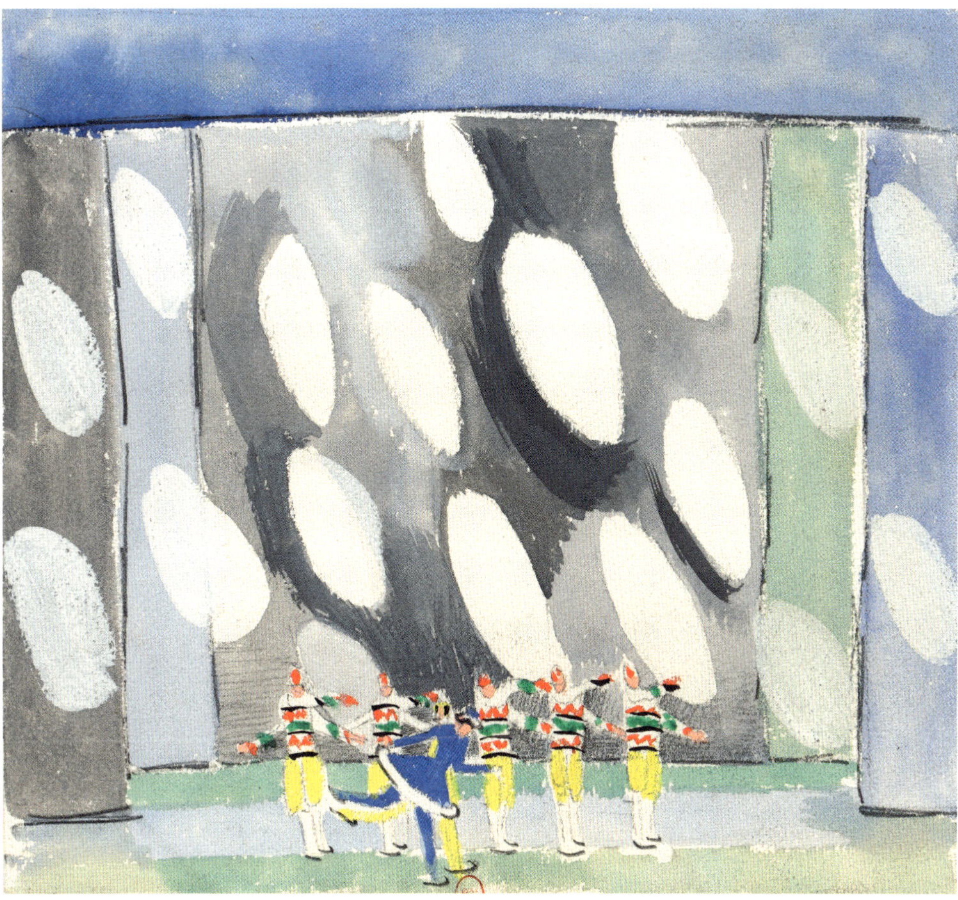

Top: Set design for the ballet *The Four Seasons*. Spring, 1928-1929
Bottom: Set design for the ballet *The Four Seasons*. Winter, 1928-1929

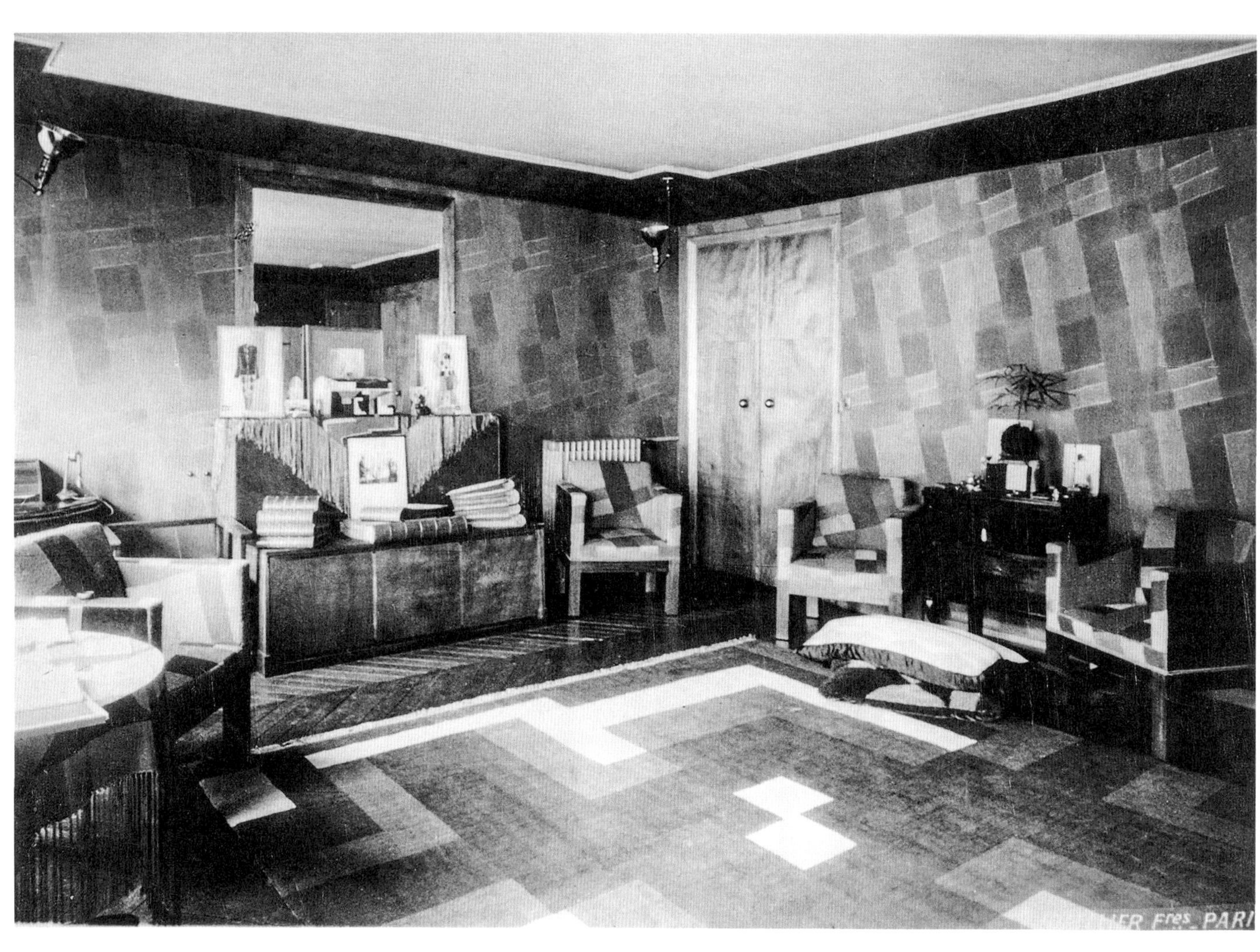

Living room in the Delaunay couple's apartment, Boulevard Malesherbes, Paris, c. 1925
Wall coverings, furniture, pillows and carpet designed by Sonia Delaunay

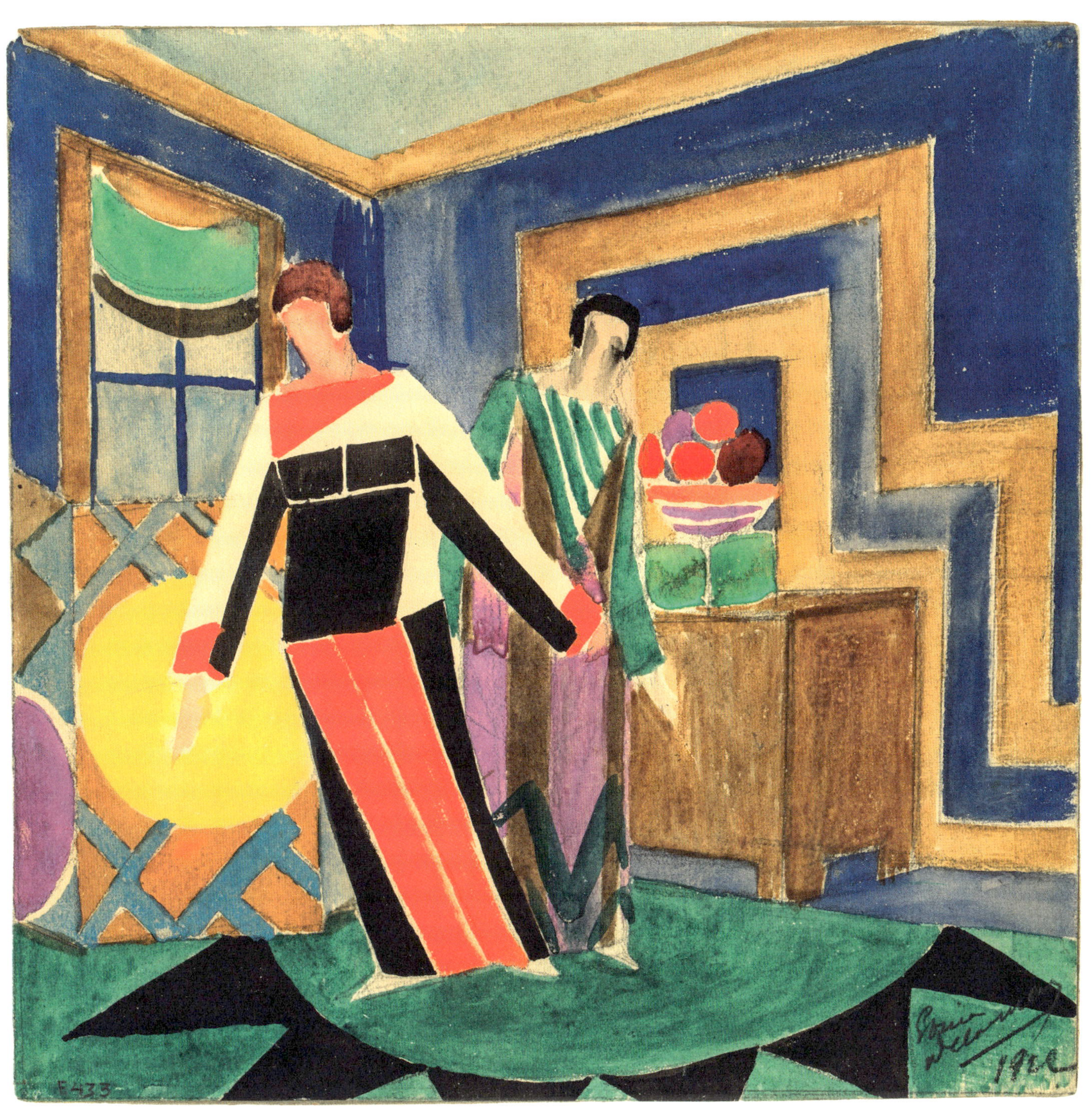

Scène d'intérieur, 1923. Indoor Scene

WHAT SONIA DELAUNAY-TERK'S PHOTOGRAPHIC PORTRAITS TELL US ABOUT THE ARTIST

Anne Montfort-Tanguy

In 1967, the Musée National d'Art Moderne devoted a retrospective to Sonia Delaunay-Terk – its first. Bringing together nearly two hundred works, it was the only major Parisian exhibition to have shown her activity in the applied arts as well as her recent paintings and youthful creations. For the artist, it was a consecration: the reviews were laudatory, she was interviewed on radio and television. It was also the culmination of a long quest for recognition. Already, in 1964, the major donation of her and Robert Delaunay's works to the Musée National d'Art Moderne, accompanied by a grand exhibition in the Louvre's Galerie Mollien the same year, should have enabled Delaunay-Terk to achieve that goal, but its results were mixed. Although in the end she donated more of her works than Delaunay's – 67 as opposed to 47 – it was the latter that seem to have captured the attention of the organisers. Jean Cassou raved in his preface about "the powerful creations of Robert Delaunay" but mentioned Delaunay-Terk only as "a creator of fabrics, bindings, and objects in the Cubist style."[30] She certainly suffered from several handicaps, not least being the range of media covered by her work. Despite the avant-gardes, the distinction between fine and applied arts persisted (the quality of the latter often being judged uniquely in terms of craft skills). And while the originality of her early works was undeniable – their dates established her as one of the pioneers of abstraction –, the longevity of her career and her fidelity to principles established before the war made the contemporaneity of her late paintings seem questionable. And finally but not all trivially, Delaunay-Terk was a woman and, moreover, the wife of a famous artist, and so, according to still prevalent misogynistic assumptions, could at best be only Delaunay's muse or epigone. The story could have ended there, but Delaunay-Terk realised that her work was being swallowed up by her husband's. A few years later, in her autobiography, she referred to all "The things they said about me – muse of Orphism, decorator, companion of Robert Delaunay – before finally admitting that the work existed in its own right."[31]

Woman With a Brush

Thirteen years later, Delaunay-Terk gave the Bibliothèque Nationale de France a substantial collection of drawings, prints, bound books, manuscripts, photographs and documents of all kinds. While the wealth of correspondence and autographed books in this donation certainly confirmed the importance of the Delaunay couple (as the nodal point of a network of artists and writers), Sonia's diaries also got across her version of the story. With the help of Jacques Damase, the following year she published her autobiography *Nous irons jusqu'au soleil* (Paris, Robert Laffont, 1978). But what is even more striking about this collection carefully prepared by the artist is the ubiquity of photographs. Of course, Delaunay-Terk lived through the golden age of photography, when every stage of life, every event, was captured for posterity by posing for a professional photographer, and then – after the ritual acquisition of a camera – for a member of the family (in this instance, Delaunay). In this abundance of photographs, the themes of which recall family archives everywhere, one particular set stands out, its purposes above all professional. It comprises fashion photographs featuring the artist's designs, reportage on the site of the 1937 *Exposition Universelle* and numerous portraits, some of them made for publication. To decipher the latter is to become aware of the way in which the artist controlled her image and the messages she sought to convey. For example, in a photograph dated 1966 (bottom page 41), Delaunay-Terk poses smiling with a telephone handset pressed to her ear. She is wearing a Chanel suit, which she made into a kind of post-war uniform. The image is intended to reassure (the artist is a very proper bourgeois woman), while at the same time signalling not only her vitality – she is so busy that, despite the presence of the photographer, she has not been able to hang up – but also her modernity, since she is using the latest means of communication. In the same vein, in December 1967 she appeared on a television entertainment show, agreeing to have the set made from drawings of hers, enlarged to the point of being psychedelic. Answering questions put by the singer Jacques Dutronc, she came across as full of self-confidence and explained that not only had she witnessed the birth of modernity, but that she was also one of its protagonists. Abstraction had long since ceased to be a matter for the initiated. Hanging on the walls of museums, its forms had been popularised by cheap design and it was on the way to becoming the official art of the 20th century. For Delaunay-Terk, it was therefore important to emphasise that she was not a follower but an initiator, that her art was not based on a formula but was the result of an original creative process. Hence the importance of another trope in her photographic portraits in which she poses standing in the studio with a brush in her hand in front of a canvas set on an easel (bottom of this page and bottom of page

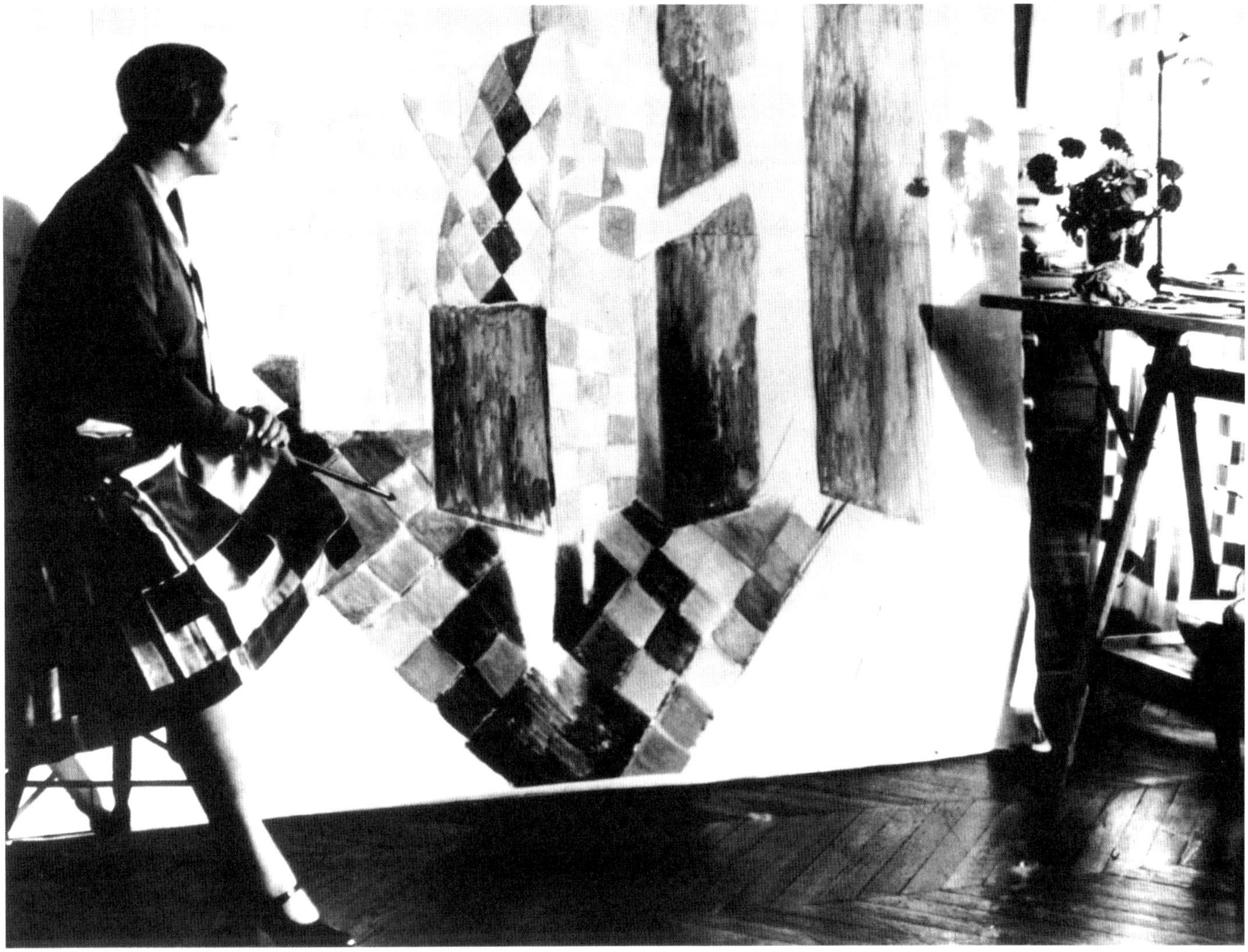

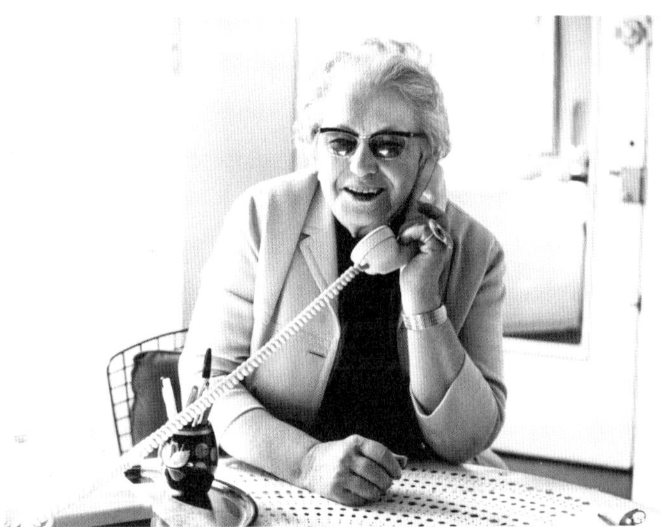

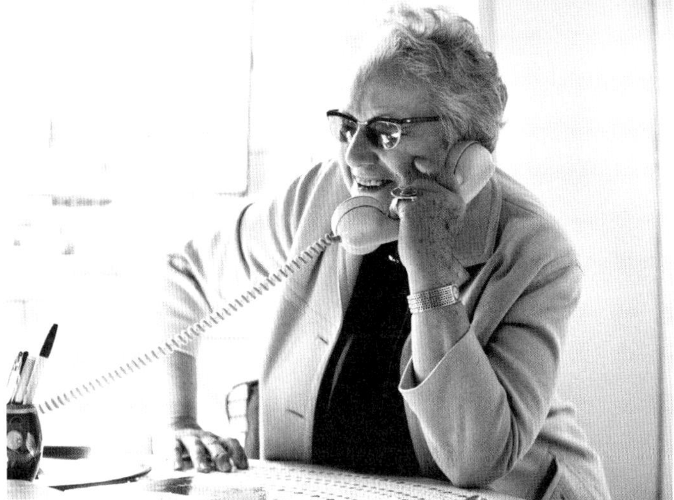

Top: Sonia Delaunay in her studio, Boulevard Malesherbes, Paris, 1925
Bottom: Wölbing-van Dyck: Sonia Delaunay, 1966

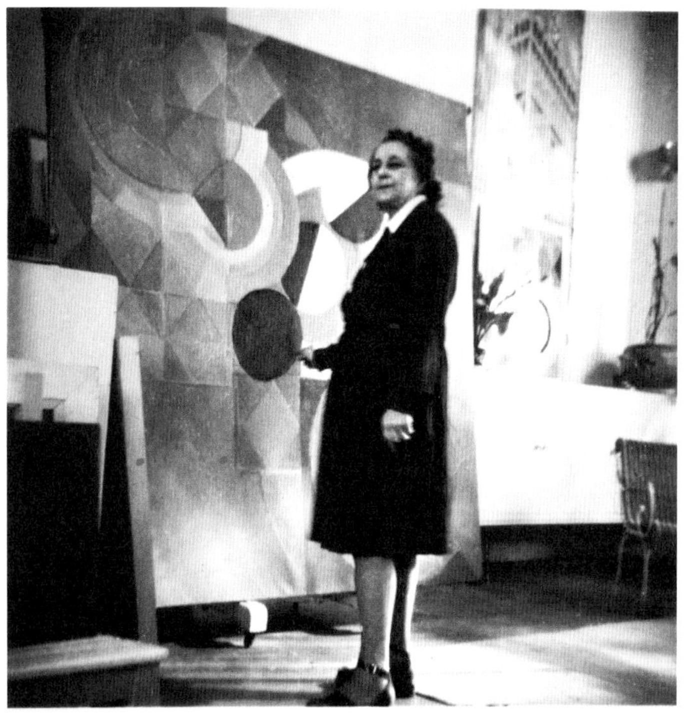

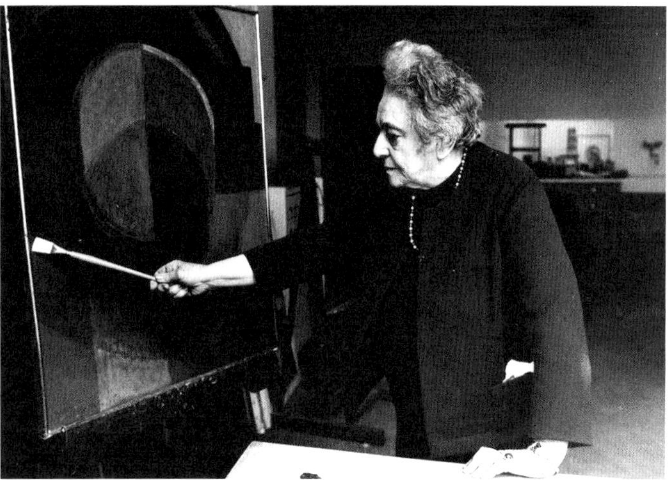

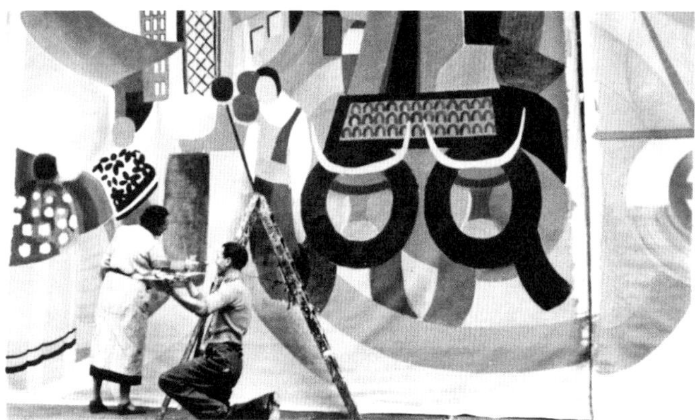

Top: Sonia Delaunay in her studio in front of the painting *Affreux Jojo*, 1947
Middle: Léon Hershtritt: Sonia Delaunay in her studio, late 1960s
Bottom: Sonia Delaunay working on the mural *Portugal* for the Palais des Chemins de Fer (Railways Pavilion) at The World's Exposition, 1937

89). These pictures[32] do not evoke the artist at work (she is always wearing a suit and court shoes, and the paintings turned towards the camera are manifestly finished), but they all emphasise her status as a painter. They are in keeping with the long tradition of self-portraits in which, emancipating himself from his condition as a craftsman, the painter represented himself in court costume and, later, formal wear, retaining only his symbolic attributes (the painting, the brush or the easel).[33] Delaunay-Terk was by now considered a painter in her own right and all the patterns she had designed were deployed in her paintings, drawings and engravings.

Thus *Rythme syncopé,* dit *Le serpent noir* (Syncopated Rhythm, known as The Black Snake, 1967, page 23) reuses both the undulating black band with which she had decorated a scarf in 1924, and the coloured squaring of the endpapers from the binding of *Pâques* by Blaise Cendrars, produced in 1913. And if she happened to design carpets, these would not be industrially produced but woven by hand using a traditional technique from the Alpajurras region in Andalusia. It is interesting to note how far the artist has come since a photographic portrait of 1947 (top of this page): although the staging is more or less the same as the one adopted at the end of the 1960s, the canvas on that occasion is unfinished and the artist, holding her brush without conviction, looks towards the lens, thus emphasising the artifice of the gesture. It is true that, in the immediate post-war period, while having resumed her painting activities with unparalleled intensity, Delaunay-Terk was also working hard to gain recognition for her husband's work. She wrote in her diary in 1946: "If one is being completely sincere with oneself, it is only Robert who brings something new and real. I don't disown my things, but they are another sensibility; they have the importance of colour studies [...]."[34]

The Woman-Painting

To find other examples of this kind of portrait of Delaunay-Terk we must go back to the 1920s. Although she occasionally appears in the reportage on the creation of the decorations for the Railways Pavilion and Pavilion of the Air at the *Exposition Internationale des Arts et des Techniques* in 1937, its main purpose was to show a group of painters at work (bottom of this page). Since the crisis of 1929, Delaunay had been thinking about a new kind of artists' association along the lines of a phalanstery, and he saw this exposition as an opportunity to put his ideas into practice. He surrounded himself with collaborators such as Leopold Survage and Delaunay-Terk, and with assistants chosen from among young unemployed artists such as Roger Bissière and Alfred Manessier. The 1920s tell a very different story. At the time Delaunay-Terk, who opened her fashion house in 1925, was more famous than her husband, a fact she liked to recall to her various interlocutors at the end of her life. In 1970, for example, she told Arthur Allen Cohen that "from 1919 to 1930, I had enormous success [...] everywhere, all over the world. With my fabrics – you saw the album from 27 – I made a lot of money."[35] In her autobiography she states that she was "a woman boss" with "a head office, letterhead, advertising leaflets, window displays."[36] In passing, we may note that she seems to single out only the attributes of this activity. She is quick to add, however, that "the business world has always filled me with horror and disgust."[37] For Delaunay-Terk, it was important to emphasise that her textile creations were not "fashion that goes out of fashion [...] women's stuff,"[38] but – and each time she is careful to mention a man whose work she esteems, be it Blaise Cendrars, Joseph Delteil or, in this case, Jacques Damase – "a collection of living paintings."[39] A photograph taken in 1925 shows Delaunay-Terk wearing a skirt and scarf made from fabrics she herself designed, posing in front of a version of *Robes simultanées (Trois femmes, formes, couleurs)* (Simultaneous Dresses (Three Women, Forms, Colours), 1925, page 51), her hand casually dangling a brush (page 41). The painting seems to prolong the scene, its geometric shapes repeating the patterns of the textiles (clothes and curtains), while the women depicted echo the artist's own form. It is not so much a question of fiction imitating reality or vice versa, as of capturing an overall aesthetic. Already, three years earlier, the poem-dresses (page 20 and 27) inspired by the poems of Iliazd, Tristan Tzara, Louis Aragon and Vicente Huidobro, presented a synthesis of the first simultaneous dress created in 1913, and the accordion-fold book *La Prose du Transsibérien et de la Petite Jehanne de France* produced that same year with Cendrars (page 19). Delaunay-Terk never hesitated to wear her own creations, whether in the 1910s or in the 1920s. The famous photograph of the artist in a simultaneous dress dating from 1913 is in itself a manifesto (page 15): more than a garment, the dress is the constitutive element of a kind of performance, the wearer, animating it, metamorphosing it with the slightest gesture. "On the dress she has a body," wrote Cendrars.[40]

Delaunay-Terk's concern to constantly control the image she projected – an issue that seems strangely contemporary today – was accompanied by an early interest in advertising. Fascinated by the spectacle of the hoardings that sprang up on façades at the turn of the last century, she tried her hand at fictitious advertisements in gouache promoting a brand or a product (page 24-25). In fact, this was not advertising in the strict sense of the word (they had no commercial purpose), but the promotional material devised by Delaunay-Terk to promote *La Prose du Transsibérien et de la Petite Jehanne de France* nevertheless shows that she was perfectly familiar with its workings. The prospectus designed by the artist (page 19) aroused the curiosity of journalists and started a controversy even before the poem was published. "We have received a strange leaflet. It is made of cardboard and has the shape of a very elongated quadrilateral. On the back are printed in six different colours these words: "First simultaneous book." The front is altogether more complicated. The cardboard background, divided into sixteen small yellow, green, blue, red, purple, etc. quadrilaterals, bears this sentence whose words vary in hue according to the shade of the quadrilaterals to which they correspond: "Prose outranssibérienne [sic] et de la petite Jeanne de France représentation synchrome peinture simultanée [sic] texte Mme Delaunay-Teyke [sic] Blaise Cendrars [...]." We know nothing more except that the smallest copy of the book announced by the prospectus described above will cost no less than five hundred francs and will be two metres high. Good business for the bookbinders." So wrote Jean de l'Escritoire in the "Gazette des Lettres" column of *Paris-Midi* on 7 October, 1913.[41] Also at this time, the artist was designing letterheads in which the name Delaunay was treated as a brand: inscribed in concentric semi-circles reminiscent of the paintings in the "Prismes" series (page 11), it was followed by a list of capitals ("New York, Paris, Petrograd, Tokyo, London, Berlin"), like so many head offices. Yet (and although she accepted the fact that she had been a businesswoman in the 1920s), Delaunay-Terk was relentless in her condemnation of what she perceived as the commercial excesses of art[42] and would never conceive of her activity as what Andy Warhol called "business art." It would be simplistic, however, to attribute this rejection to her loyalty to traditional values, for ever since her adolescence Delaunay-Terk had tried to escape her condition as a Jewish woman, and asserting her status as an artist was the first way of freeing herself from her original milieu, claiming to be an artist of the international avant-garde, capable of working in all media, of emancipating herself from the milieu in which she lived, of escaping all forms of categorisation. A free woman to the end, she saw herself as one of the heroines of modernity who, in the spirit of Charles Baudelaire's "Beacons," opens the way for future generations.

Anne Montfort-Tanguy is curator at the Musée National d'Art Moderne in Paris. Historian of 20th century art and specialist in graphic arts, she has curated many exhibitions, and is particularly interested in artists who have been marginalized by their unconventional creations (Sonia Delaunay, Stephane Mandelbaum, Wols, Saül Steinberg). She co-curated with Cécile Godefroy the retrospective *Sonia Delaunay* at Musée d'Art Moderne in Paris and Tate Modern, London, in 2014-15. She publishes articles in magazines and catalogues on abstraction and on the making of its history on a regular basis.

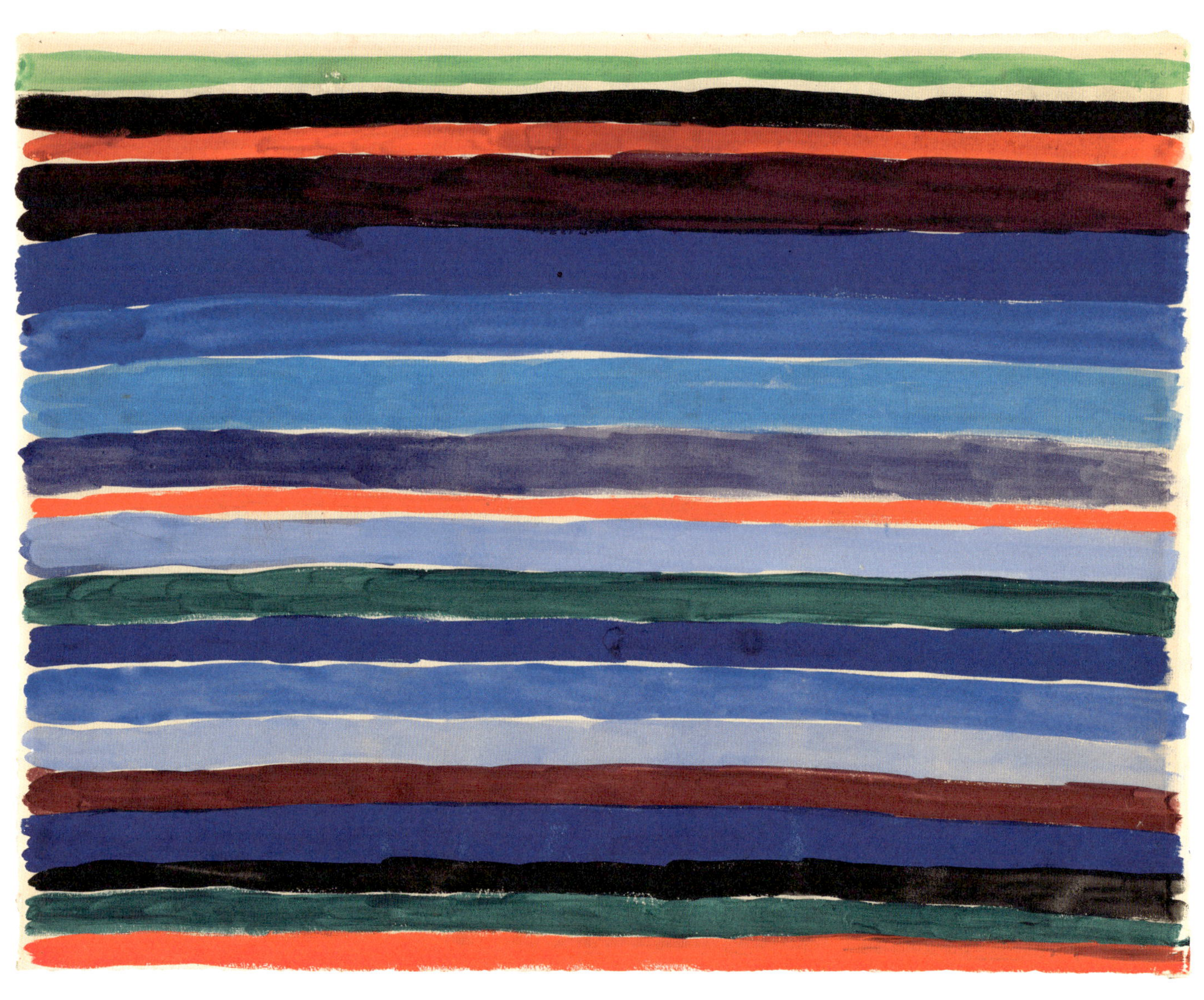

Design for Simultané fabric, 1937
Right page: Top: Design for Simultané fabric, No. 186, 1926
Bottom left: Design for Simultané fabric, No. 156, 1926
Bottom right: Design for Simultané fabric, No. 170, 1926

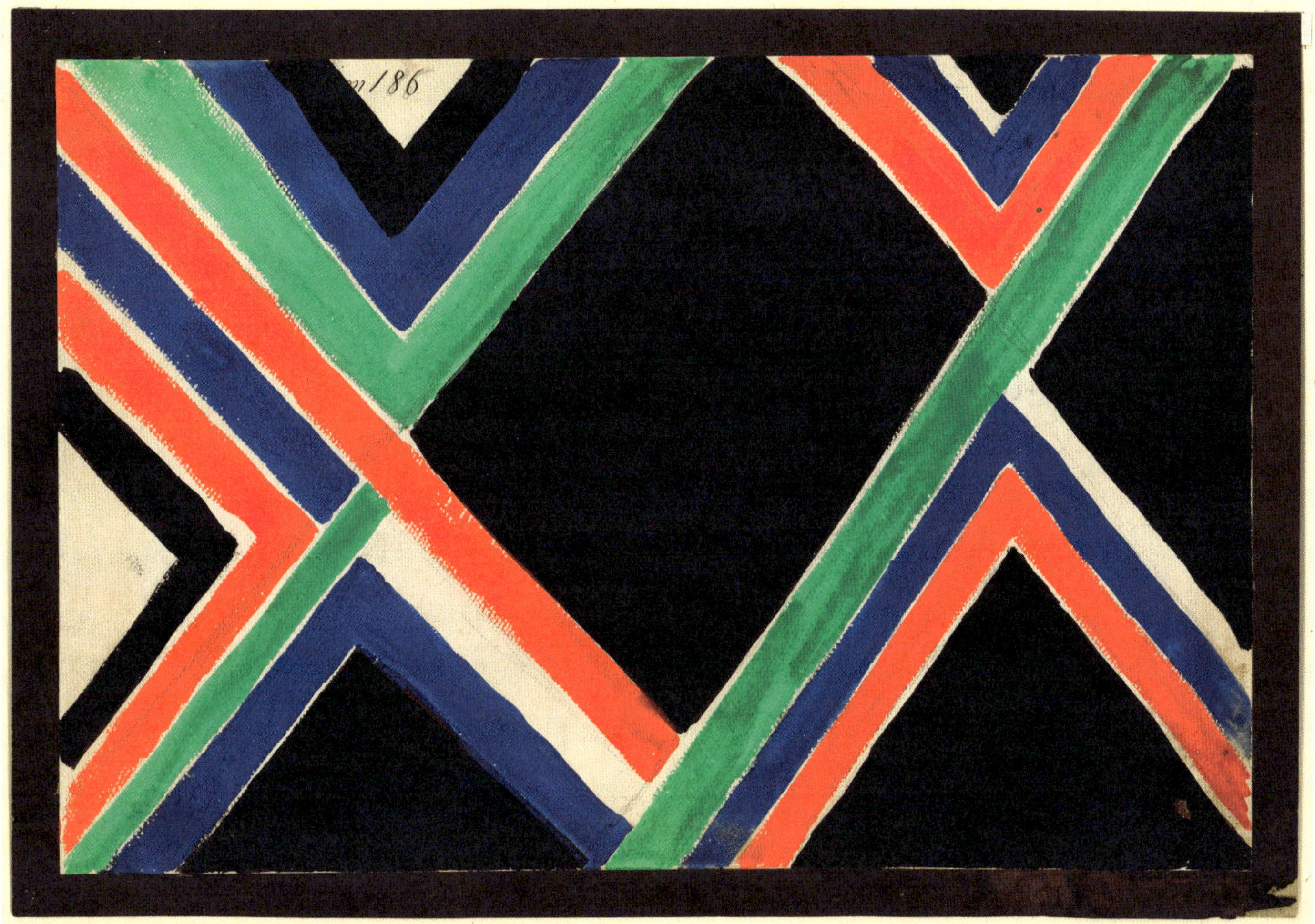

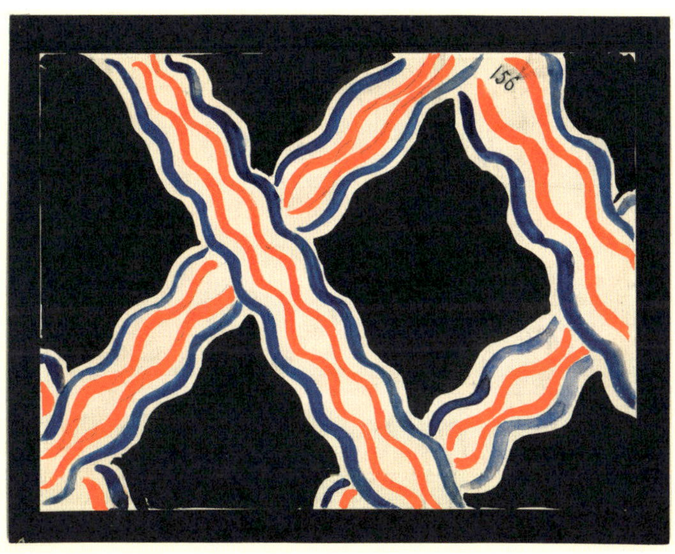
156

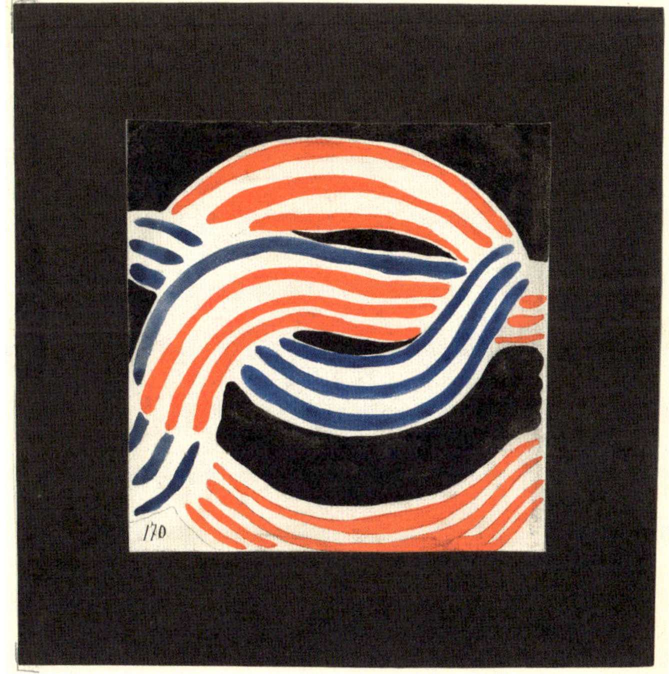
170

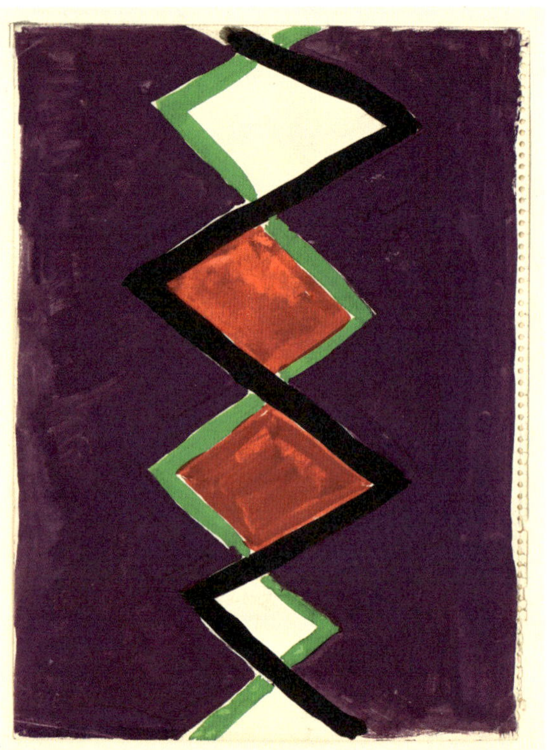

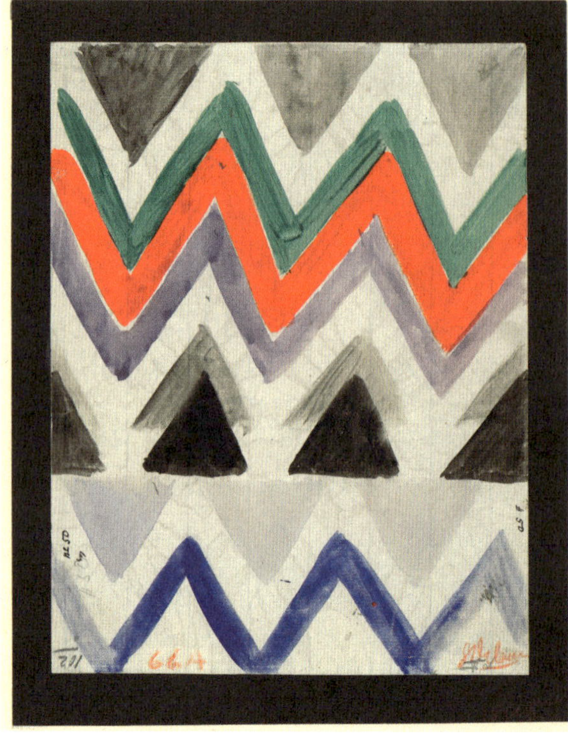

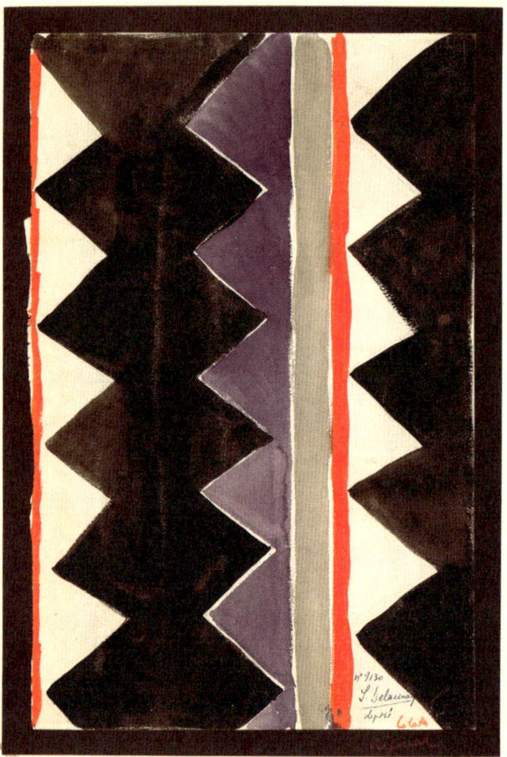

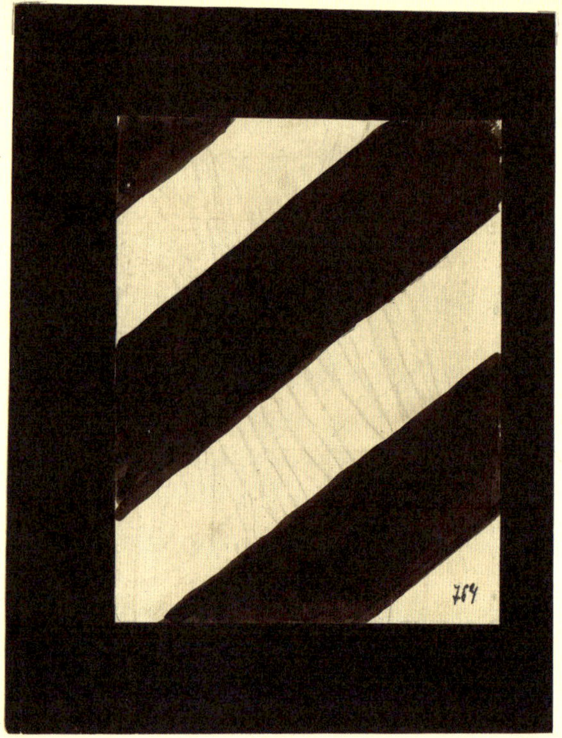

Top from left: Design for fabric F 1425, 1948/1949. Design for Simultané fabric, No. 50, 1924
Bottom from left: Design for Simultané fabric, No. 30, 1924. Design for Simultané fabric, No. 764, 1928
Right page: Design for Simultané fabric, No. 33, 1924

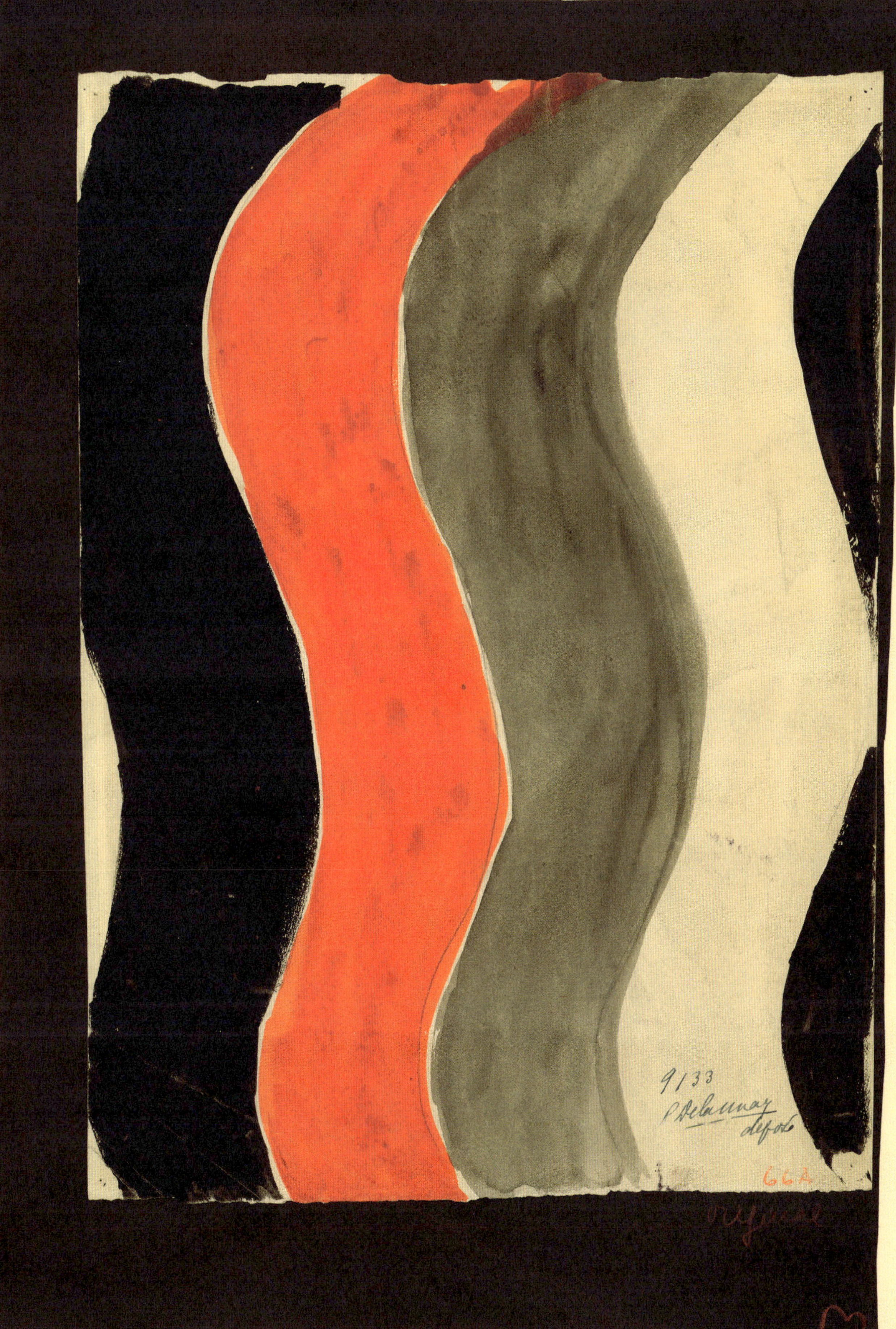

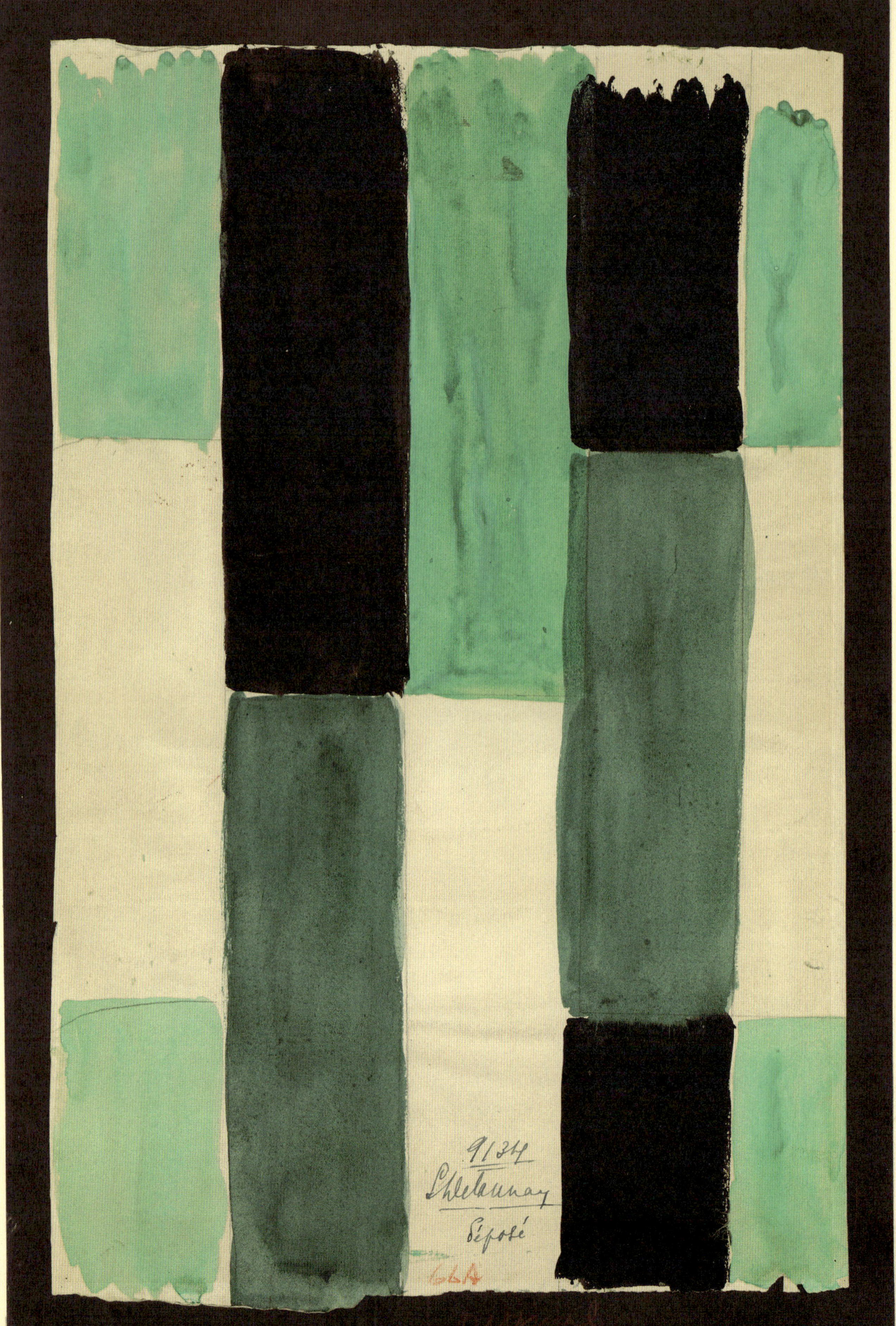

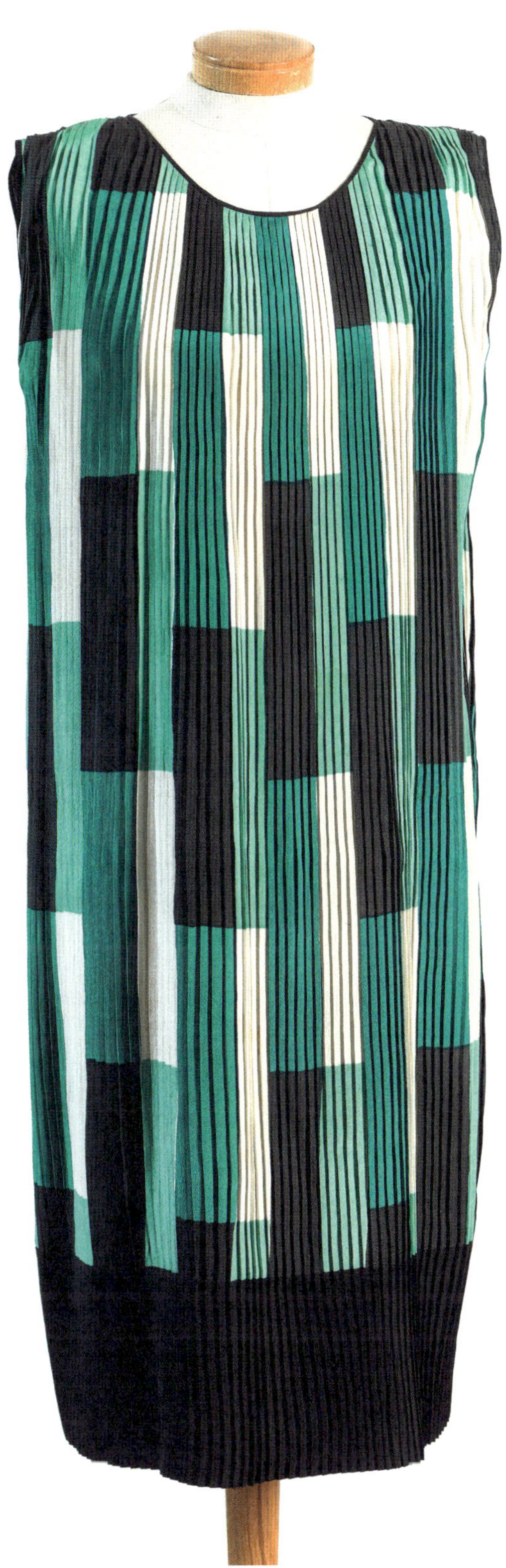

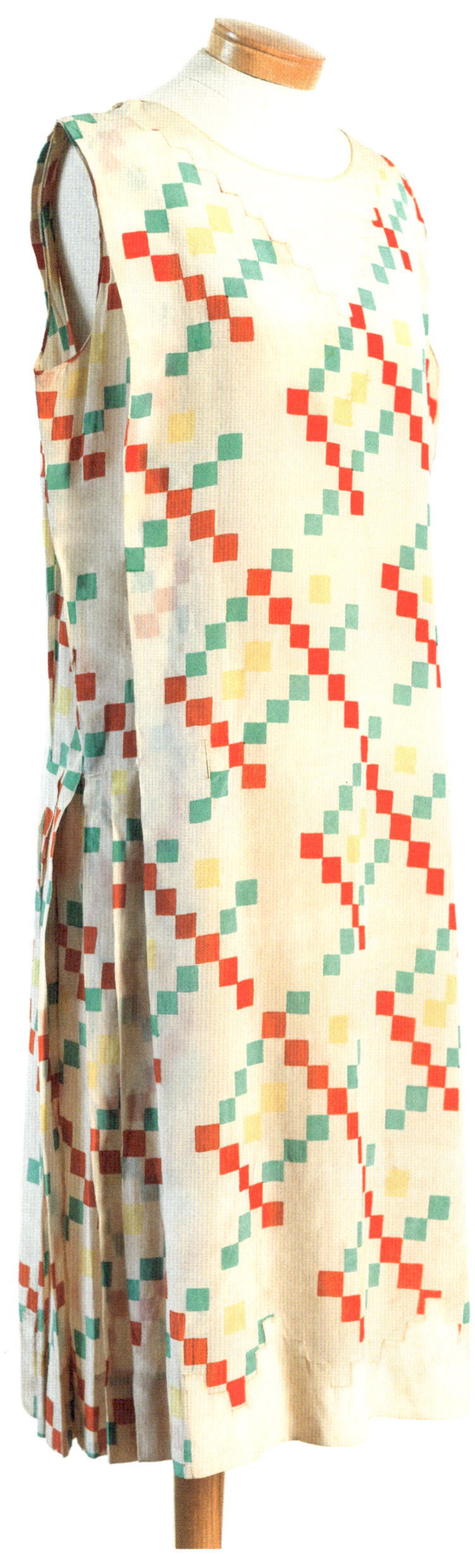

Two dresses, c. 1926
Left page: Design for Simultané fabric, No. 34, 1924

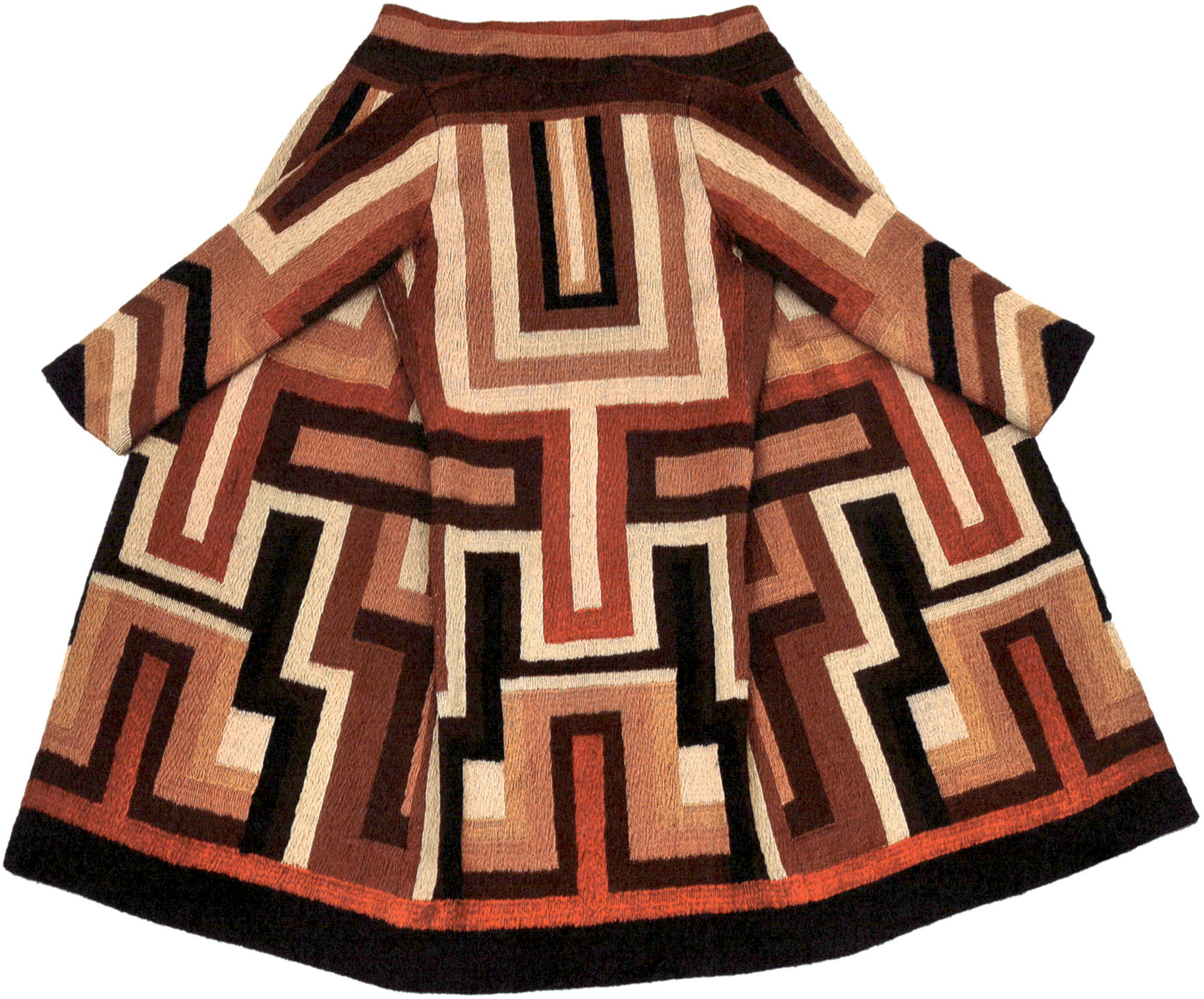

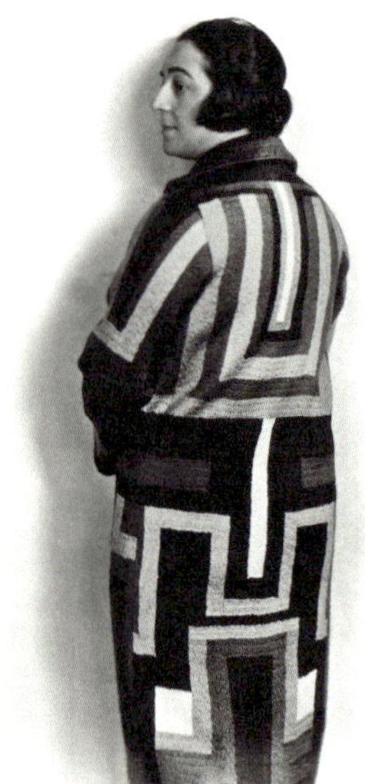

Top: Coat for Gloria Swanson, c. 1925
Sonia Delaunay in an embroidered coat of her own design
Right page: *Robes simultanées (Trois femmes, formes, couleurs)*, 1925. Simultaneous Dresses (Three Women, Forms, Colours)

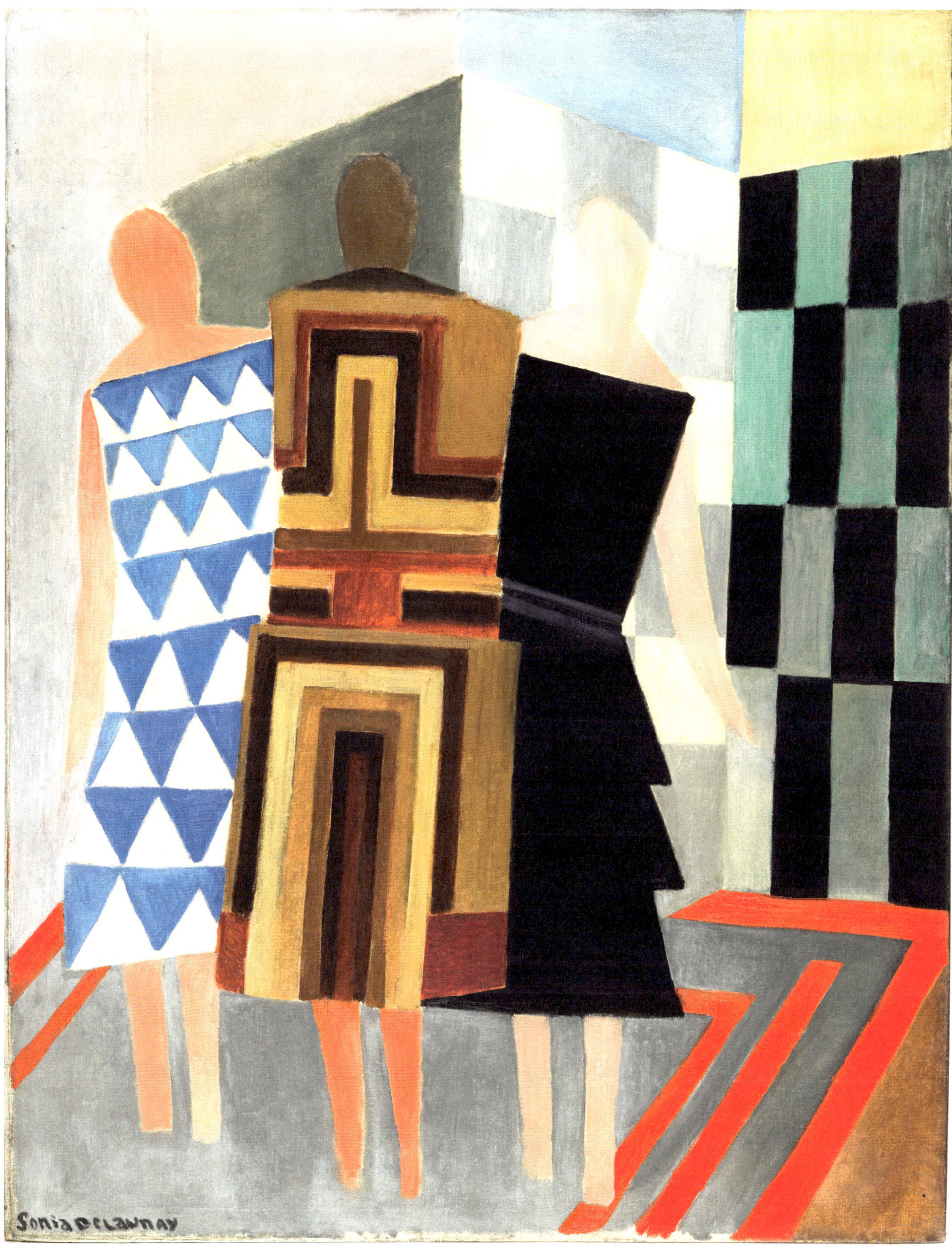
Sonia Delaunay

COLOUR, LIGHT, RHYTHM, MOVEMENT

AN INTRODUCTION TO SONIA DELAUNAY AND HER DESIGNS FOR METZ & CO

Matteo de Leeuw-de Monti[43]

The young artist that just arrived in Paris in 1906, determined to be a painter, had a long prolific life ahead of her. But she had already come a long way too.

She was born Sara Stern in Odessa in 1885, daughter of Elia Stern, reserve soldier, and his wife Hana Terk.[44] Lack of employment and the danger of pogroms forced the young Jewish family to move to Gradizk, a squalid village on the river Dnjepr, some 500 km northeast, where her father took up a job in a nail factory. Much to the chagrin of her mother, who came from a simple artisan family where the parents obviously cared little for the daughters and invested only in the sons. Hana's three brothers were given a better fate, especially the eldest, Genrikh Terk. He became a successful lawyer in St. Petersburg with good international connections. His wife Anna, a gifted literary translator, was the daughter of the banker and writer Israel Sack,[45] whose older brother Abraham Sack,[46] one of the wealthy bankers and influential financiers in St. Petersburg, had enabled him a brilliant career. Genrikh Terk owned several companies and was on the board of Brockhaus & Efron, encyclopaedic dictionary publishers, a Russian counterpart of the Leipzig publishing house F.A. Brockhaus.

To improve her chances in life, Sara Stern was given away by her parents as a young girl into the care of her uncle Genrikh and aunt Anna in St. Petersburg, who were childless. And so, Sofia (Sonia) Terk, as she was called from now on, although never adopted, grew up in an assimilated, upper middle-class environment of art, literature, and music, instead of in a desolate backwater or in a ghetto. She never saw her mother again.

She had a Fräulein, a Nanny, and a Mademoiselle as governesses and learned German, English, and French. Summer holidays were spent in the country house in Finland and with travels through Europe with her foster parents. They often visited Heidelberg, where Aunt Anna's eldest brother, Dr. Arnold Sack, was a renowned dermatologist and director of a sanatorium.[47] Her uncle Genrikh's art collection, visits to the Hermitage and to the most important museums in Germany, Italy and Switzerland awakened her interest in art. The painter Max Liebermann, an acquaintance of her uncle, presented her with her first paint box. Her drawing teacher in St. Petersburg recommended an art education.

With Arnold Sack able to keep an eye on her from Heidelberg, it was decided in 1904 she would study at the Malerinnenschule[48] in Karlsruhe. Women were not yet admitted to the Academy of Fine Arts at that time. Sonia Delaunay appears there in the register of the study years 1905 and 1906 as "Fräulein Sophie Terk-Stern, Petersburg." She received a solid basic education in Karlsruhe, but her urge for independence and adventure fuelled her decision to settle and further her studies in Paris in 1906.

Early years in Paris

One can imagine the impressions of the colour explosions that were engraved on the retina of this much-travelled young woman, who had seen the world rolling by for miles in constant movement of carriages and trains. These impressions were put into practice in early oil paintings of 1907/1908, such as *Jeune Finlandaise*, *Nu Jaune*, *Philomène* (page 9) or *Mme Minskaya* (page 8).[49]

These are not just paintings influenced by Gauguin, as is so often claimed, they are 'pure Sonia'. The seeds of abstraction had already clearly sprouted: the movement of the colours, the interplay of her palette – so much her signature in both her painting as well as in her fabric designs over the many years to come – everything is there.

She studied the technique of woodblock printing and etching with Rudolf Grossmann,[50] which would be of great importance later for her fabric designs and lithographs. Through him she met Wilhelm Uhde,[51] a German author, art critic and contemporary art dealer. To elude the Terks' call to return to St. Petersburg, Sonia and Uhde, who was gay, agreed to enter a marriage of convenience, which enabled her to remain in Paris. Although Sonia never returned to Russia, she never broke her ties with her homeland, and always maintained close contact with Russian artists and writers.

Uhde had introduced her into the new Parisian literary and art scene of Guillaume Apollinaire, Marie Laurencin, Georges Braque, Pablo Picasso, Henri Rousseau, Gertrude and Leo Stein and her future husband Robert Delaunay. After an amicable divorce Sonia married Robert Delaunay in November 1910, just two months before the birth of their son Charles.

Simultaneous Contrasts – the Expressive Language of Colours

Their apartment became a meeting place for the international avant-garde. It was here that Sonia Delaunay began to 'live her art': not only pictures on the wall, but also book covers, blankets, boxes, cradle covers, cushions, lampshades, clothes, fabrics, furniture – without any hierarchy,

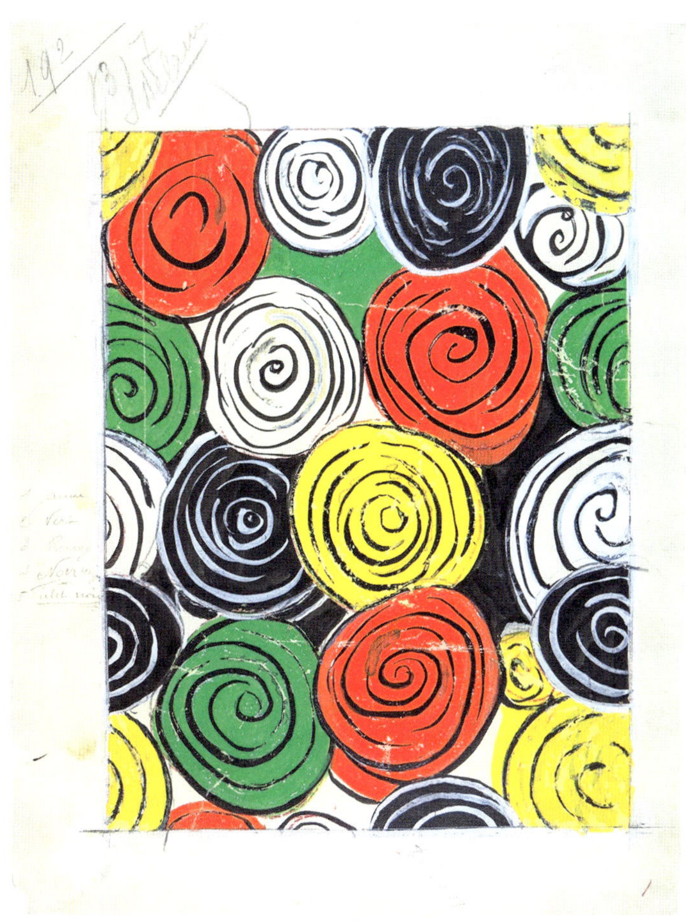

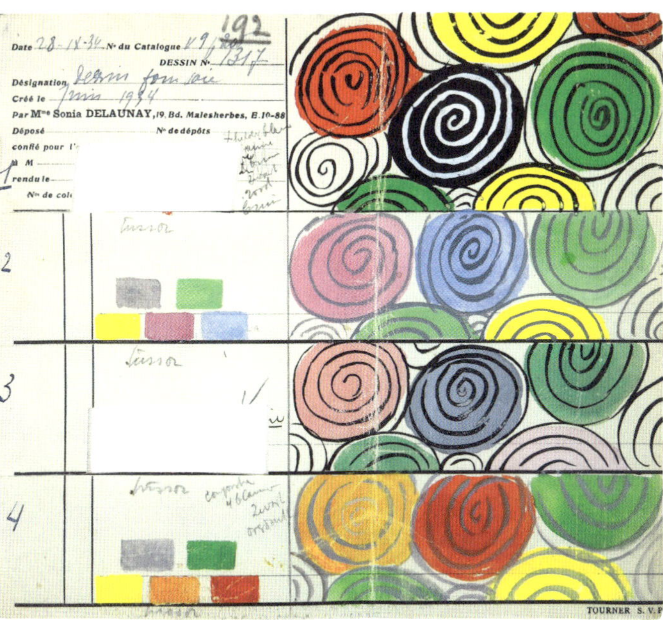

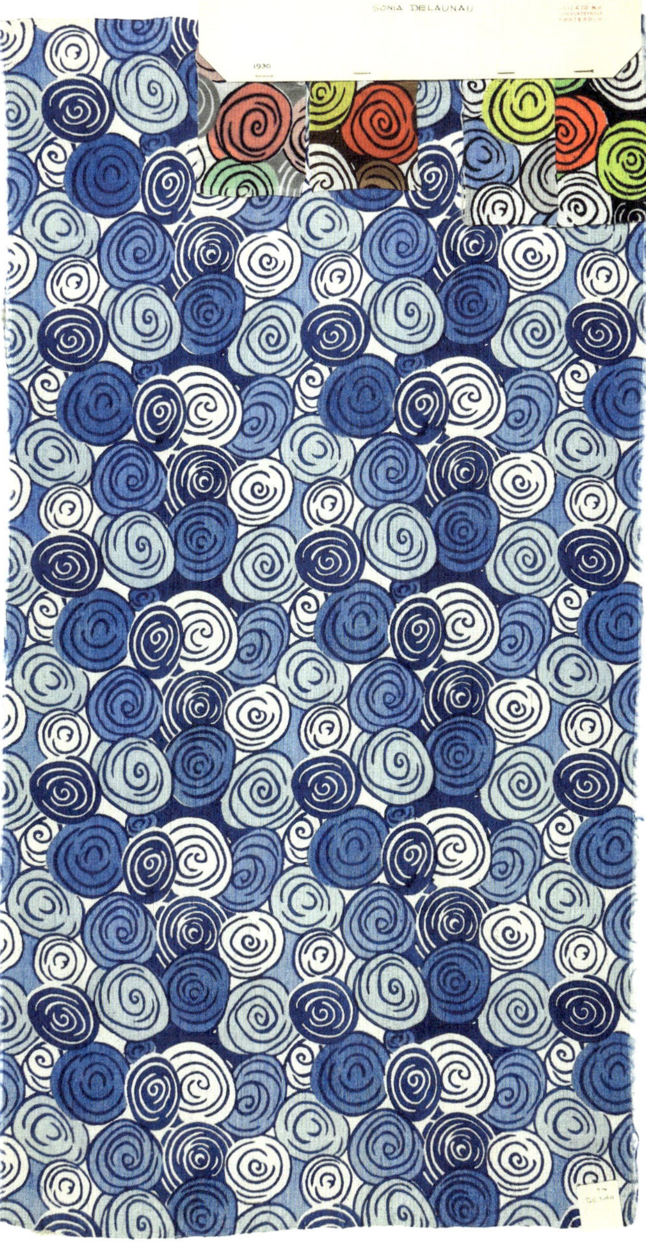

Top: Dessin 1317 (Design 1317), 1934
Bottom: Sonia Delaunay's pancarte for Dessin pour soie 1317 (Design for silk 1317), 1934
Right: Set of 5 Metz & Co fabric samples, Dessin 1317 (Design 1317), 1934

everything became a collage of colour compositions. What initiated the new painterly experiments, the *contrastes simultanés*, was the influence of the chemist Michel Eugène Chevreul (1786-1889), who had published his studies on colour in 1839 in *On the Law of Simultaneous Contrast of Colours*, which had become an important colour manual for painters.[52] As director of the dye works at the Gobelin Manufactory in Paris, Chevreul had observed that although yarns were dyed a desired colour, the result could look faded when used in tapestry. He found that this was not a chemical problem but an optical one. His research into the optical mixing of colours drew his attention to different types of colour and tone contrasts: side by side, colours can reinforce or also weaken each other, influence each other, each colour imposing its own complementary colour on the other.

What was a theory put into practice for Robert Delaunay came to Sonia Delaunay naturally.

She had an instinctive awareness that every colour has a life of its own, that the infinite colour combinations have their own expressive language. *Simultané* became the key word.

Sonia tailored her first simultané dress and waistcoat from colourful pieces of fabric for regular visits to the Bullier dancing establishment. She captured the tango in a dance of light and colour in her large-scale masterpiece *Bal Bullier* (MNAM, Paris). This painting, almost four metres wide, was exhibited in Berlin in 1913 at Herwarth Walden's *First German Autumn Salon*. Whereas in this painting one can still perceive hints of dancing figures, the smaller version (Kunsthalle Bielefeld) is a truly abstract work, only the colours move (page 16).

Sonia Delaunay received generous financial support from her foster parents since her marriage to Robert Delaunay. This continued after Anna Terk's death in 1911. Her financial independence made it possible for her to paint and experiment at leisure. Thus, when the First World War broke out in August 1914 while they were on holiday in Spain, it enabled them to stay in Portugal and Spain for the next few years and paint without worry, mixing simultanism with new figurativeness.

The Russian Revolution, however, put an end to the carefree existence: the Terk properties were confiscated, and all income from St. Petersburg ceased. Sonia realised that she could not live from painting alone. This marked a turning point in her career: for the next thirty years, she was to focus her art mainly on design. She met up with Sergei Diaghilev who offered her to design new costumes – and Robert Delaunay new scenery – for the London production of *Cléopâtre* for his Ballets Russes.[53]

In Madrid, she set up a small fashion and interior decorating enterprise: Casa Sonia. She successfully attracted attention with her revolutionary colour-contrasting simultaneous designs. This Madrid period was an important dress rehearsal for the next chapter in her life, when she returned to Paris with her husband in 1921, yearning to be part of the exciting new art scene there.

'Sonia', 'Simultané' and 'Tissus Delaunay'

They settled into a large apartment on 19, Boulevard Malesherbes, which was soon furnished in the 'Simultaneous' style. Sonia Delaunay continued where she had left off in Madrid. Embroidered, woven or appliquéd scarves, costumes, coats, dresses, and waistcoats all met with an enthusiastic response from an insider audience. Sonia Delaunay had carved out a niche for herself in fashion with her art and set up her own atelier in her apartment. An abundance of Russian seamstresses stood at her disposal. On 20 March 1925, she registered her business under the name 'Sonia', she trademarked the name 'Sonia Delaunay', and the fabrics were given the registered trademark 'Simultané'.

Her real breakthrough came in 1925, when she showed her *Simultané* creations during the *Exposition Internationale des Arts Décoratifs et Industriels Modernes* in the boutique Sonia Delaunay Simultané – Heim Furs – Girau-Gilbert Maroquinerie[54] on the Pont Alexandre III.

Her reputation grew rapidly, she was involved in theatre and film, but her fashion clientele consisted mainly of artists, intellectuals, and ladies of the haute bourgeoisie: Gloria Swanson, Nancy Cunard, Claire Goll, Florence Henri; the wives of Leopold Stokowski, Igor Stravinsky, Walter Gropius, Marcel Breuer, Erich Mendelsohn,[55] even Mrs. Solomon Guggenheim.

Despite artistic recognition, from a business point of view things did not prove easy in the long run. She was admonished by her financial advisors and urged to be more commercial to keep the atelier out of the red, but Sonia Delaunay refused to turn into a mere businesswoman. She had never run a fashion house like Coco Chanel, Jeanne Lanvin, or Elsa Schiaparelli.

Delaunay saw herself as an artist, a painter who sought new ways with fabrics as her medium.

Eventually, the 'Sonia' project was abandoned. On 1 January 1929, she registered a new enterprise: Tissus Delaunay. The situation improved, thanks to substantial sales of her fabrics in the USA, but soon the economic crisis hit her hard too. In 1930, the remaining employees were laid off and, with considerable debts on hand, she faced financial ruin.

It has often been asserted, erroneously, that the closure of her workshop was the moment when Delaunay left her design period behind and returned exclusively to painting. This misconception stems in part from post-war biographical notes, including her own, where there is a noticeable 'gap' in her career in the 1930s. This easily led to the

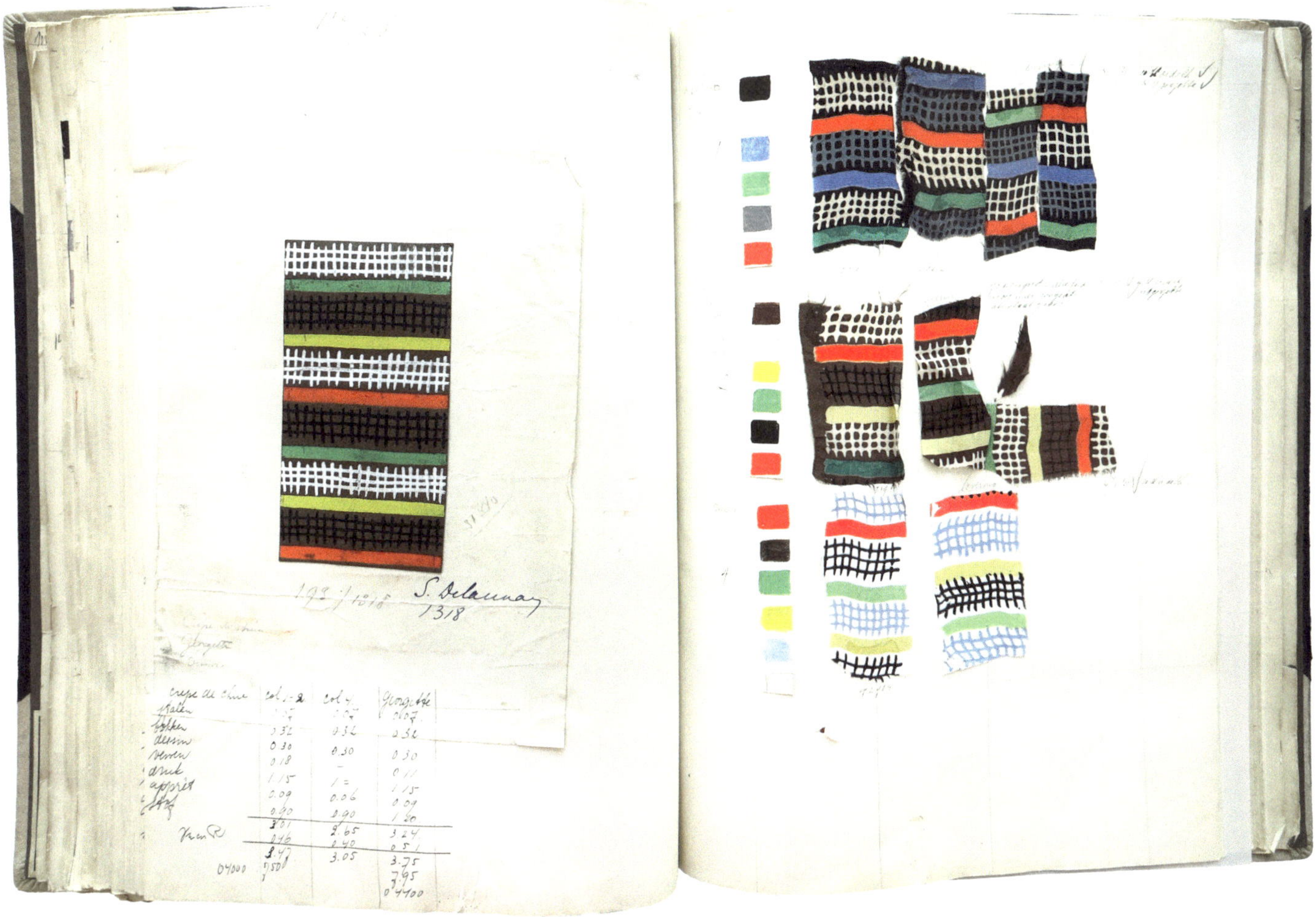

Dessin 1318 (Design 1318), 1934, in Metz & Co fabric book, 1931-1935

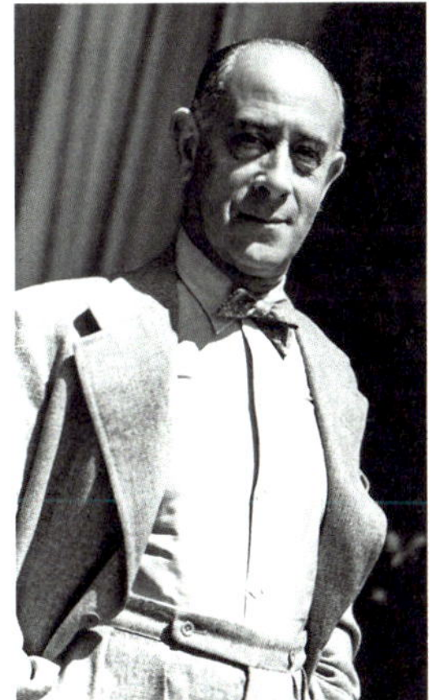

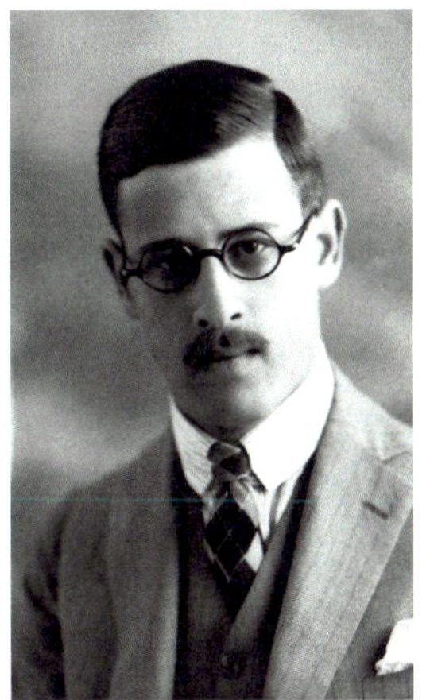

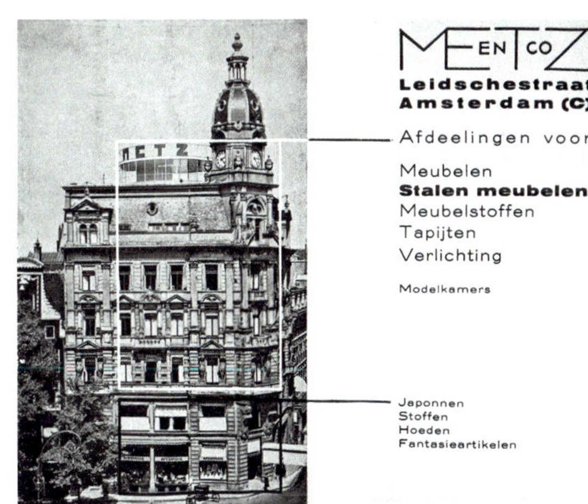

From left: Joseph de Leeuw with bow tie designed by Sonia Delaunay
Hendrik de Leeuw with tie designed by Sonia Delaunay
Right: Advertising flyer for Metz & Co, 1935

misinterpretation that she stopped designing fabrics after 1930.

The opposite was the case: with the elemental force of a survivor, she continued to design and became a one-woman show, supported by the Dutch firm she had already been collaborating with for five years: Metz & Co.

The Designs for Metz & Co

Metz & Co was a unique luxury department store for textiles, furniture, interior design, decorative arts, and fashion in Amsterdam.[56]

The owners Joseph de Leeuw (1872-1944)[57] and his son Hendrik de Leeuw (1908-1978) were constantly looking for new ways to bring art into everyday life and commissioned designs from many international artists.[58] Joseph de Leeuw met Sonia Delaunay in 1925 in Paris at the *Exposition internationale des Arts Décoratifs*, where Metz & Co was also exhibiting. It was the beginning of a long-lasting collaboration and friendship. For over 30 years, Metz & Co commissioned around 200 designs. Delaunay fabrics were sold at Metz & Co up until the 1960s.[59]

As of 27 February 1933, Sonia Delaunay had begun to keep a diary.[60] Reading her journal of that time one encounters an overwhelmingly active person with a loaded schedule and an iron discipline. Without employees, she kept the Delaunay household going, only assisted by a few seamstresses or a lady to embroider the appliqués, and occasionally by her son Charles, who was in fact a talented artist before he set out to become a jazz and record producer.

Metz & Co appears already on the very first page of her diary and one gets a clear picture of the enormous care and energy she and De Leeuw *père et fils* spent working together over the many years. Countless letters, telephone calls, and visits were noted down. Contrary to most other clients, to whom she simply sold a design, with Metz & Co she was very much the pivot of the entire procedure.

She kept meticulous records of her designs with numbering and sketches in her so-called *Livres Noirs*: ten volumes of black linen-bound books, covering the period from 1924 to 1940. By then she had created no less than 1,500 designs. From 1940 onwards, several hundred more were added, indicating the important position they occupy within her oeuvre.

From the diaries, the account books, the *Livres noirs* and especially Metz & Co's own fabric books (page 55) one can reconstruct the exact dating and get a clear insight into the various stages of the process, from the original design to the final result, a unique way to watch her 'at work'.

For numerous designs she sold, she created a *pancarte*, her special design card. On it she added a miniature gouache of the design, as well as the design number, the date of creation, and the various colour samples that were to be matched. Sonia Delaunay had developed her very own palette of over 400 colours, each with its own name and reference number.

Occasionally, Metz designs were sent back and forth by mail, folded in half or in four, with instructions or comments penciled in. Sometimes pieces of the design or fabric were cut out and were glued into Metz's or Sonia Delaunay's fabric books for reference. The designs did not always receive the museum treatment they enjoy today: they were working material.

The dress fabrics were mostly hand-printed luxury silks – crêpe de chine, crêpe georgette, tussore, twill, or voile. Artificial silk was also very fashionable. There were roll-printed cotton fabrics, but also woollen fabrics, woven fabrics, linen for upholstery and curtains. They were made in France, Germany, England, the Netherlands and even in Japan for the most luxurious scarves. Some of the silk fabrics were so exclusive that only 30 metres were ordered.

Calligrams in Colour – the Painter at Work

The designs for Metz & Co cover the entire spectrum of Delaunay's artistic diversity. The large geometric, contrasting colour blocks of the mid-1920s gave way to finer structures. She played with squares, oblongs, circles, crosses, dots, stripes, strokes, and zigzags in countless combinations of poetic rhythms and themes that in themselves form new motifs in ingenious repeats: Delaunay turned them into calligrams in colour. Often, her Russian roots clearly shimmer through in abstracted folkloristic motifs. Florals are also abundantly represented: some delicately stylised, others of an explosive freshness that leaps out of the black or dark blue background, even an Op Art bloom, far ahead of its time.

The Metz & Co designs from 1936 to 1939 again show a new side: austere geometrics or softer, impulsively painted compositions in Monet style, as well as miniature chequerboard patterns with shades of red, pink, purple, blue, and green that one would normally associate with the 1960s. One immediately recognises the stroke of her brush, the painter at work. She was skilled at transferring her ideas from one medium to another. In this sense, she found ideal partners in De Leeuw – father and son –, who were equally fastidious in their efforts to transform the final product into a work of art in its own right, to ensure that colours and colour contrasts turned out exactly as intended and that the painterly flow in the fabric was maintained.

Joseph de Leeuw had become a widower in 1930, so it is not surprising that their relationship intensified, both on a professional and personal level. At some point he wanted to marry her and proposed to her. Though she turned him down, it did not affect the continuing friendship with the Delaunays.

As much as he appreciated Sonia Delaunay's artistry and potential, Joseph de Leeuw was also aware of her financial

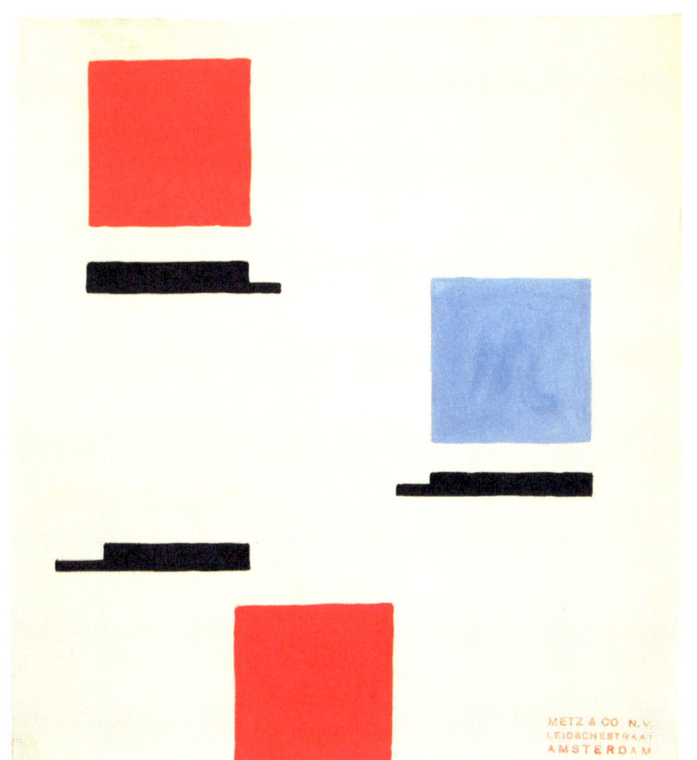

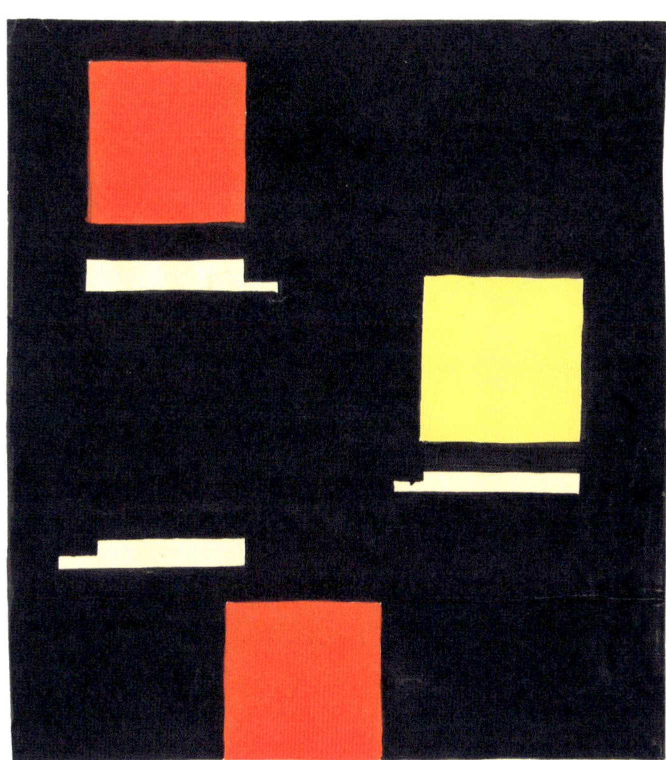

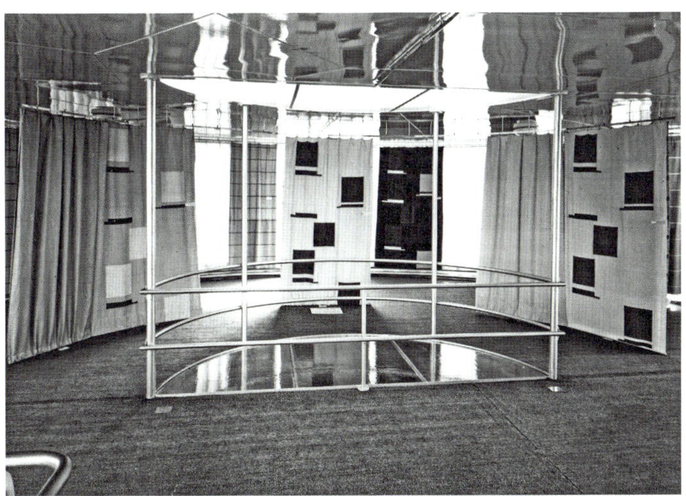

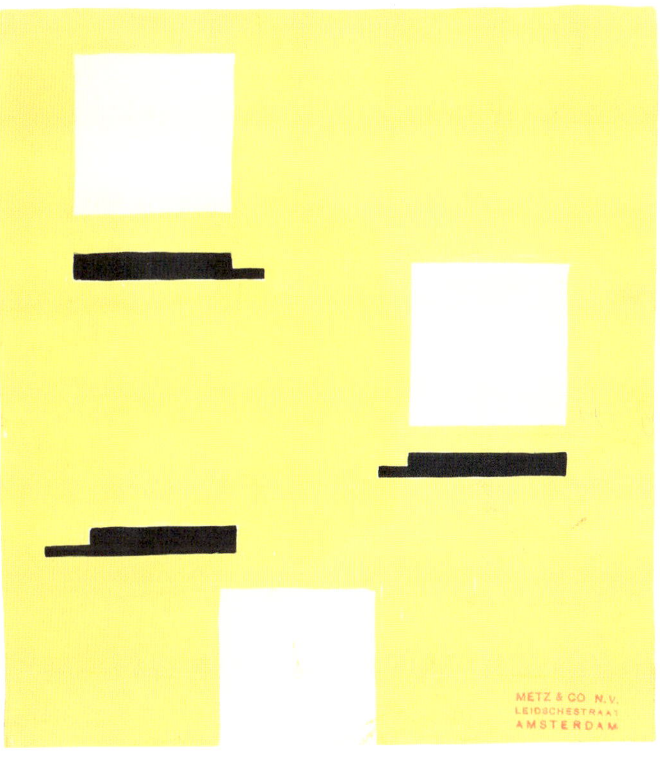

Three versions of Dessin 1177 (Design 1177), 1933/1934
Bottom left: Dessin 1177 in the exhibition *Machinale Weefsels voor de Woning* in the Rietveld cupola on the roof of Metz & Co, Amsterdam, 1934

worries. The economic crisis had been taking its toll, and Robert did not sell. Sonia's ideas of setting up a Metz type boutique in her apartment[61] or a new fabric printing business, which De Leeuw tried to help her with, did not materialise.[62]

In 1936, the Delaunays left the Boulevard Malesherbes and moved into the much smaller apartment at 16, Rue de Saint-Simon where Sonia lived for the rest of her life.

For a while she worked as a colourist for the young architect Félix Aublet.[63] According to her diary a frustrating period, but Robert and Aublet had set up a new company, Art et Lumière, to prepare their participation in the Paris World's Fair of 1937. Her large scale works for the Palais de l'Air and the Palais des Chemins de Fer were highly acclaimed.[64]

She had begun to paint in oils again, something she had hardly done for 20 years. She also created new gouaches – similar in style. *Gouache 1938 no. 1* of 1938 sums up the artist Sonia Delaunay: colour, light, rhythm, movement (page 70).

1940-1945

The outbreak of the Second World War changed everything. The Delaunays fled to the south of France. Robert, who had been ill with cancer for some time, died in Montpellier on 25 October 1941. Those were hard, uncertain times for Sonia, financially and emotionally. Miraculously, her Jewish origins were not revealed or betrayed. She had dealt with this threat very early on and had consciously managed to suppress it. Even her son Charles did not know about it. Apart from a series of designs in 1942 for Robert Perrier,[65] which were never produced, work was scarce and near impossible.

Metz & Co had become out of the question: Joseph de Leeuw, dispossessed and forced to relinquish Metz & Co, was deported, and died in the Theresienstadt concentration camp.

Gradually, Sonia Delaunay returned to painting. "I began to work and started on a gouache. I would like to link the principle of fabrics with painting, which Robert always advised me."[66] Though her gouaches display great strength and reveal enormously expressive clarity, she seemed to have developed a certain inward timidity when it would come to showing them.

In Toulouse, on 8 August 1944, she noted: "My work is completely separated from me, I never talk about it, or show it, because I never think of it, I have no assertive craving for recognition. Took along the album 10 and my notebook of fabrics of 1942 and everyone liked it a lot."[67]

After the War

The challenges of the post-war period were met with renewed energy. Back in Paris, she painted again, participated in exhibitions, and worked tirelessly to gain recognition for Robert Delaunay's work, which would purposefully become her main task for the next few years.

"I'm not worried about R. Nor about me, because for me art is a personal luxury and I do it for myself without consideration for anyone else. I don't care about fame either, because I have realised what its vanity does to people's lives. After my death it's something else, people can say about me what they want."[68]

From 1946 onwards, she again regularly created designs for Metz & Co. Hendrik de Leeuw, who had managed to escape during the war, gradually regained control of the company.

The post-war designs for Metz & Co differ from Sonia Delaunay's *Rythmes colorés* and similarly titled paintings of the period but contain the same bold freshness in the flow of colour. The compositions became larger again, powerful, and confident. In 1953, she also created new carpet designs: "After tea I had made three carpet models for Metz, very successful in my opinion!"[69] She rarely praised herself.

Her tireless commitment to Robert Delaunay's work had begun to bear fruit. Now it was her own turn. To colleagues, especially also to those amongst the younger generation, she had long been an inspiration as an abstract painter. Still, she recognised the need to free herself from what the mainly male-dominated art market viewed as her "decorative artist image."

Her artwork of the 1950s, however, spoke for itself. The inner strength and her self-confidence are reflected in majestic, almost pensive paintings. Indeed, Delaunay continued to paint with tireless vigour and joie de vivre until her death on 5 December 1979. By then she was highly recognised and celebrated. The oil paintings and gouaches of the 1960s and 1970s testify to her artistic confidence. Of course, this did not stop her from making numerous lithographs or designing books, tapestries, mosaics, playing cards, and occasionally fabrics and scarves.

Sonia Delaunay was never a designer in the usual sense. Her designs were not subject to the whims of fashion. The power of her colours made them timeless. As a painter, she remained true to herself. She lived for her art.

Matteo de Leeuw-de Monti first met Sonia Delaunay as a little boy in her atelier in Paris in 1956. Delaunay's longstanding friendship and collaboration since 1925 with his grandfather and father, the owners of the former department store Metz & Co in Amsterdam, led him to an intensive study of her textile designs and paintings. For 30 years, he has contributed to numerous exhibitions and publications on Sonia Delaunay.

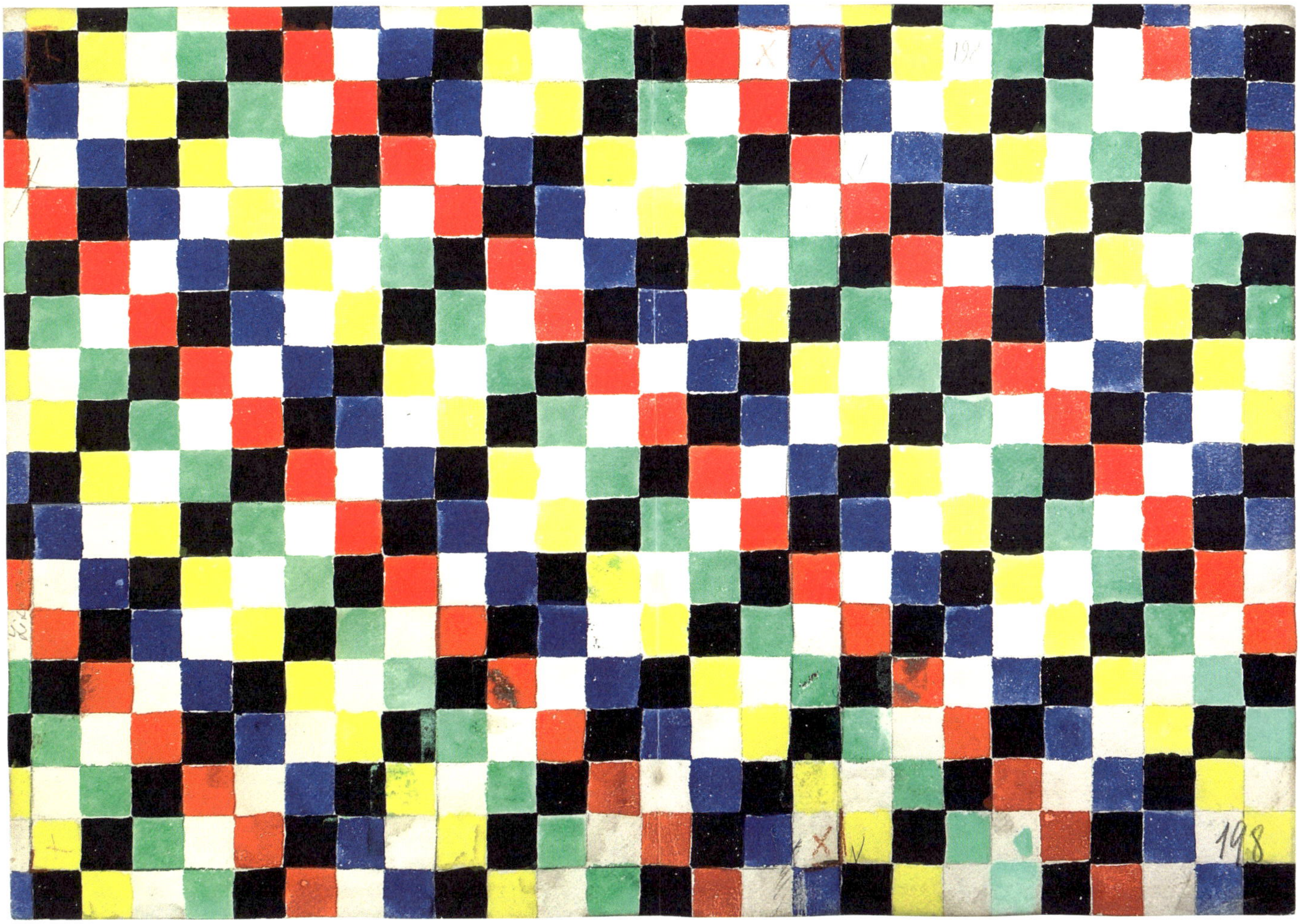

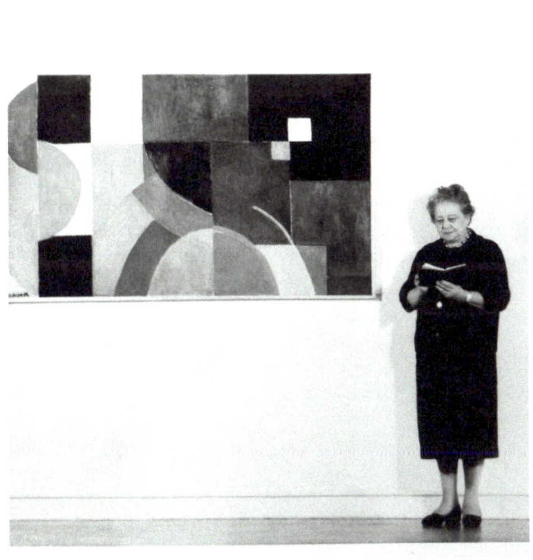

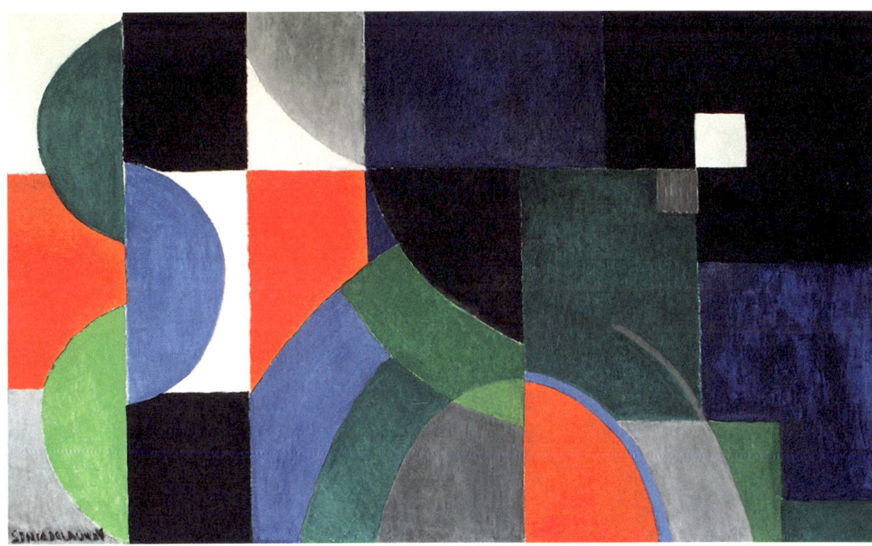

Top: Dessin 198 (Design 198), 1927
Left: Sonia Delaunay in her retrospective exhibition at Städtisches Kunsthaus, Bielefeld, Germany, 1958
Right: *Rythme coloré (694)*, 1958. Coloured Rhythm (694)
Next spread: Details of Sonia Delaunay's textile designs and fabrics for Metz & Co

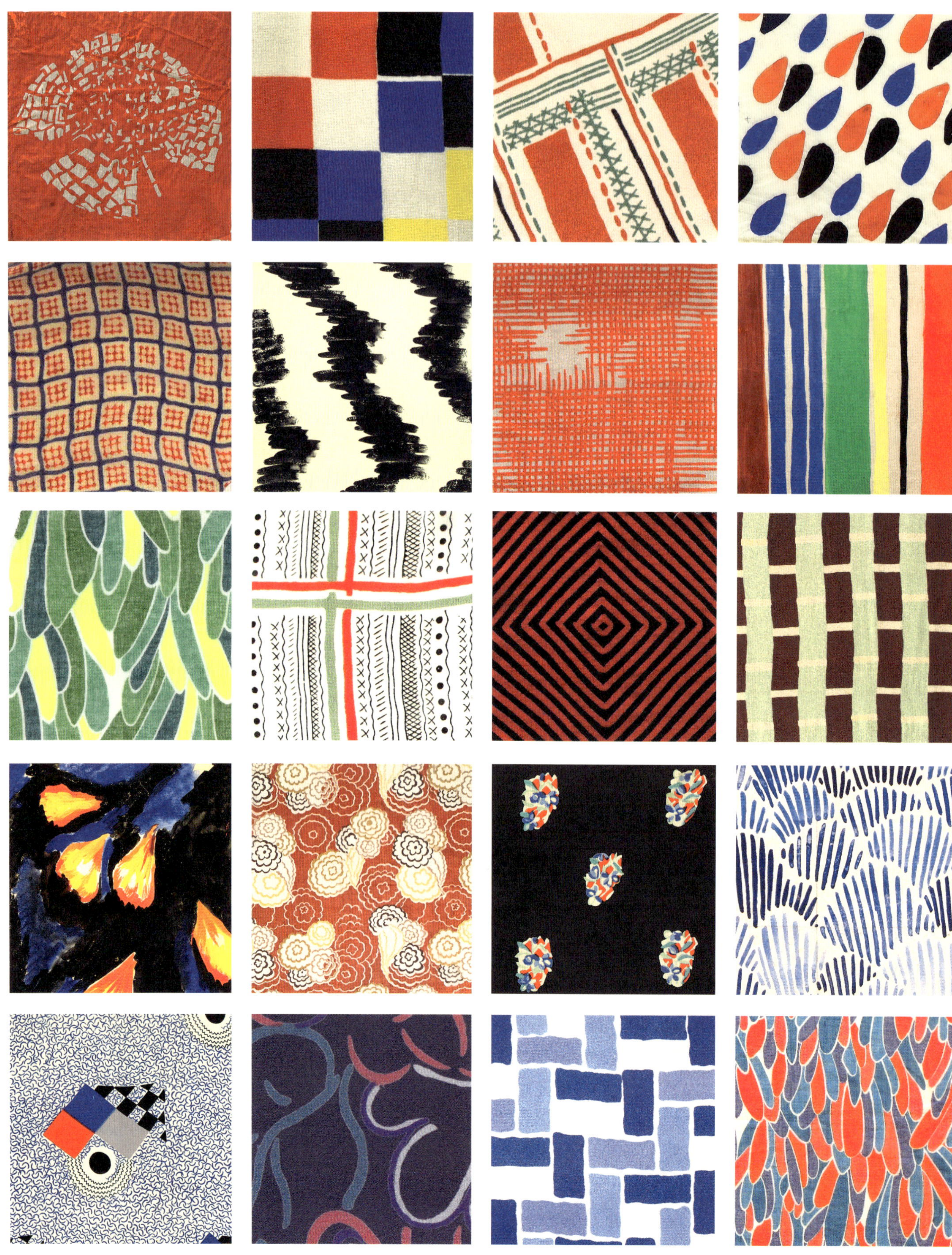

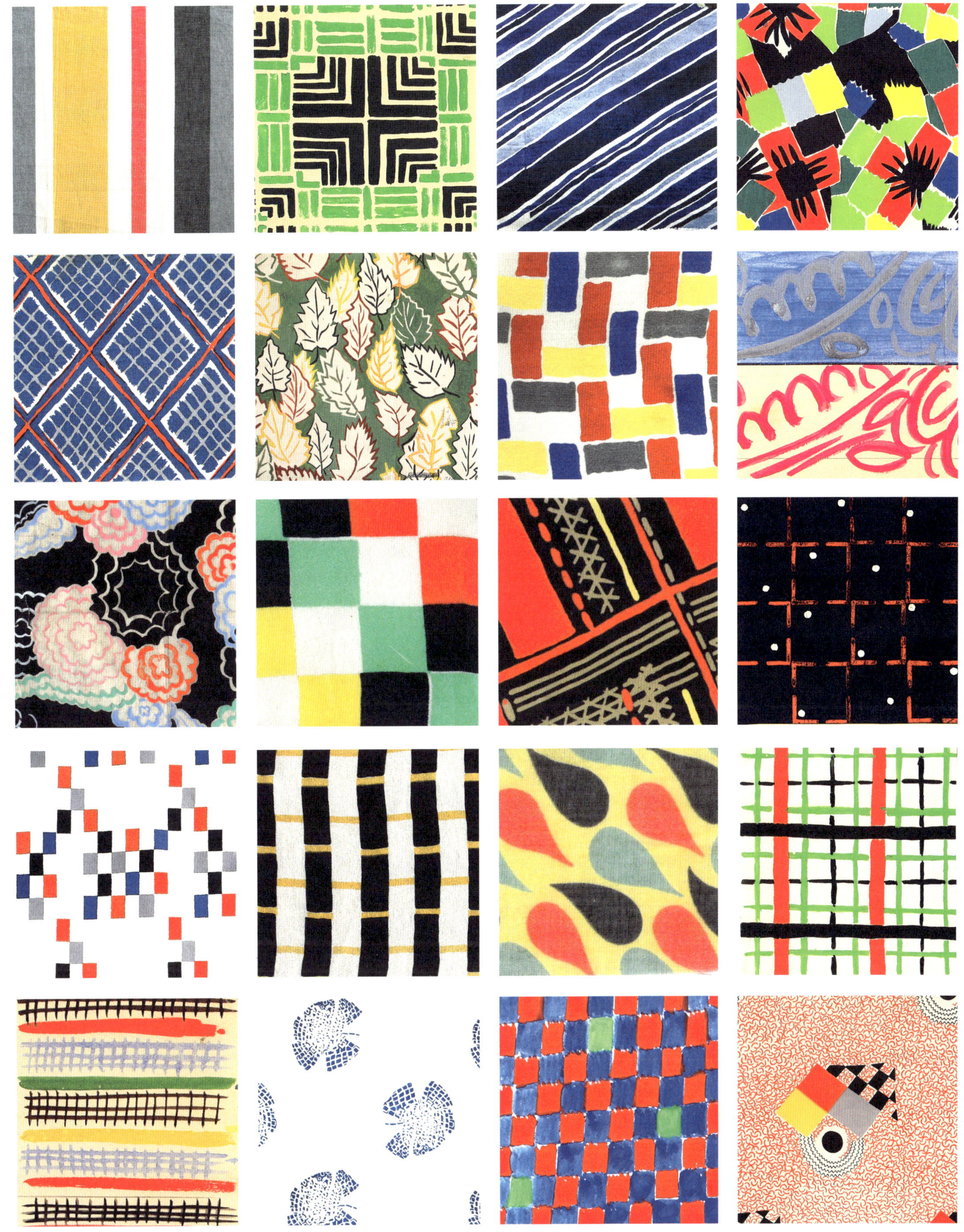

FROM FASHION TO ITS IMAGE: SONIA DELAUNAY'S TOTAL ART

Cécile Godefroy

A key figure in the arts of the 20th century and one of the pioneers of abstraction in painting, Sonia Delaunay also occupies a special place in the world of fashion and the decorative arts.[70] Far from subscribing to the established hierarchy of genres, she considered each of her activities as an extension of painting and as a means of emancipation from the limits of the easel and of bourgeois interiors, allowing her to enter the vital space of the city and illuminate the modern world. This form of theatricalisation, combined with the desire to enliven life generally by means of colour, was grounded in the artist's Russian roots and is what characterises her work as a whole, in which painting is intimately bound up with the arts of theatre, poetry, fashion, textiles and architecture, in a fully deliberate search for visual correspondences. The connection between painting and fashion was particularly strong in the period from 1913 to 1930. As the witness and mirror of these experiments, photography was an integral part of Delaunay's effort to unite the arts.

Reforming Costume

Born Sarah Stern in the city of Odessa in 1885, Delaunay always remembered the colourful *izbas* (traditional Russian wooden cabins, ed.) of her childhood and the actions of the female workers composing their patchworks out of remnants of fabric to decorate walls and objects with colour. Raised in St. Petersburg by her mother's brother, Henri Terk, whose name she took, the young girl became familiar with the ideas championed by *Mir Isskusstva* (World of Art), an independent structure directed by Sergei Diaghilev and Alexandre Benois which promoted art in all the variety of its forms – painting, sculpture, architecture, theatre sets, posters, furnishing, illustrated books, ornamentation, sewing, toys and postcards – in accordance with a principle of "dramatic unity"[71] close to that of Richard Wagner's *Gesamtkunstwerk* and later shared by all the Russian avant-gardes. Sonia Terk moved to Paris in 1906. There she exhibited her paintings for the first time and met the French painter Robert Delaunay. In 1911 the young married couple moved towards abstraction and developed simultanism, an aesthetic movement that rejected traditional means of representation and was based instead on the constructive and dynamic power of colour. This entry into the realm of non-figuration was celebrated in Robert's art by pure painting, and in Sonia's by painting and the decorative arts. In 1913, basing herself on the quilt made for her son Charles in 1911, Sonia Delaunay created a simultaneous dress by assembling fabrics in different sizes, materials and colours (page 15 and 17). This first simultanist garment was followed by a small collection of colourful clothes that the couple and their friends used to wear at Parisian openings and balls. Described by the poet Guillaume Apollinaire as "Reformers of Dress,"[72] with these initiatives the Delaunays were responding to the sartorial offensive launched by the Italian Futurists and disseminating by means of colour the aesthetic principles of a tendency that was not limited to the field of painting, or to its Parisian context: simultanism was resolutely cosmopolitan in its intentions. Sonia Delaunay also decorated the couple's apartment in Rue des Grands-Augustins: she painted a toy chest for Charles, made lampshades and cushions, bound the avant-garde books and journals that were important to her, designed posters, and produced the first poem-painting with Blaise Cendrars, *La Prose du Transsibérien et de la Petite Jehanne de France* (Prose on the Trans-Siberian Railway and of the Little Jehanne of France, 1913, page 19). A few photographs showing the artist wearing a simultaneous dress bear witness to the visual dialogues that took place in the apartment between semi-abstract paintings, textiles and objects in the pursuit of a general aestheticization reminiscent of certain Art Nouveau interiors.

In Portugal, then in Spain during the war, the Delaunays worked on various simultaneous exhibition projects and contributed to the costumes for the ballet *Cléopâtre* (1918, page 32) with the Ballets Russes troupe. In 1918, Sonia Delaunay inaugurated the Casa Sonia in Madrid where she sold fashion accessories and decorative objects, based on the model of La Maison Martine and Atelier Martine.[73] In 1919 she presented her designs at the Majestic Hall in Bilbao, and opened three branches of Casa Sonia in Barcelona, San Sebastián and Bilbao. Their success with the Spanish aristocracy was reported and illustrated in the national press and encouraged the artist to extend the experience in Paris, which had recovered its status as "capital of the arts and of fashion." There she opened a shop more specifically dedicated to the arts of fashion.

The Simultané Brand

Returning to Paris in 1921, Delaunay presented her first creation at the Dada evenings and Bals Russes. With the collaboration of the Romanian poet Tristan Tzara she designed poem-dresses (page 20 and 27) and conceived the interior decoration of Au Sans Pareil, the Dadaist bookshop in Neuilly-sur-Seine, in 1922, as well as dance costumes for

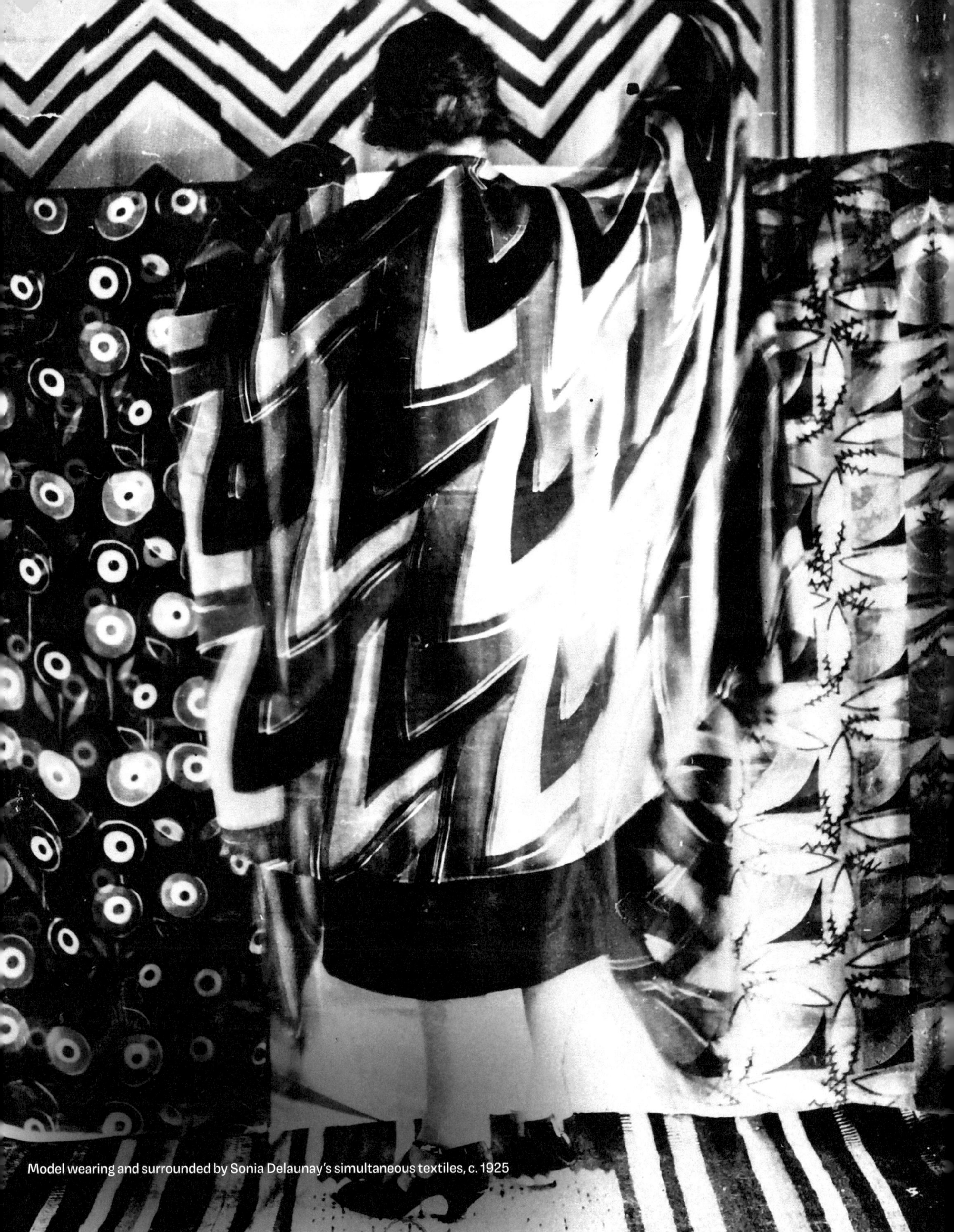
Model wearing and surrounded by Sonia Delaunay's simultaneous textiles, c. 1925

Lizica Codreano and two of the costumes for the play *Le Cœur à Gaz* (The Gas Heart, page 20).

In 1924 she opened the *Simultané* workshop in the family apartment on Boulevard Malesherbes where, as in Spain, she employed Russian seamstresses to create her models, reproduce the designs for the fabrics and the embroidery for scarves and dresses, and make woollen coats. A few months later, she exhibited her first textiles at the *Salon d'Automne* (The Autumn Exhibition) in an original display. Presented at the heart of a public square, the Simultané stand was imbued with movement based on a patented "Simultaneous Cinematic Presentation" devised by Robert Delaunay: the "ordered and living" spectacle of the chevron, tortoiseshell, chequerboard, zigzag motifs, the coloured rectangles and stripes produced by Maison Godau Guillaume – Arnault set up a host of vibratory effects, exemplifying the hypnotic qualities of simultanism.

Advertisements for Maison Sonia, which was inaugurated in March 1925 and located, like the simultané workshop, in the family apartment on Boulevard Malesherbes, signal a business selling fabrics, clothes, accessories and furniture and emphasise the products' artistic dimension.[74] After the avant-garde poems on the walls of the entrance hall[75] the living room, used to host customers and the Parisian intelligentsia, featured "all the elements of the modern interior": a wall tapestry, furnishing fabrics, curtains in crêpe de chine, cushions, a carpet, shawls, watercolours, photographs and painted and embroidered objects. In the same year, the Simultané brand was patented in France and the United States for its fabrics, objects and advertising devices. The opening of two branches in London and Rio de Janeiro was announced in the press: Simultané became a trademark. The artist took part in the 1925 *Exposition Internationale des Arts Décoratifs et Industriels Modernes*, where she presented the Simultané boutique with the furrier Jacques Heim and the leather specialist Girau-Gilbert. Following the model of department store windows with their carefully arranged "novelties," Delaunay composed her displays with fur coats laid out flat, fabrics and accessories. The presentation was enthusiastically greeted by the French and international press.

As in any other fashion company, the artist used photography as a vital tool for recording registered models, publicising products in the press and experimenting with the possibilities of the visual image with the cooperation of photographers. While very few of Delaunay's textile and clothing designs have survived the ordeals of time,[76] we do have nearly five hundred prints bearing witness to her production.[77] Up until 1925, when Delaunay's fashion activities were marginal, the photographic records mainly take the form of portraits of the artist wearing her own designs, as in 1913. When the boutique opened, the fashion portraits continued and gave rise to a "gallery" of photographic portraits built up around the Simultané brand: Sophie Taeuber-Arp, Florence Henri, Eyre de Lanux, Nelly Walden-Heimann, Paulette Pax, Nancy Cunard, Violette Napierska, Gloria Swanson, Lucienne Bogaert, Gabrielle Dorziat and Lizica Codreano, the cream of Parisian female society, artists, gallerists' and architects' wives, publishers, actors, dancers, socialites, combined simultaneous fashion with the worlds of the stage and dance, architecture and interior decoration, poetry and the visual arts. Playing on the gender ambiguity made possible by "geometric" fashion, the photographic portraits of the poet René Crevel, architect Ernö Goldfinger and the artists Theo Van Doesburg and Jean Arp wearing simultanist garments, as well as portraits of Tristan Tzara (page 20), Madame Heim, Thérèse Bonney, Maria Lani and Michel Seuphor painted during the same years by Robert Delaunay, celebrated simultanist fashion as the "visual and constructive" art of the day, and were a tremendous tool for promoting simultanism.

The *Parisienne* of the 1920s

While continuing with amateur photography and fashion portraits, Delaunay also worked with professional photographers.[78] The studios (Henri Manuel, the Frères Manuel) and reporters (Paul Géniaux) she called on were known mainly as artistic portraitists; for them fashion photography was a secondary activity and they published their prints in specialist magazines such as *Femina, L'Illustration des Modes, L'Officiel de la Mode, Minerva, L'Excelsior-Mode* and *Le Petit Bleu*, which still limited photography to a documentary function, using it essentially for photogravure. Other studios (Photo Rep, Studio Iris), in contrast, did make use of the resources and specificities of photography, with fashion models, whose own activity was also becoming professionalised, posing for similarly specialist photographers. While most of the photographs were taken in the studio, some sessions were held outdoors and juxtaposed the designs with the great symbols of modernity embodied by Paris and modern architecture. Encouraged by the increasing prominence afforded to photographic images in specialist and artistic magazines (*Vogue, L'Art et la mode, La Revue de la Femme, L'Art vivant*, *L'Amour de l'art*), fashion photography was gradually breaking free of the dominance of the fashion portrait and fashion prints, using new techniques offered by the medium and developed by the proponents of the Nouvelle Vision Photographique.

The *Exposition Internationale des Arts Décoratifs et Industriels Modernes* in 1925 was the most spectacular demonstration of this desire to conjoin fashion and Parisian modernity. Parked in front of the French Embassy Pavilion by Mallet-Stevens, a Citroën B12, covered with colourful geometrical chequers, painted after a drawing by Sonia Delaunay, set the scene for the fashion models bedecked with sumptuous fur coats from the Sonia fashion house. Praised by the women's press as the chic and showy accessory of the new woman, the car – a veritable "mobile mannequin"

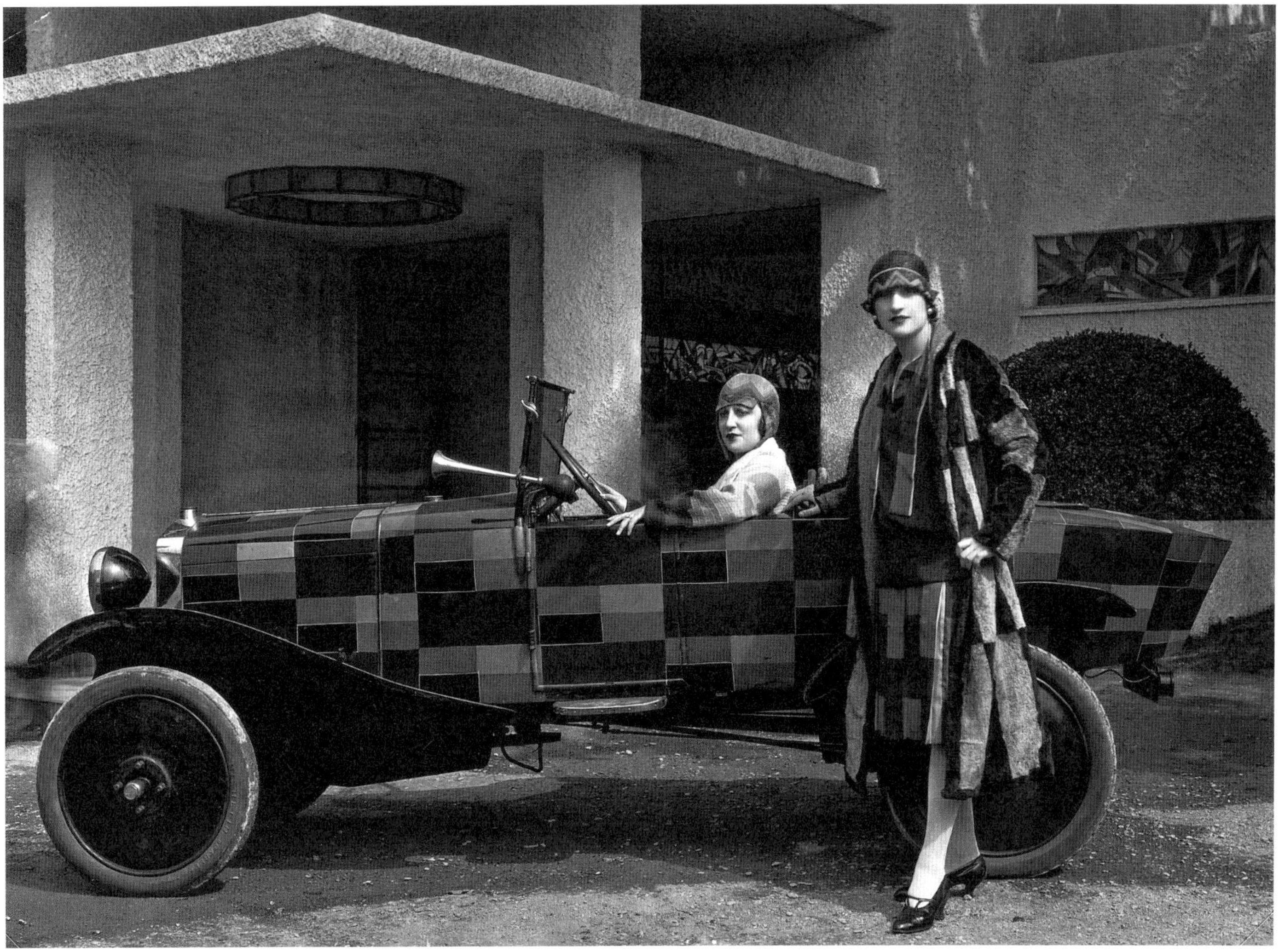

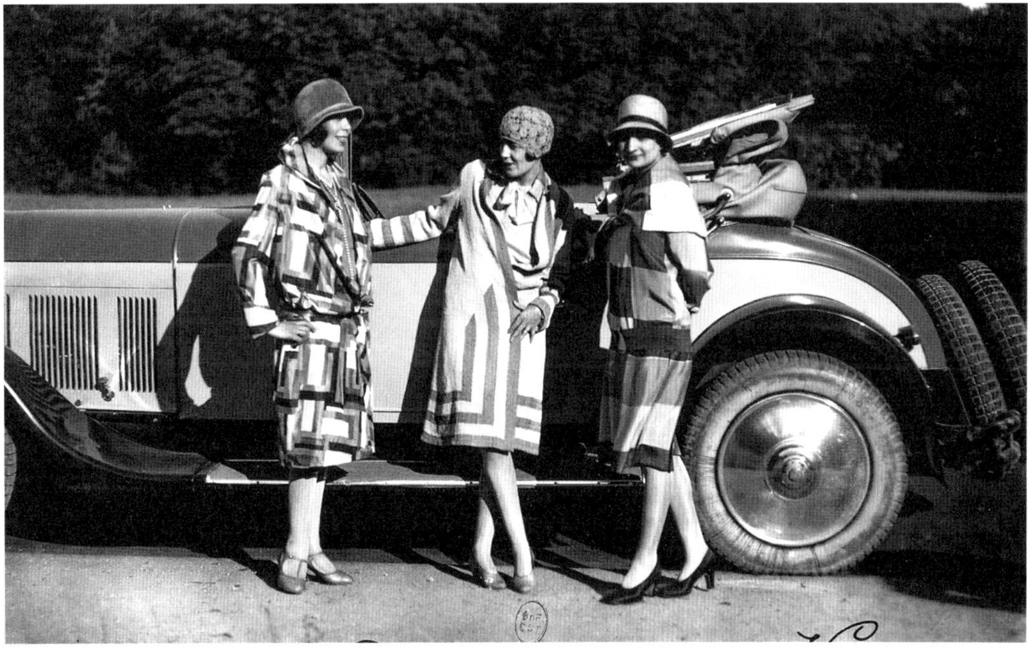

Top: Two models in design by Sonia Delaunay and Citroën B12 decorated by the artist, 1925
Bottom: Three models in coats by Sonia Delaunay in Bois de Boulogne, Paris, c. 1927

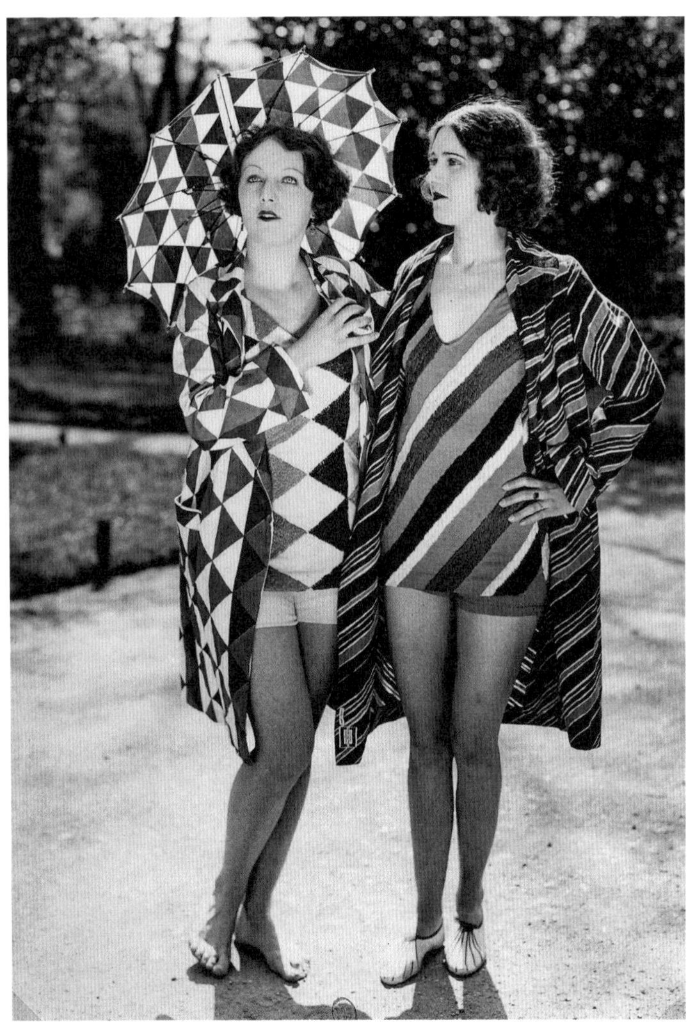

– turned the *simultanist* woman into a modern and independent figure. The bob-haired *garçonne*, that legendary figure of the Roaring Twenties, was extensively illustrated in photographs by the Simultané boutique, exalted by the power of the new clothing and placed in modernist environments. "Representing a new *social type*, that of the *liberated* woman,"[79] the *garçonne* was presented smoking, her short hair swept back wearing a "gender-neutral" outfit and displaying a certain casualness in front of the lens. Celebrated by the modernist setting, she embodied the "type" of the Parisian woman of the 1920s: in Francis Jourdain's gymnasium, in front of the Cubist trees by the brothers Jan and Joël Martel, in the Guévrékian garden, or in Rue Mallet-Stevens, inaugurated in 1927 in Auteuil, simultanist fashion flirted with the most modern architecture of its day.[80]

As Delaunay brought in a number of renowned photographers such as the American Thérèse Bonney and the French Florence Henri, the German photographer Germaine Krull produced a series of fashion pictures for Maison Sonia.[81] These images were published by the foreign press, especially in Germany, where newspapers and periodicals such as *Frankfurter Zeitung, Für die Frau, Illustrierte Textil-Zeitung* and *Bilder Courier* presented them in carefully conceived layouts and with a high quality of reproduction. In plain but skilfully composed compositions, portraits of Sonia Delaunay by Germaine Krull introduced the new visual language to the public. Some of the photographs, set in the apartment-boutique on Boulevard Malesherbes, presented "artistic models" in a decor wholly designed by the artist. The models merged with the simultanist setting and the general effect was that of a total wallpaper inscribing fashion in the ultimate modernity of the day. These photographs were given a novel extension in the rare paintings executed by Sonia Delaunay in the 1920s *Robes Simultanées (Trois femmes, forms, couleurs* (Simultaneous Dresses (Three Women, Forms, Colours), 1925, page 5).

Despite the different backgrounds and specialisations of the photographers, the collection of images relating to the history of Maison Sonia reveals a singular homogeneity, and the iconography that it conveys offers a telling illustration of the Jazz Age. While the fashion images of course publicised Maison Sonia by virtue of their dissemination in the international press, they also ratified the synthesis of the arts pursued by the Delaunays since 1913 and, along with theatre, poetry, advertising, fashion shows, cinema, animated win dow displays and "modern films in colour," constituted a way of staging fashion and, through fashion, painting.

Cécile Godefroy is an art historian, PhD, and an independent curator. Author of several essays on Sonia Delaunay, as well as a book dedicated to *Sonia Delaunay. Sa mode, ses tableaux, ses tissus* in 2014 (Paris, Flammarion) and co-curated with Anne Montfort-Tanguy the retrospective Sonia Delaunay at Musée d'Art Moderne in Paris and Tate Modern, London, in 2014-15.

Models in swimwear and with a parasol designed by Sonia Delaunay, c. 1929
Right page: Model wearing silk tunic designed by Sonia Delaunay, 1925

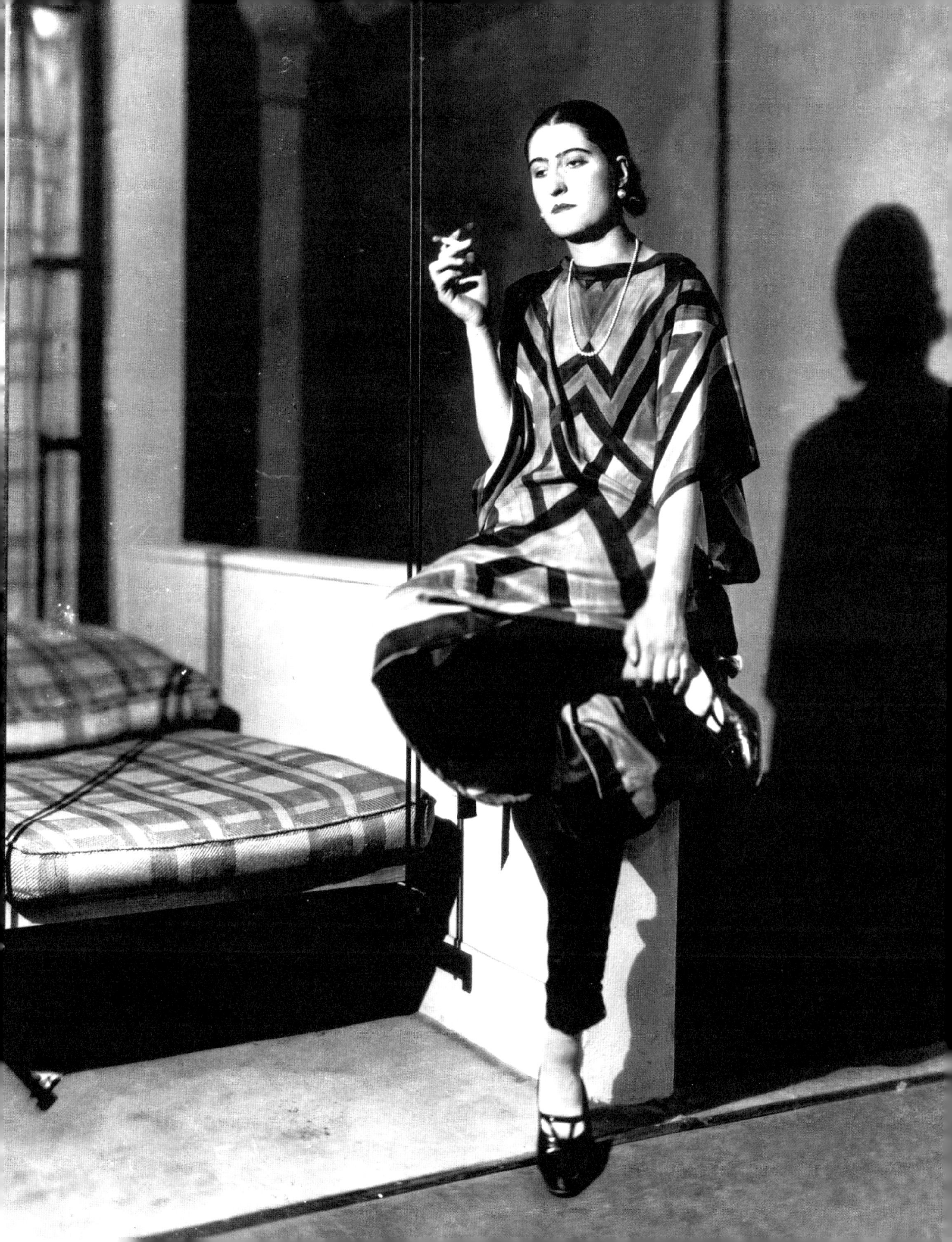

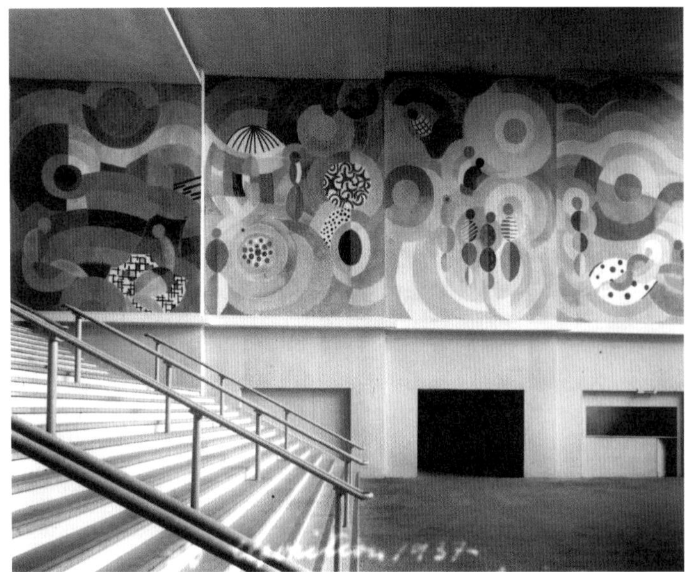

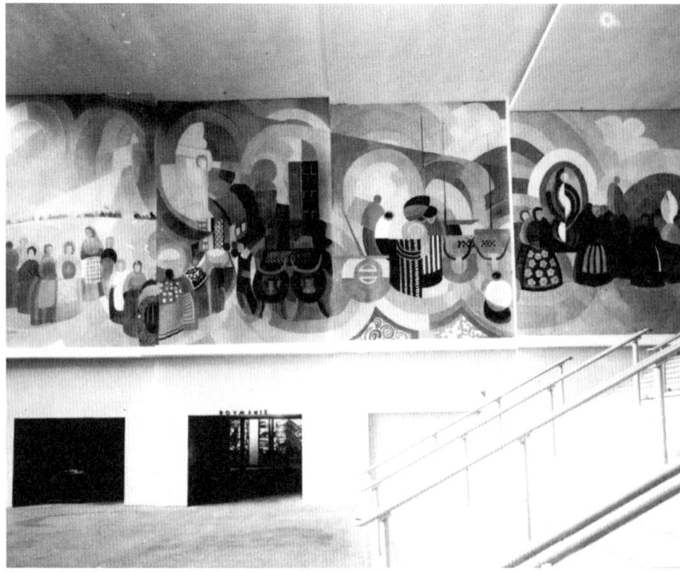

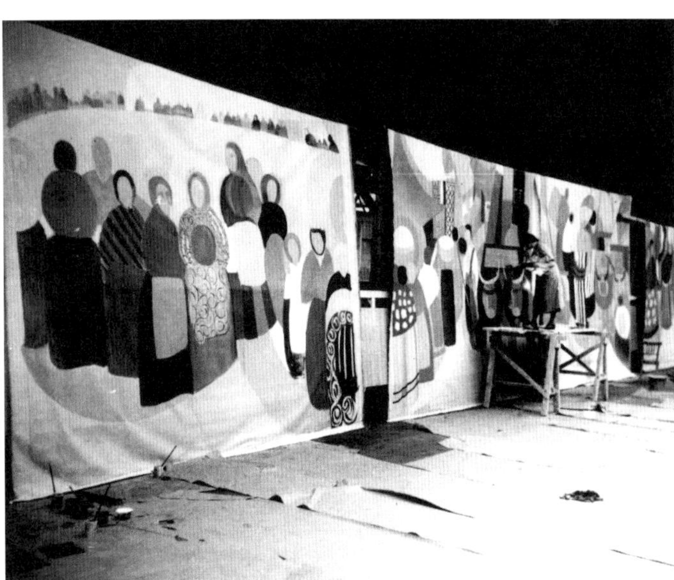

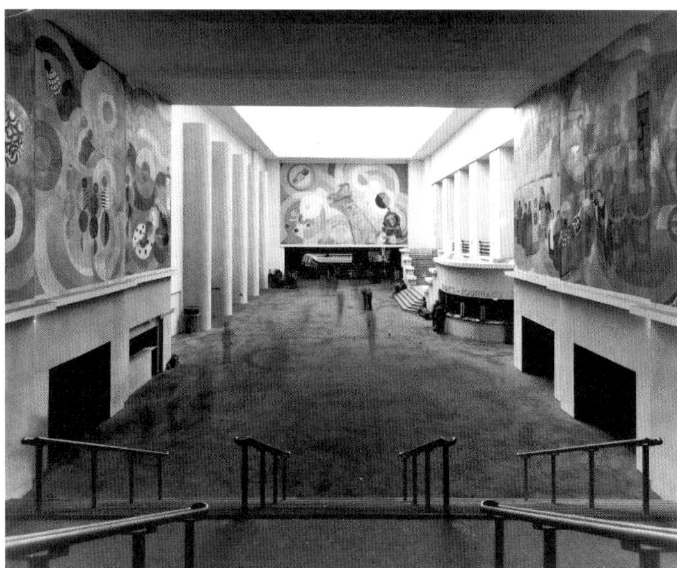

Sonia Delaunay's large paintings *Voyages lointains* and *Portugal* created for the Palais des Chemins de Fer (Railways Pavilion) for The World's Exposition in Paris, 1937. The sketches can be seen on the opposite page

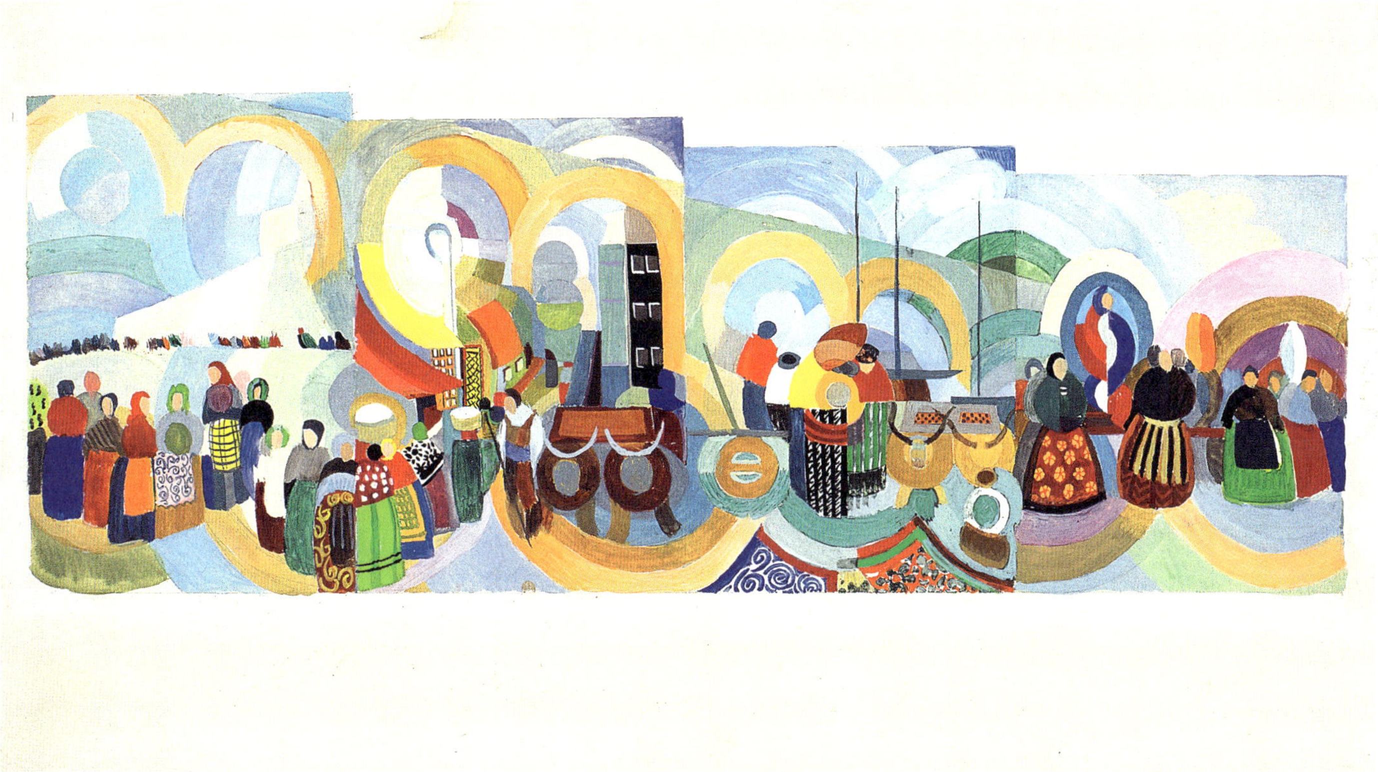

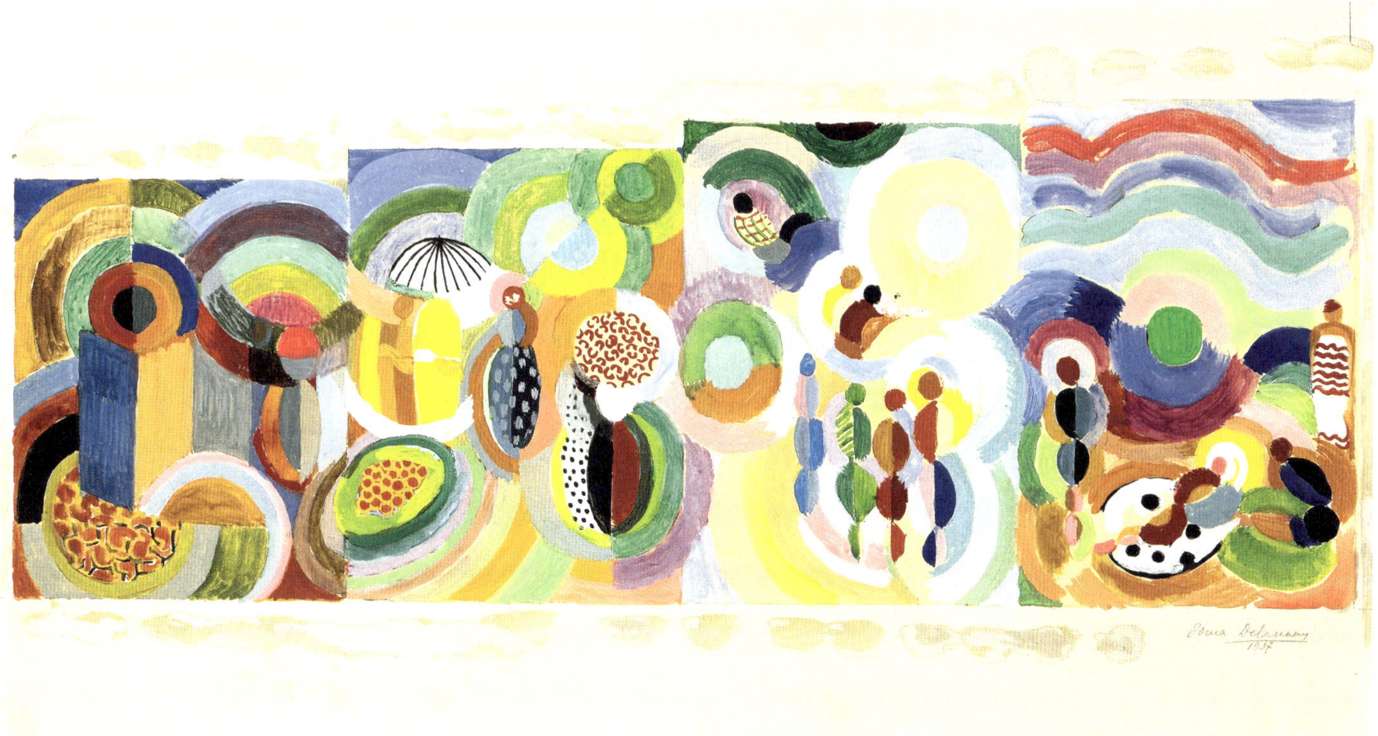

Top: *Portugal*, 1937
Bottom: *Voyages lointains*, 1937. Distant Journeys

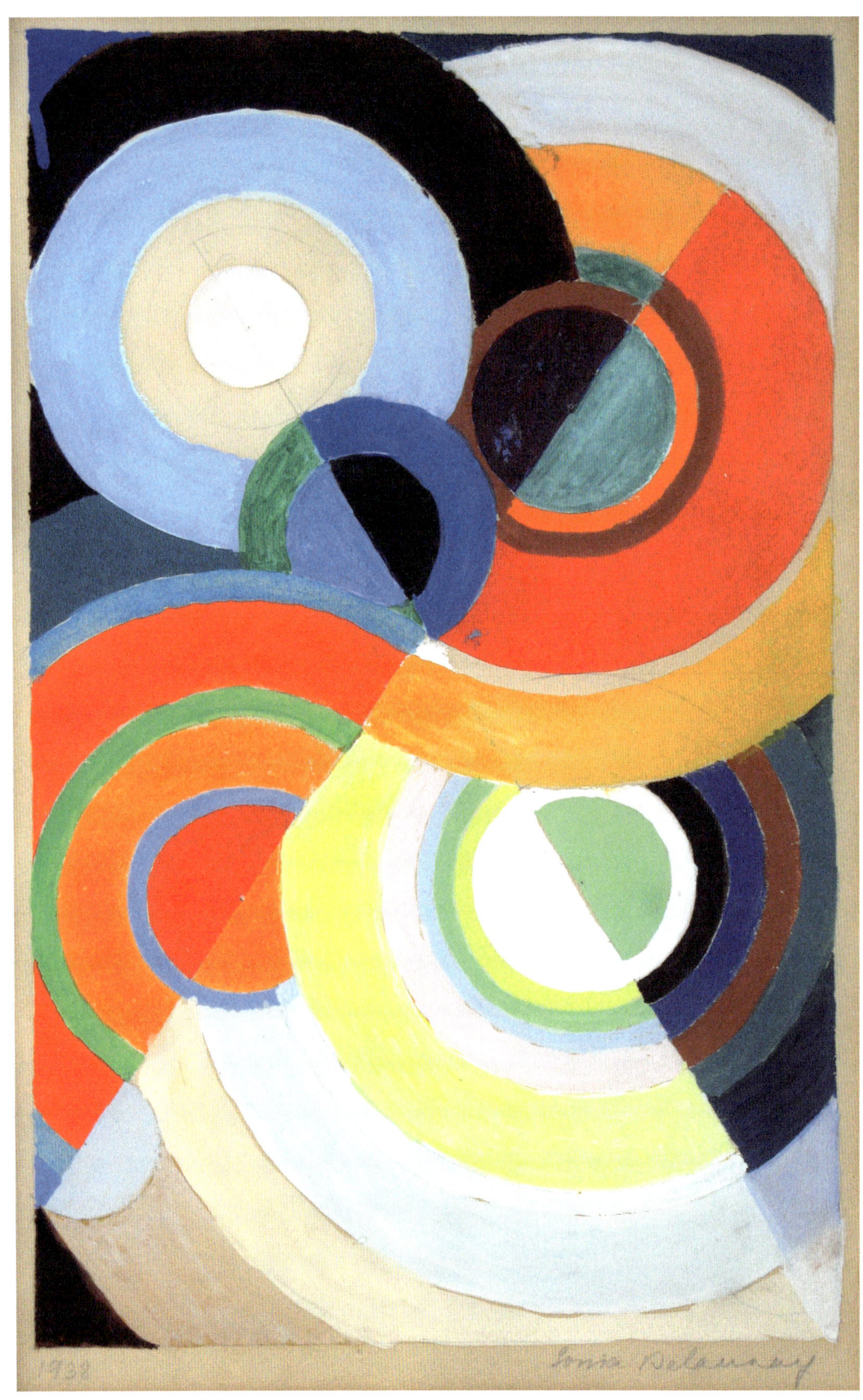

Gouache 1938 no. 1, 1938. Gouache 1938 No. 1
Right page: *Rythme*, 1938. Rhythm

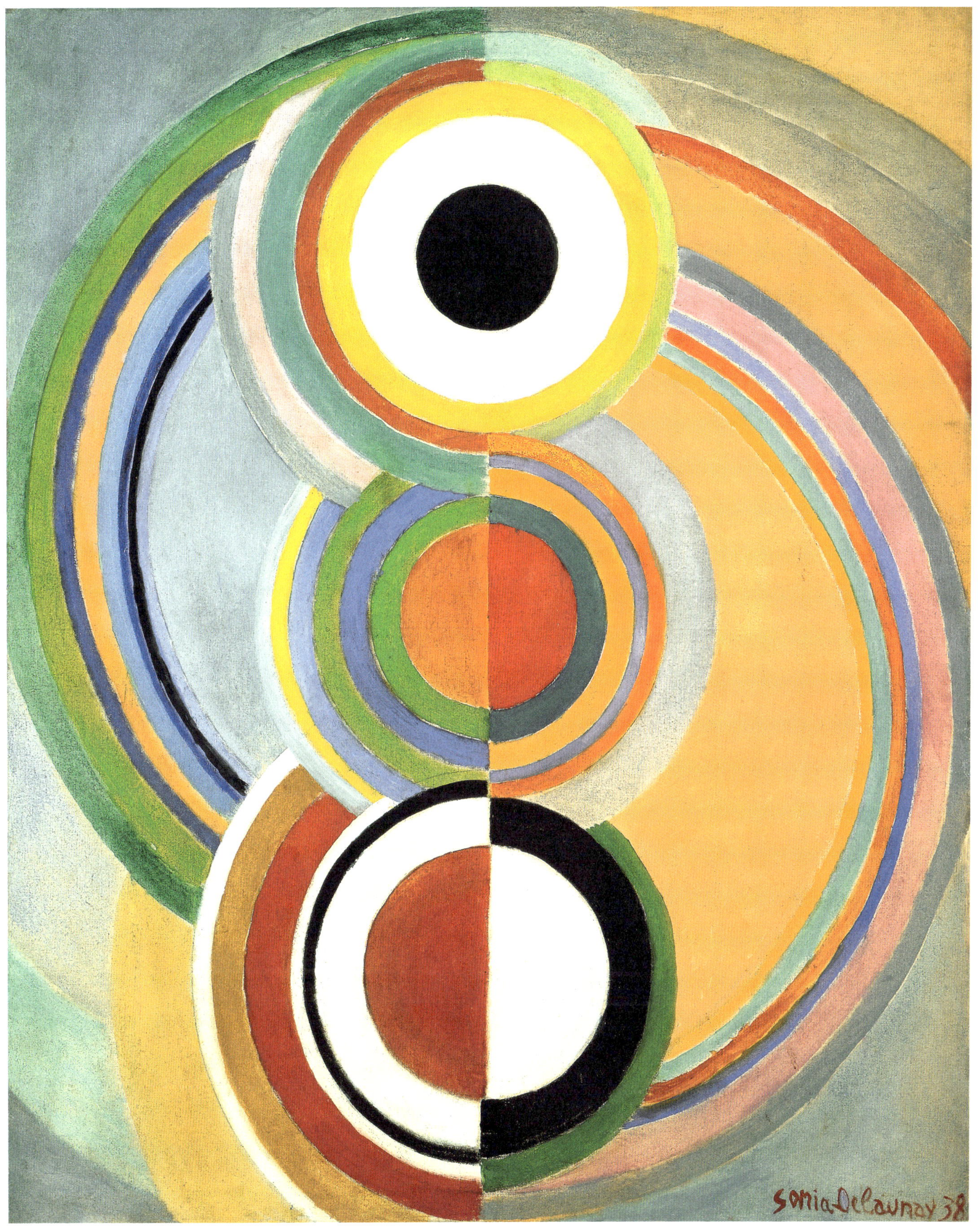
Sonia Delaunay 38

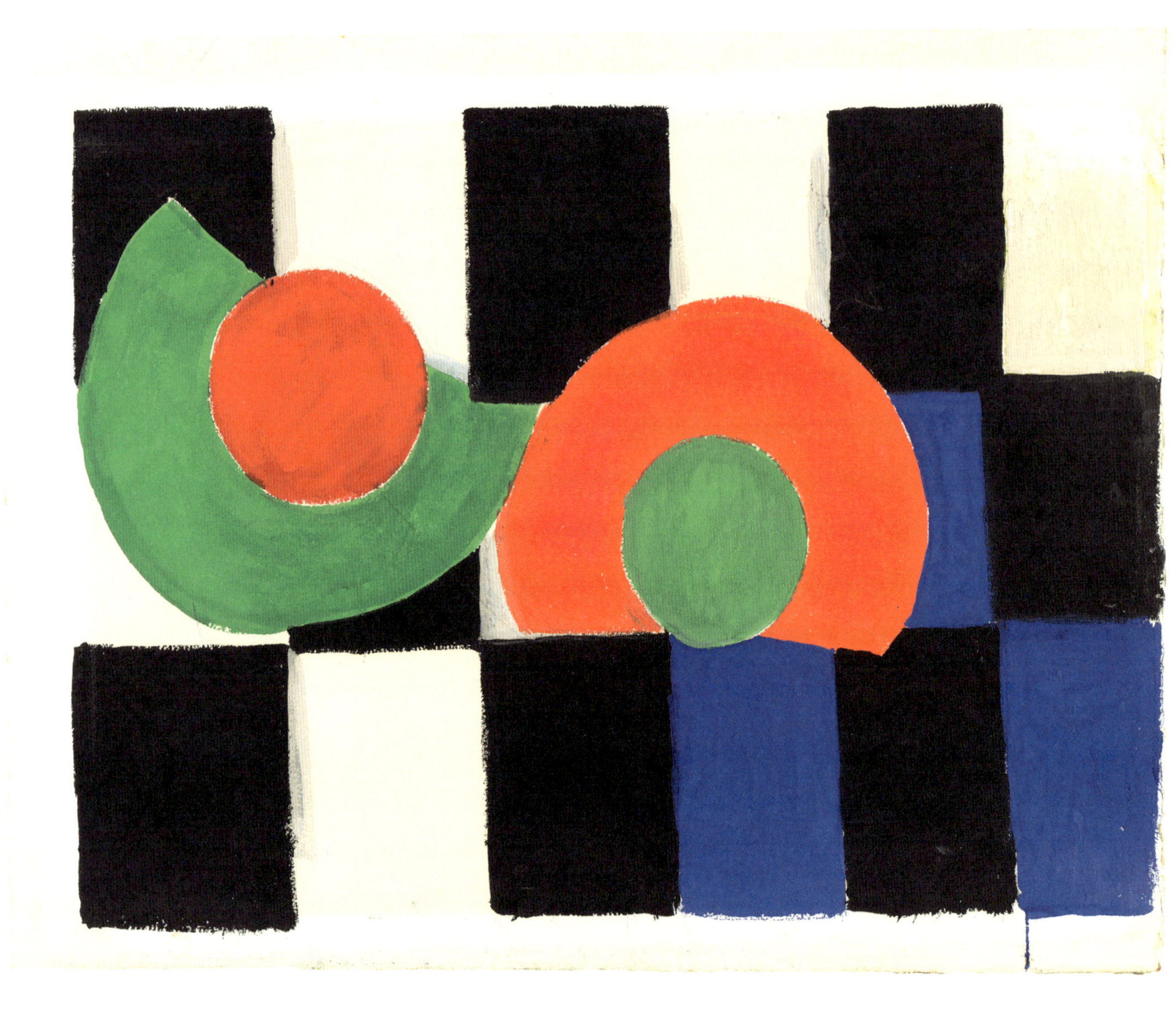

Coloured Rhythm, 1953
Right page: Top: *Rythme coloré*, *Paris*, 1954. Coloured Rhythm
Bottom: *Rythme coloré*, 1952. Coloured Rhythm

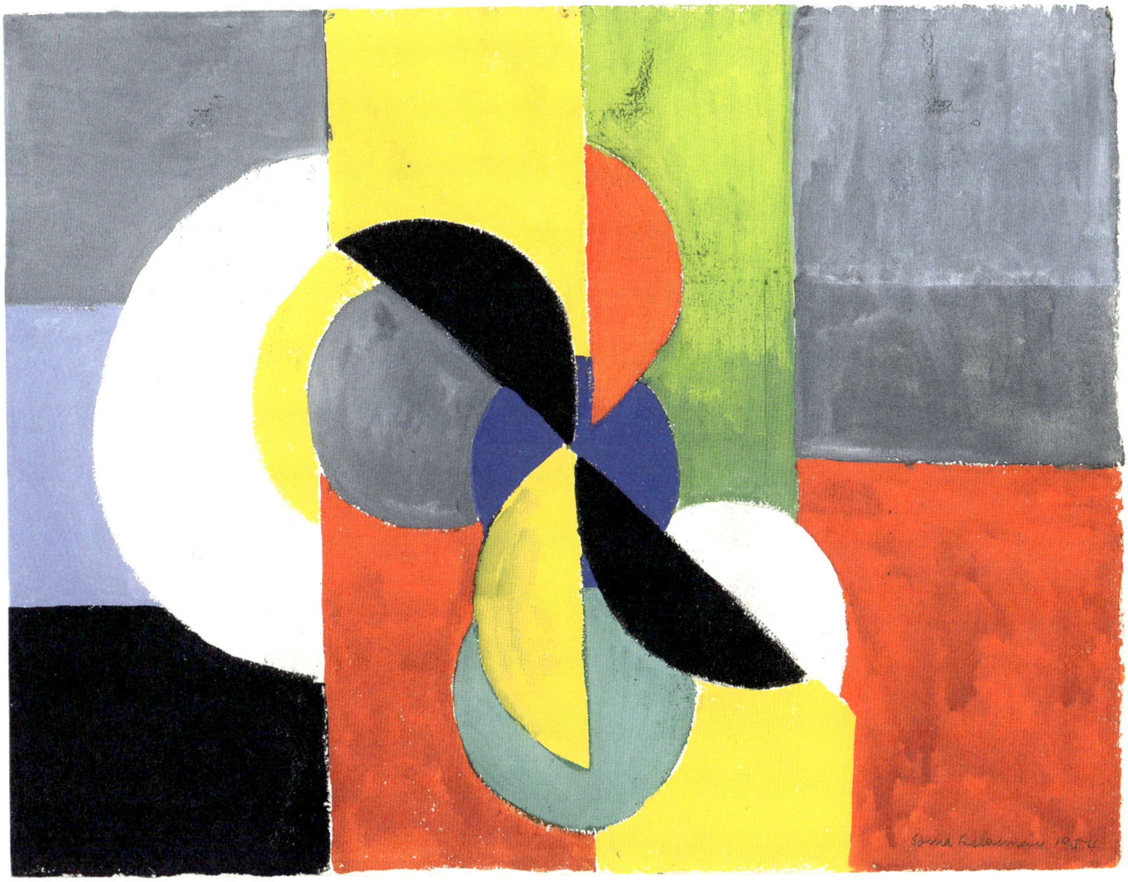

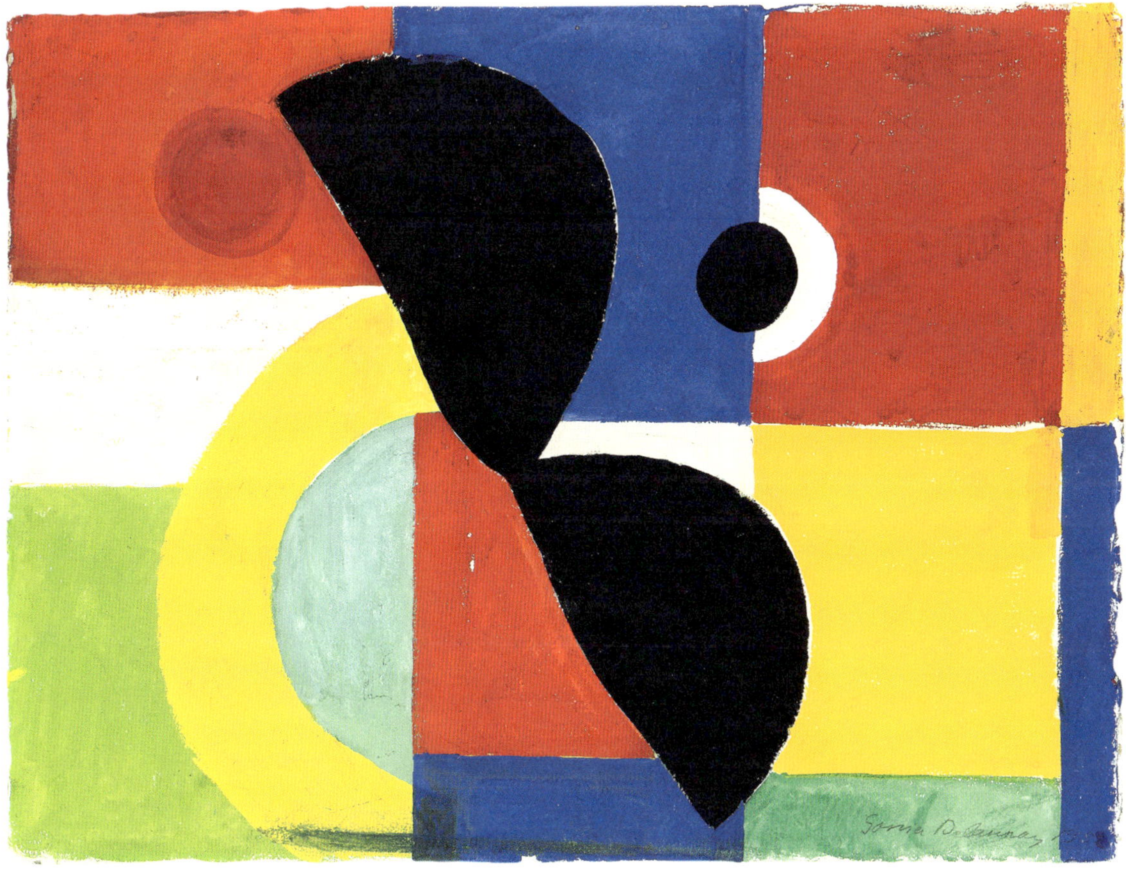

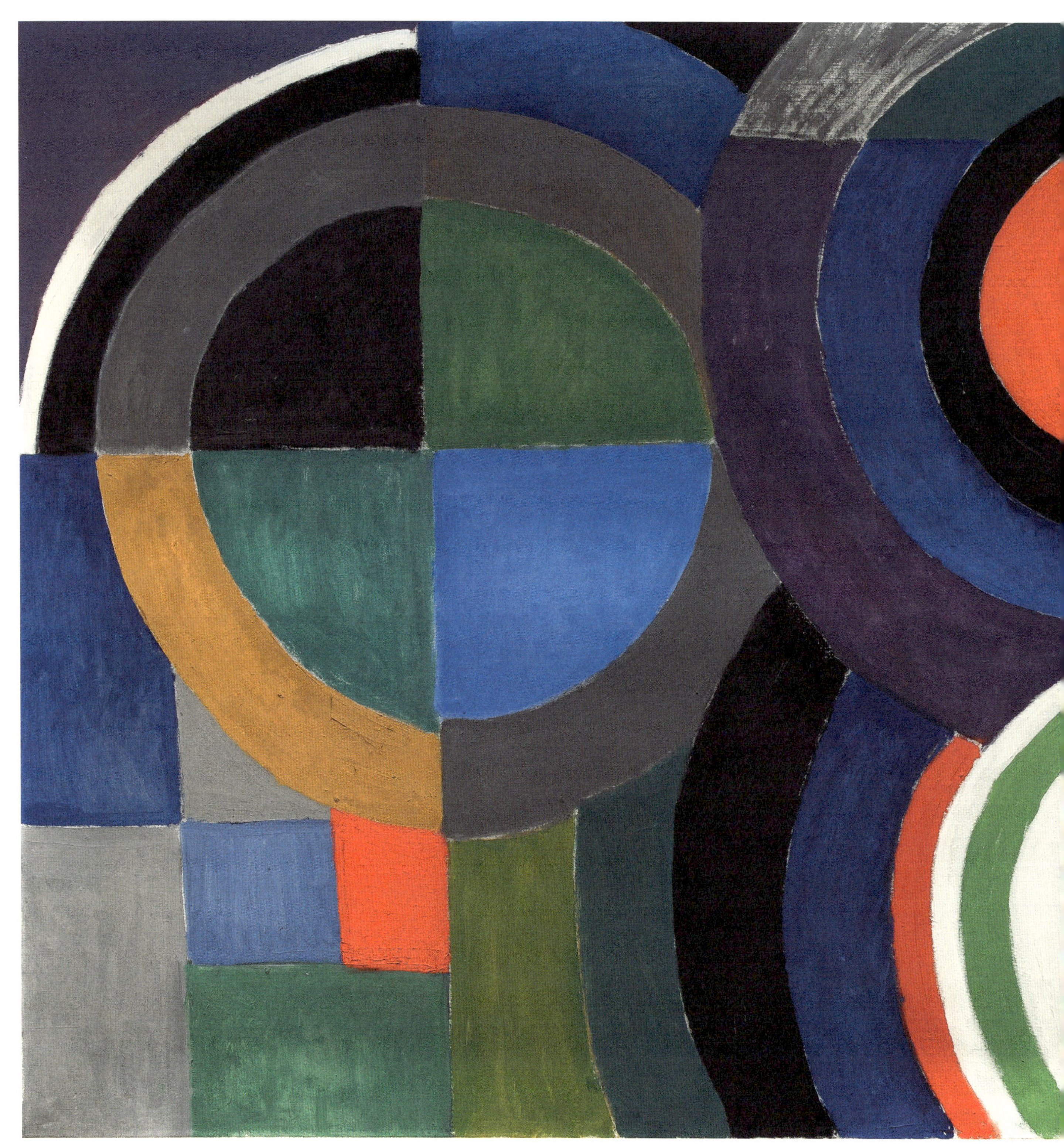

Rythme couleur, 1964. Rhythm Colour

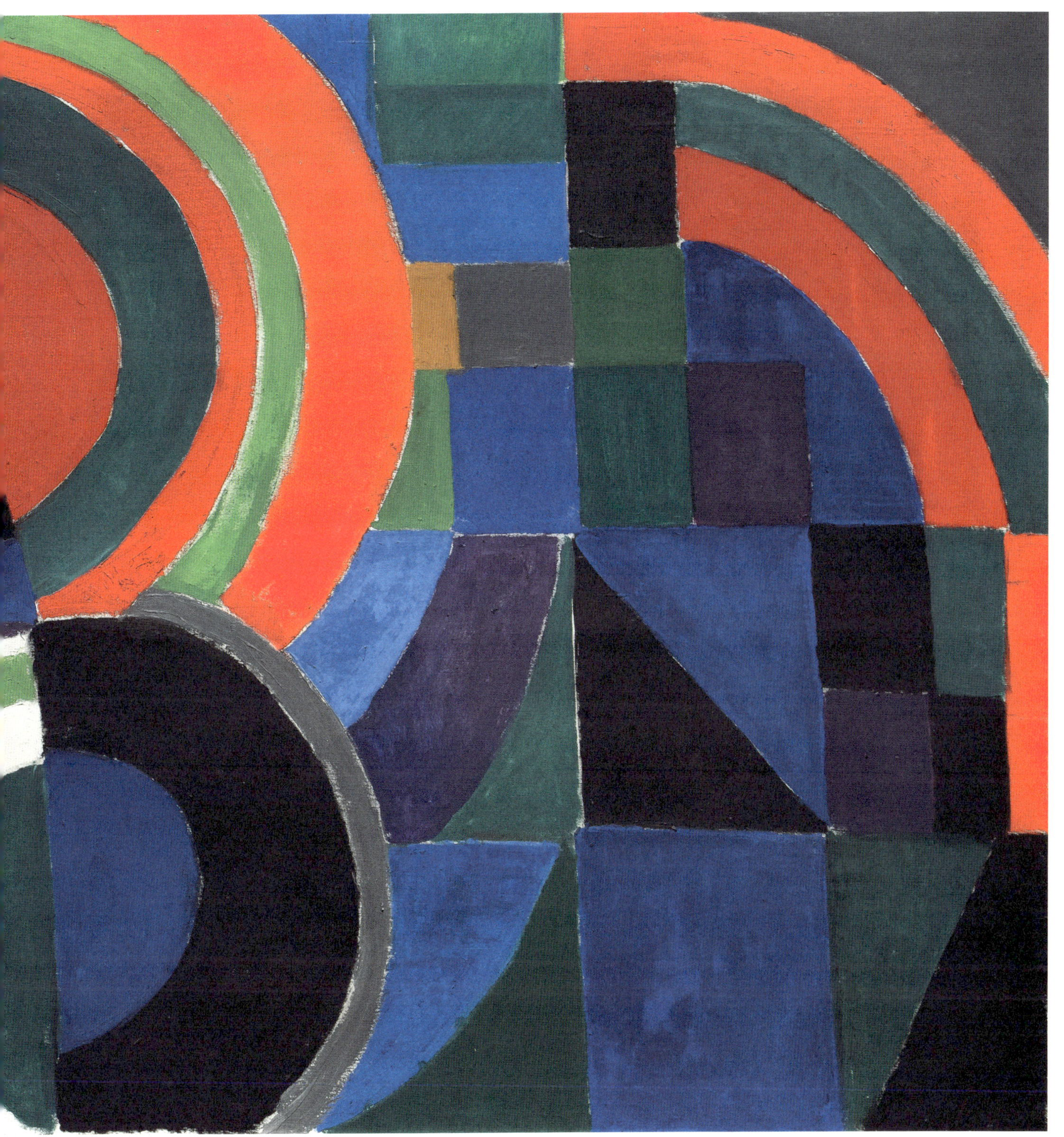

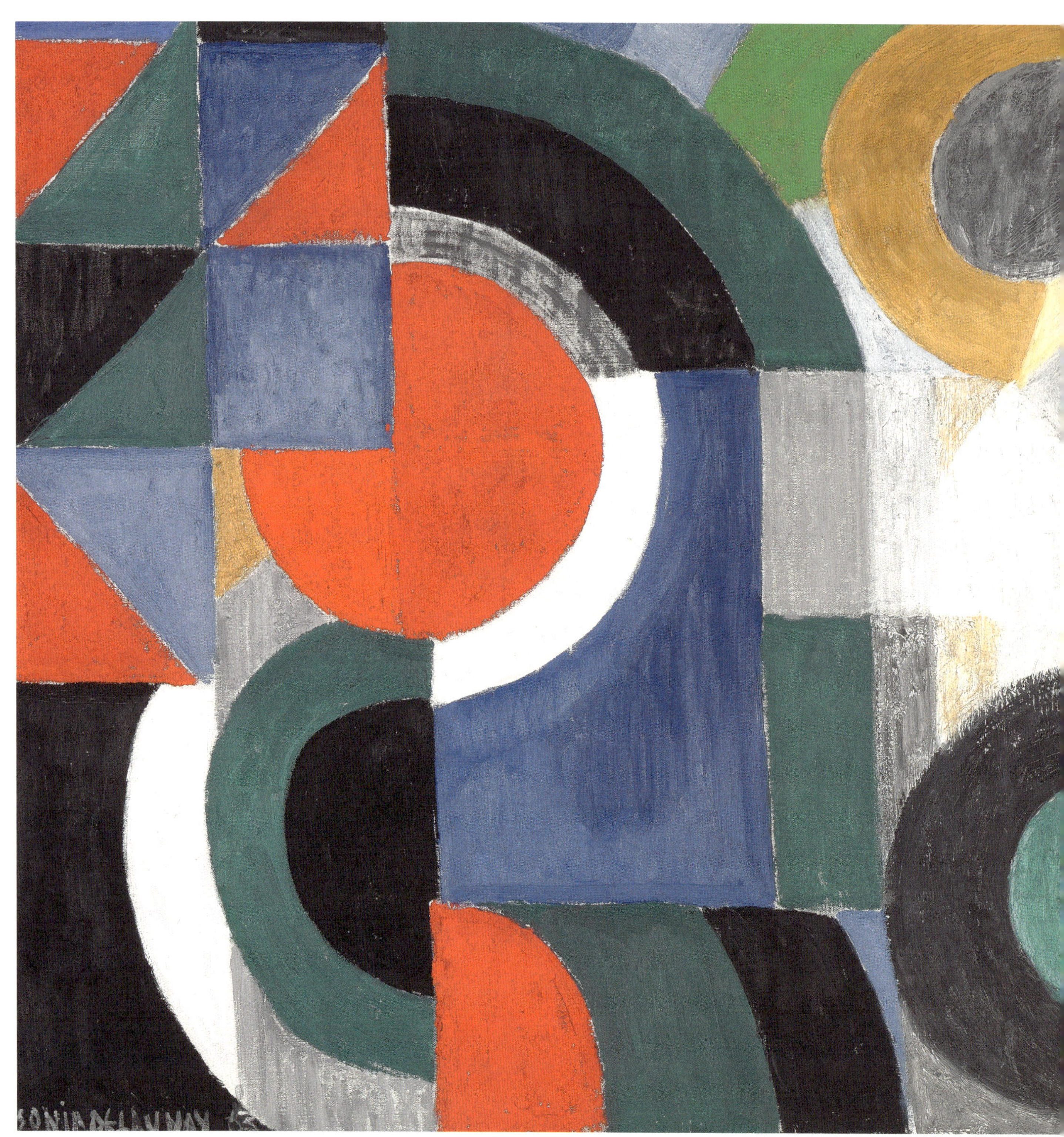

Triptyque, 1963. Triptych

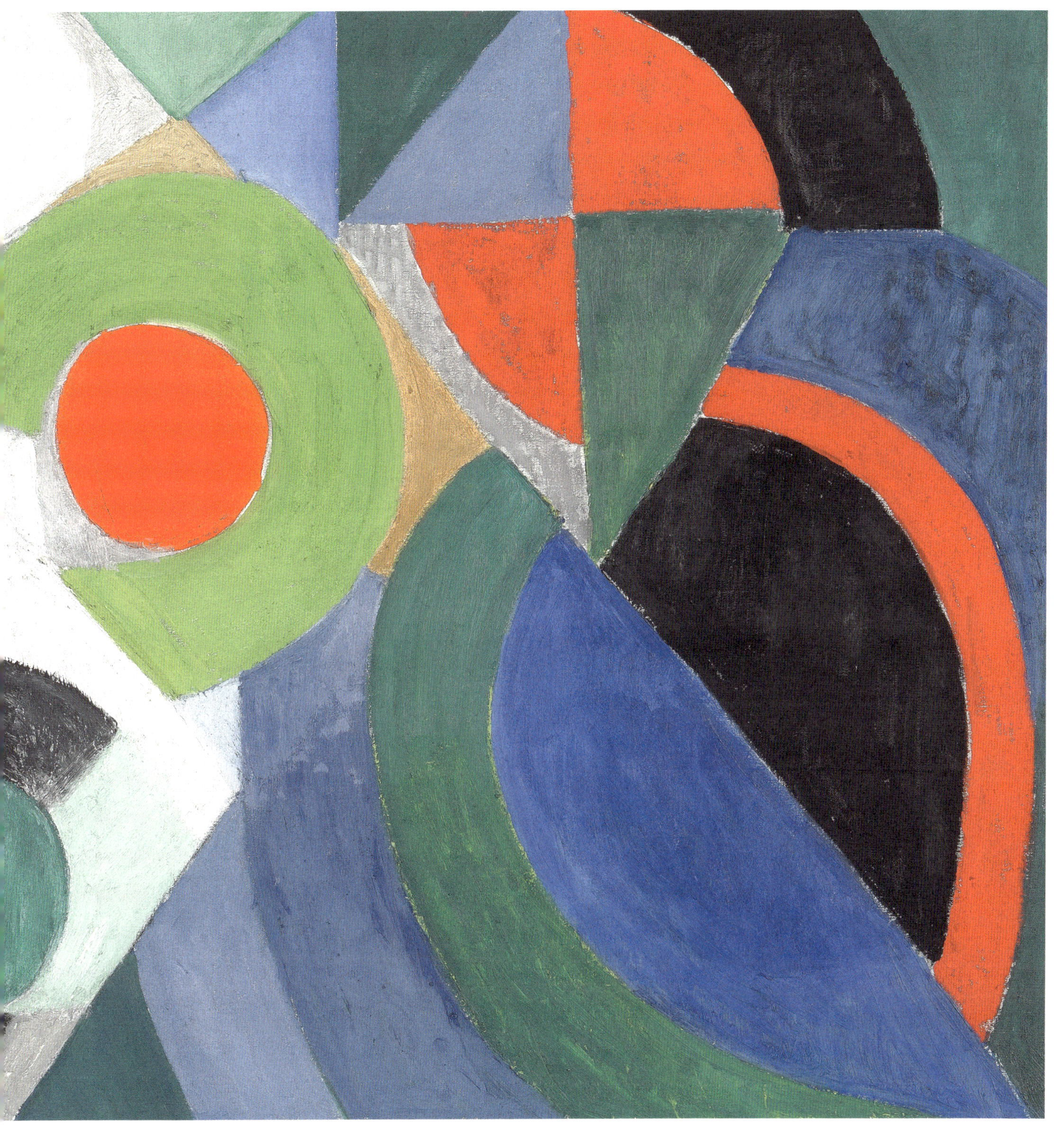

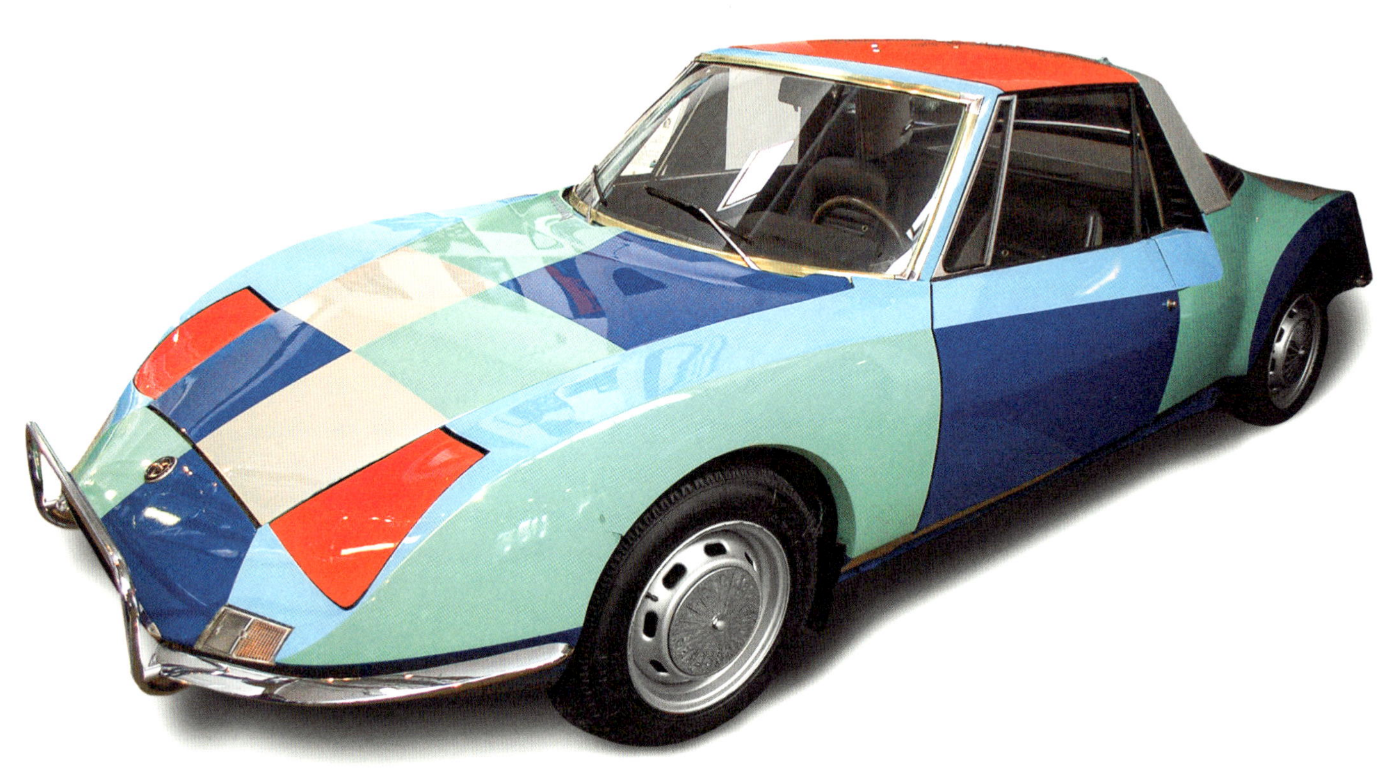

Matra 530 A, 1967
Right page: *Rythme couleur*, 1967. Rhythm Colour

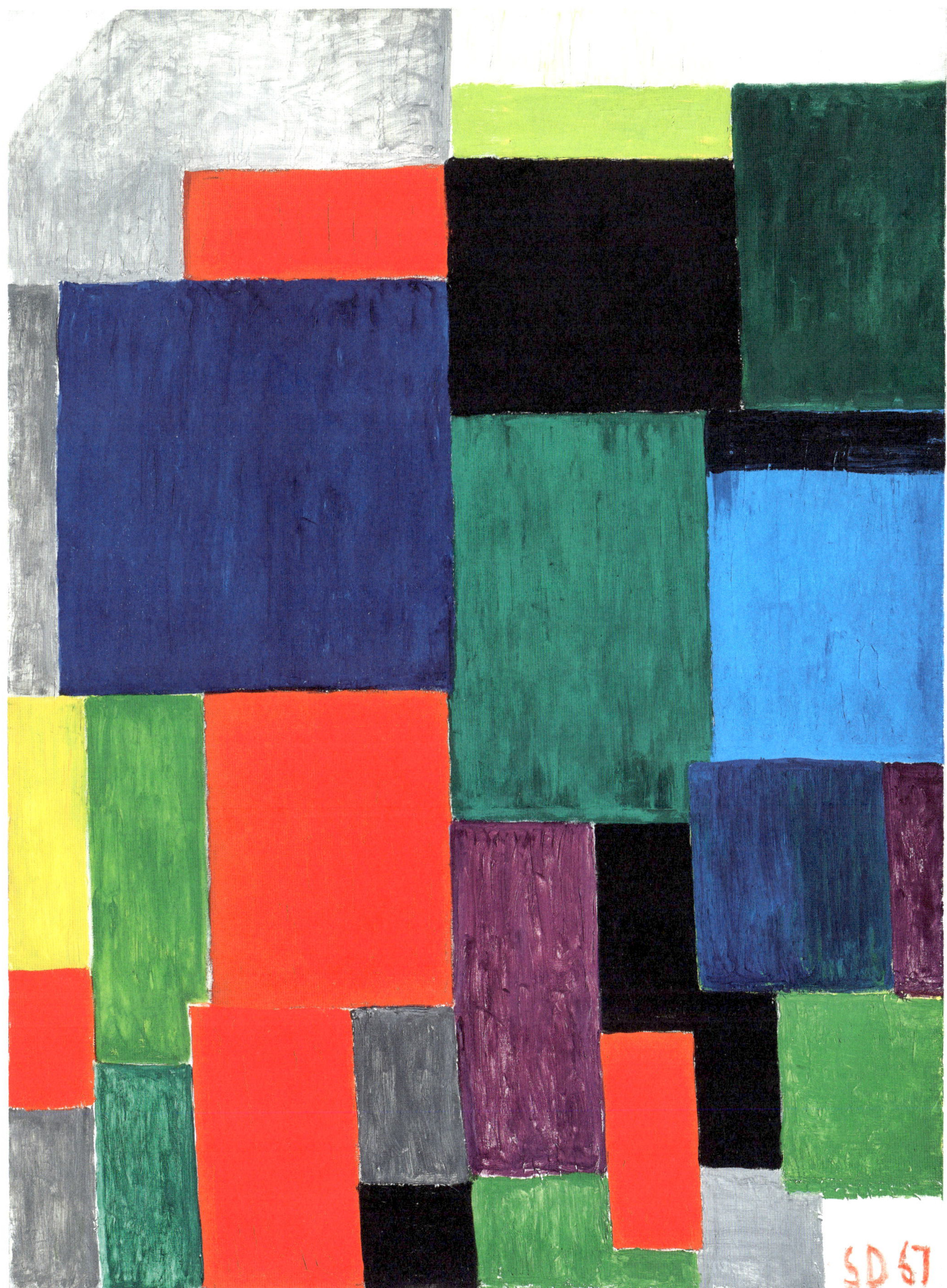
SD 67

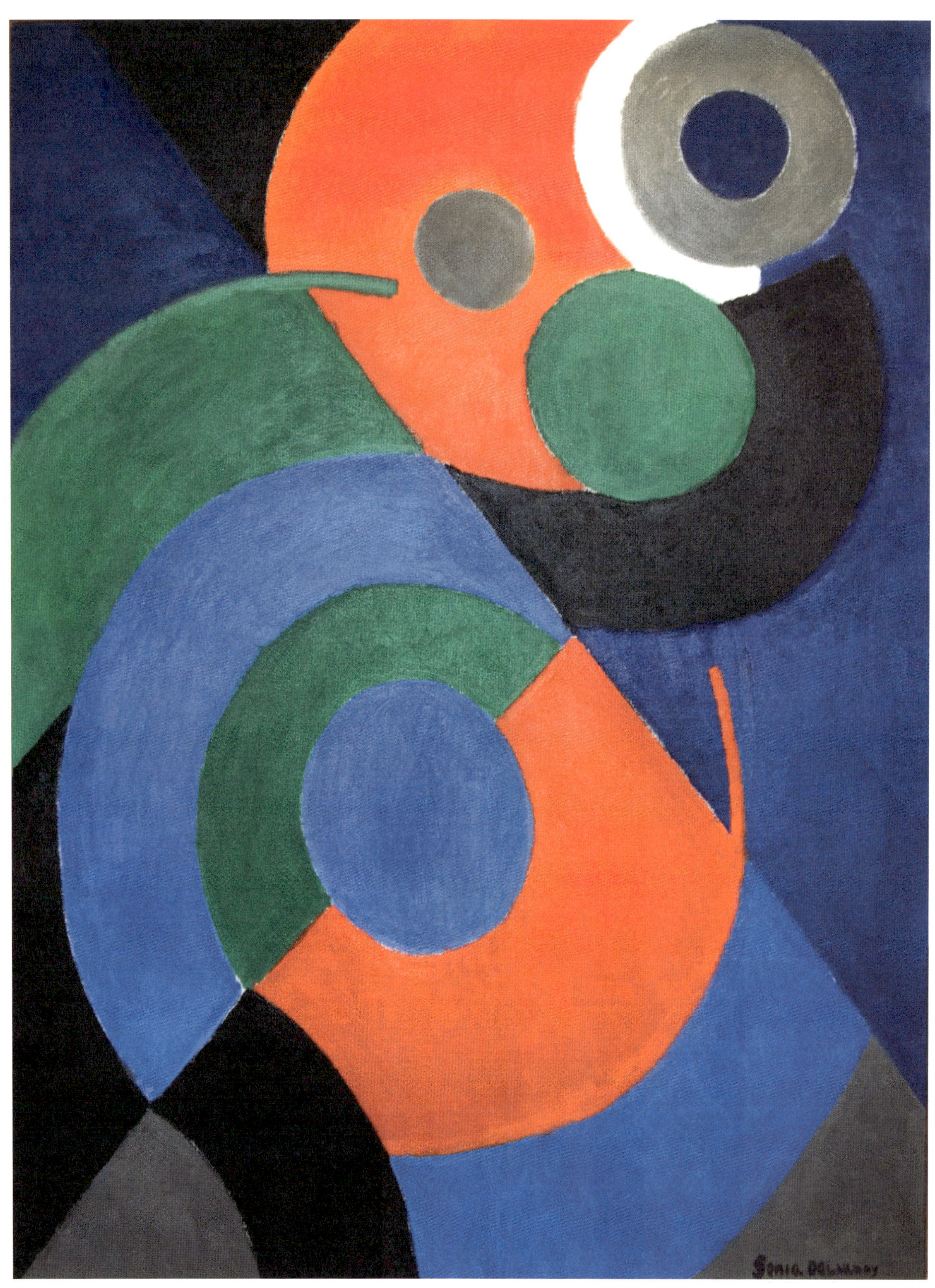

Rythme coloré (no. 614), 1954-1957. Coloured Rhythm (No. 614)
Right page: *Disques*, 1968. Discs

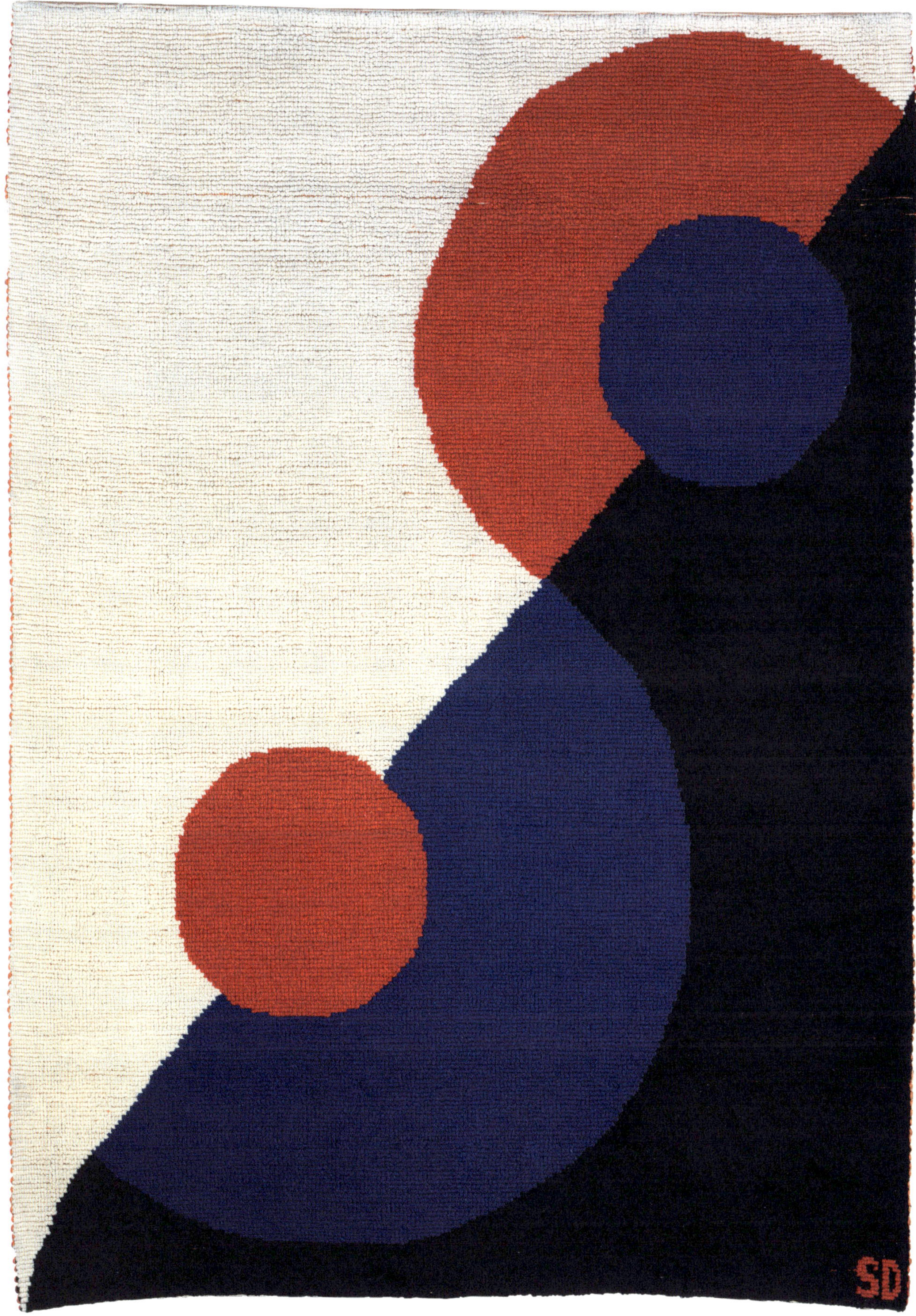
SD

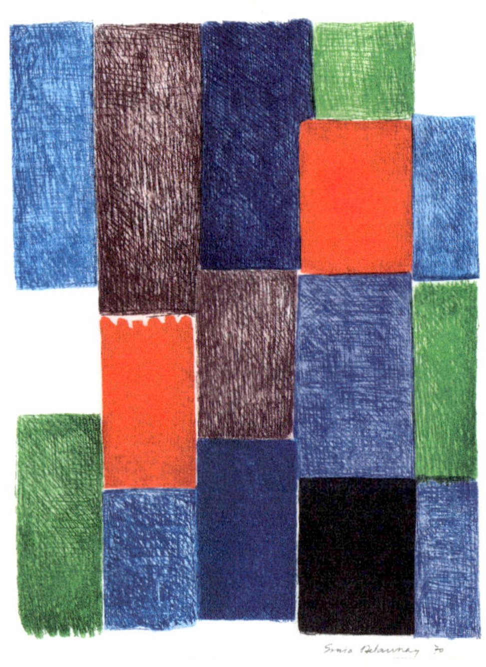

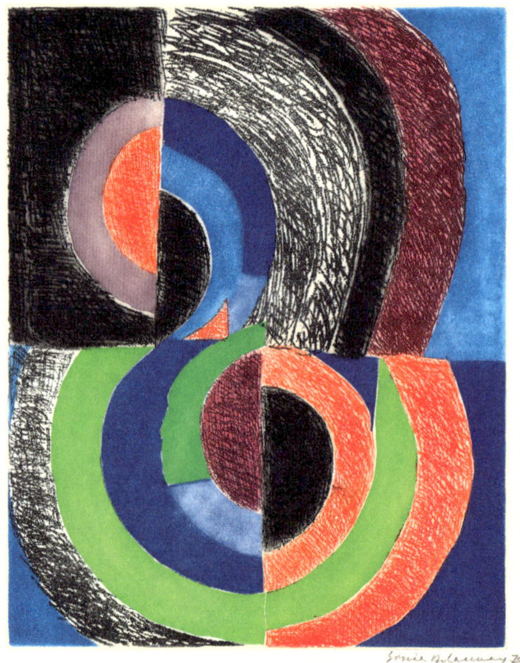

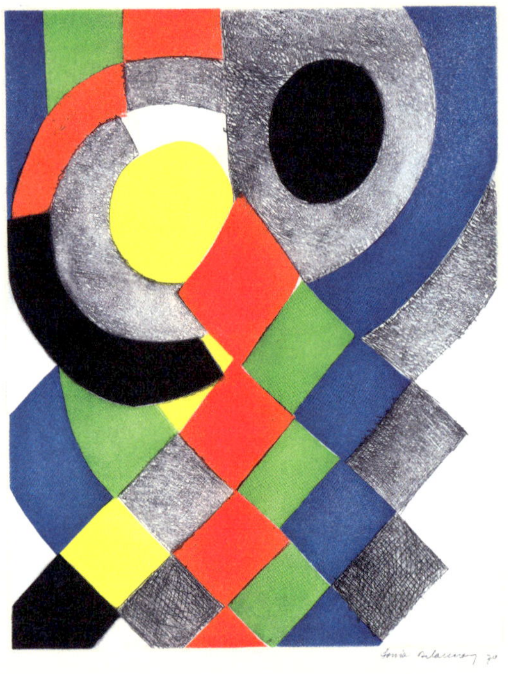

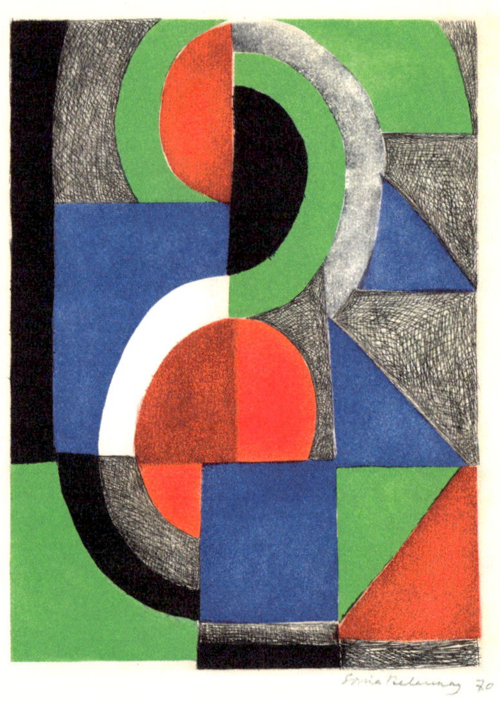

Four works from *Avec moi-même (Portfolio de seize éléments dont dix planches)*, November 1970
With Myself (Portfolio: sixteen elements, containing ten etchings)

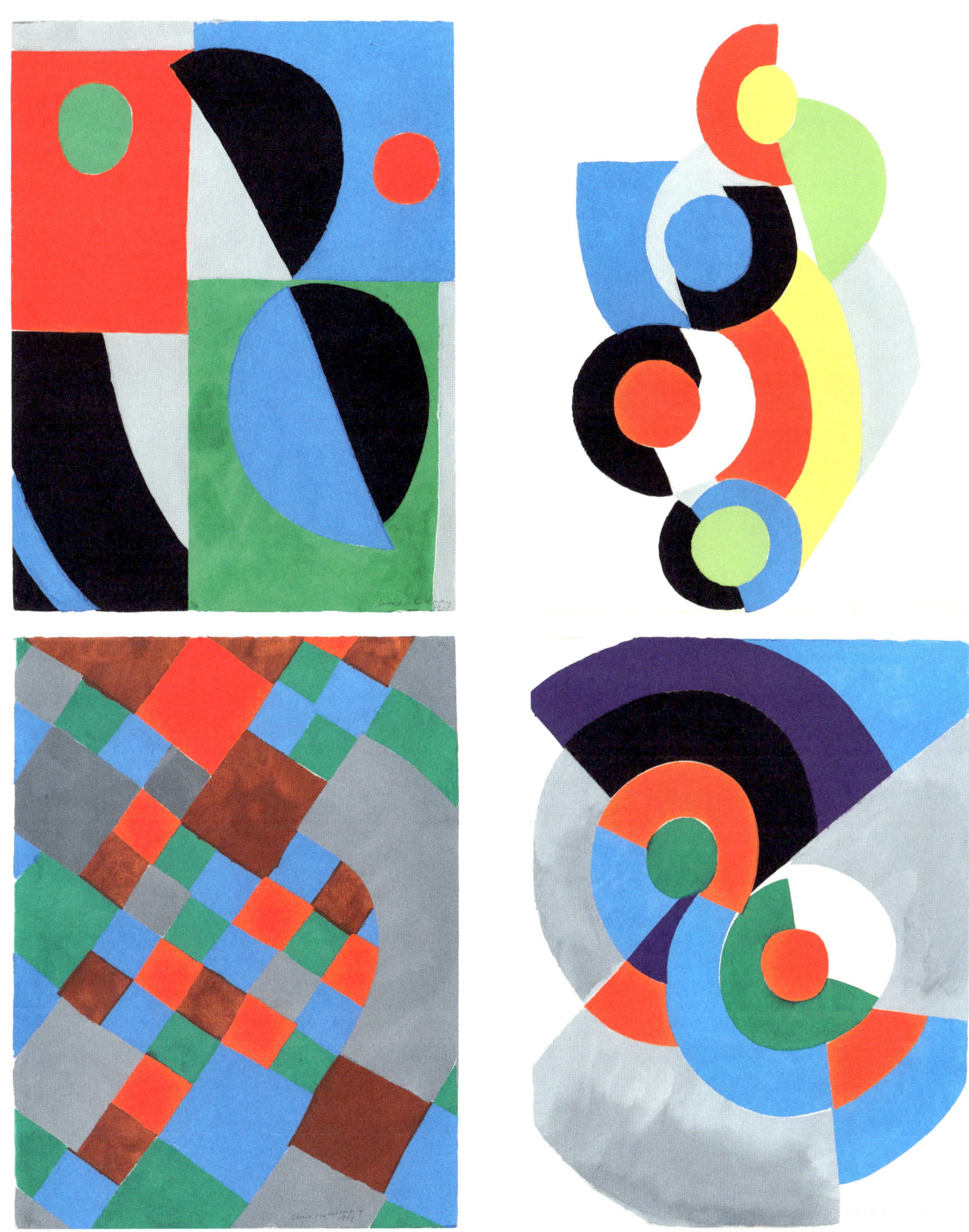

Four works from the portfolio *Poésie de mots, poésie de couleurs*, 1961/1962. Word Poetry, Colour Poetry

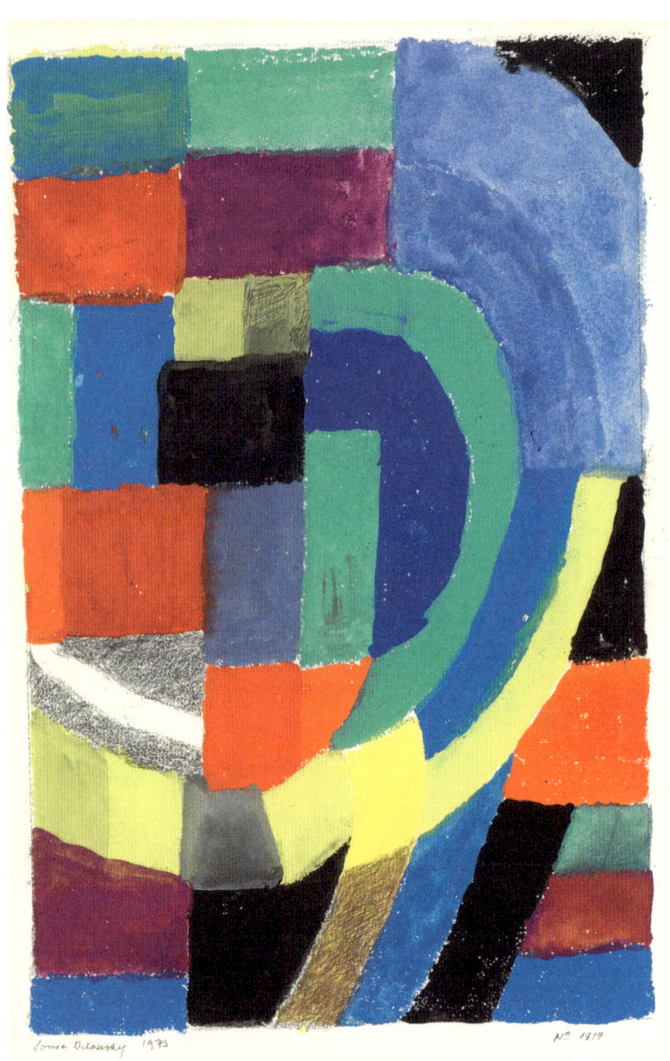

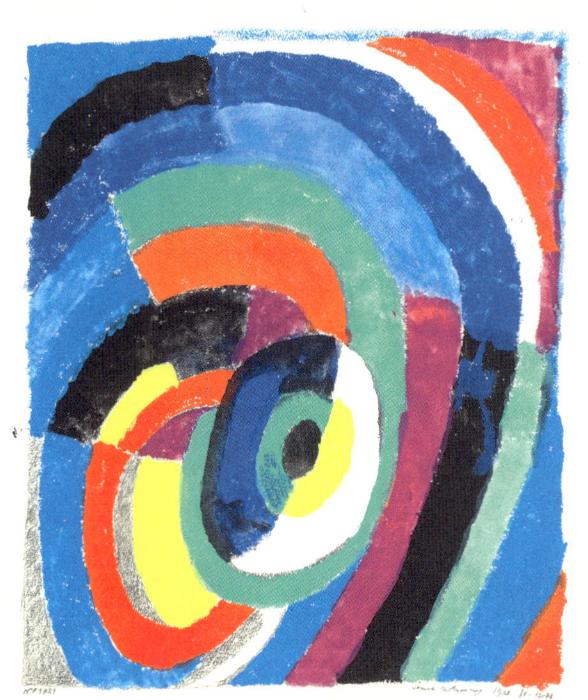

Top: *Rythme Couleur no. 1919*, 1973. Rhythm Colour No. 1919
Right: *Colour Rhythm No. 1921-1973*, 1973
Right page: *Rythme Couleur no. 1916*, 1973. Rhythm Colour No. 1916

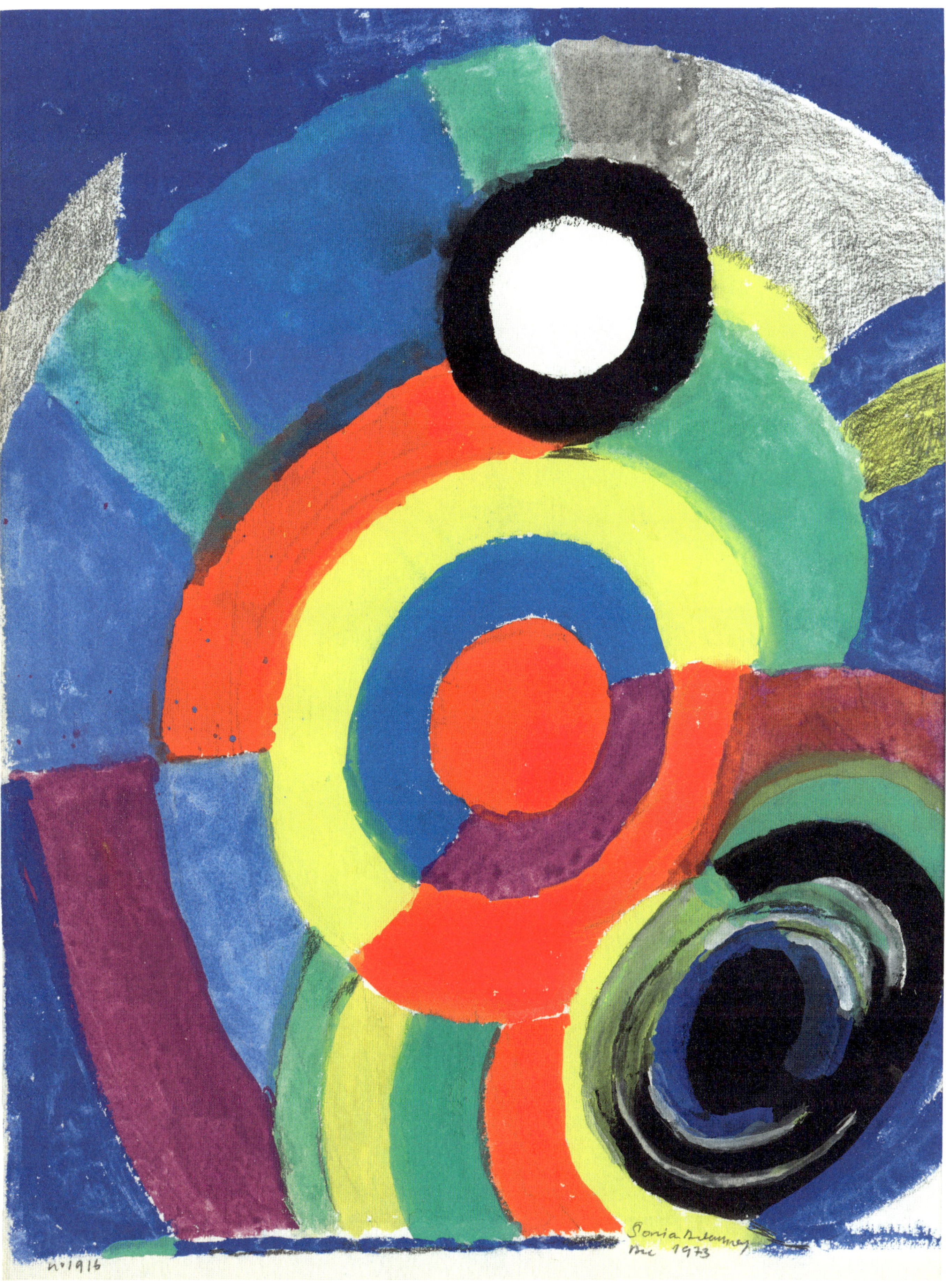
n°1916
Sonia Delaunay
1973

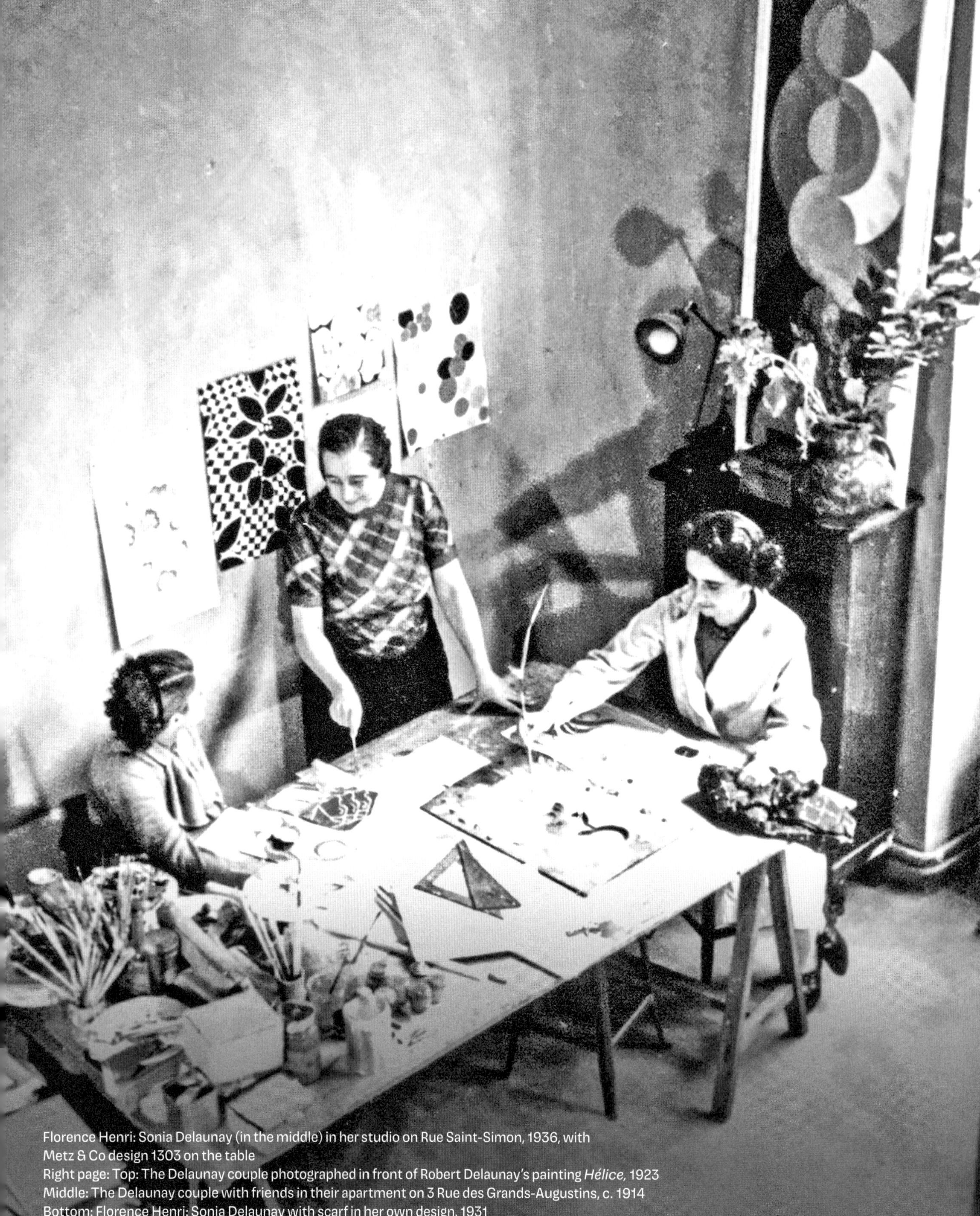

Florence Henri: Sonia Delaunay (in the middle) in her studio on Rue Saint-Simon, 1936, with Metz & Co design 1303 on the table
Right page: Top: The Delaunay couple photographed in front of Robert Delaunay's painting *Hélice,* 1923
Middle: The Delaunay couple with friends in their apartment on 3 Rue des Grands-Augustins, c. 1914
Bottom: Florence Henri: Sonia Delaunay with scarf in her own design, 1931

BIOGRAPHY

1885
Sara Stern is born on 14 November in Odessa, Russia (now Ukraine), the youngest of three children in a Jewish working-class family.

1890
At five years old she is sent to St. Petersburg to be raised by her wealthy uncle and aunt, Henri and Anna Terk. She takes their surname and is always called Sonia. The Terk family takes her along on trips to museums and galleries in Europe.

1904
She moves to Karlsruhe, Germany to study painting and drawing with Professor Ludwig Schmid-Reutte.

1906
Sonia Terk travels to Paris to study at the Académie de la Palette. She experiences the period's colourful Fauvist painting style and is inspired by artists such as van Gogh, Gauguin and Matisse.

1907
In Paris she meets the German art critic Wilhelm Uhde, who runs the Galerie Notre-Dame-des-Champs. She becomes part of Uhde's network and exhibits at his gallery alongside Braque and Picasso, the pioneers of Cubism. She also meets the painter Robert Delaunay.

1908
She exhibits vividly coloured portrait paintings at her first solo show at Uhde's gallery. She defies the Terk family's wish for her to return to St. Petersburg by entering into a marriage of convenience with Uhde, who is homosexual.

1910
She divorces Uhde in order to marry Robert Delaunay. She uses the surname Delaunay-Terk for some years, but then calls herself Sonia Delaunay. Over the next few years the couple develop an abstract mode of expression based on colour contrasts. Taking inspiration from the French colour theorist Michel-Eugène Chevreul, they name the style *Simultané*. Their home becomes a lively meeting point for avant-garde artists and writers.

1911
Sonia Delaunay gives birth to their son Charles, and a patchwork blanket for his cradle becomes her first geometric textile work. From her aunt she inherits a steady monthly income from property rentals in St. Petersburg.

1913
Sonia Delaunay and the poet Blaise Cendrars create the poem-painting *La Prose du Transsibérien et de la Petite Jehanne de France*. She sews her first simultaneous dress from pieces of geometric fabric in contrasting colours, which she wears to the Parisian ballroom Bal Bullier. She furnishes the family's apartment with simultaneous objects. She shows the breadth of her practice by exhibiting paintings, decorative book covers and functional objects at the important exhibition *Erster Deutscher Herbstsalon* at the Berlin gallery Der Sturm.

1914
The First World War breaks out while the family are holidaying in the Basque country. They take up residence in Madrid and spend the next six years in Spain and Portugal.

1918
She opens the fashion and interior-design store Casa Sonia in Madrid. Her income from St. Petersburg had come to an end as a result of the October Revolution, and her business now provides for the family. She creates costumes for the ballet company Ballets Russes' production of *Cléopâtre* in London. Robert Delaunay is responsible for the scenography.

1919-1920
She decorates the Petit Casino variety theatre in Madrid and creates costumes for some of the dancers. She also designs costumes for the staging of Verdi's *Aida* at the Liceu in Barcelona. She exhibits alongside Robert Delaunay in Bilbao as well as solo at Der Sturm in Berlin.

1921-1922
The Delaunay family moves back to Paris and re-joins the avant-garde milieu. Sonia Delaunay decorates the family apartment on Boulevard Malesherbes with her designs,

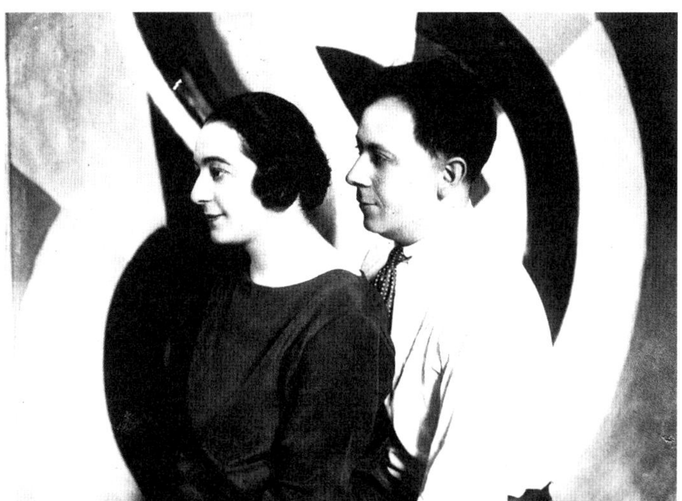

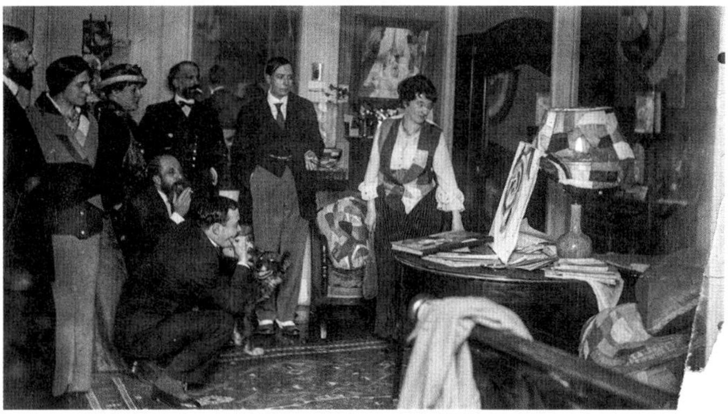

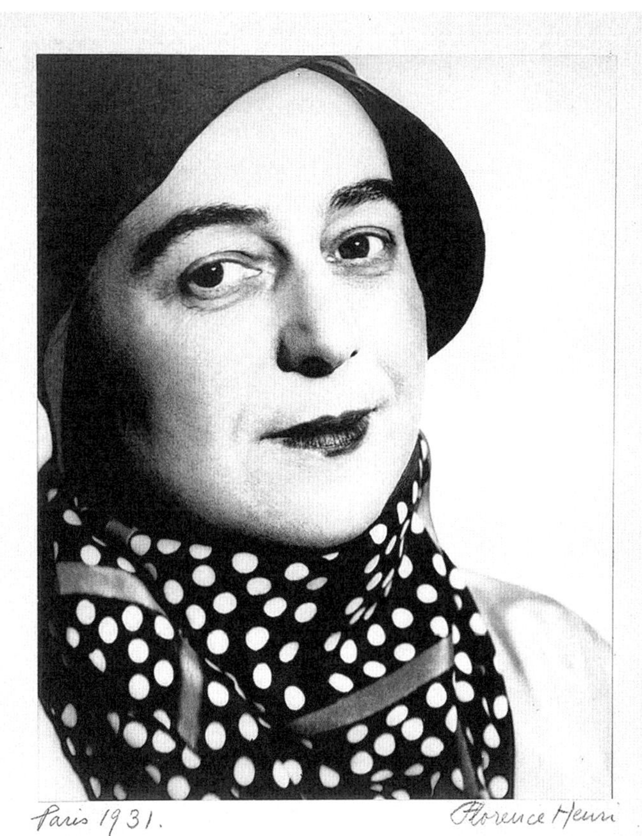

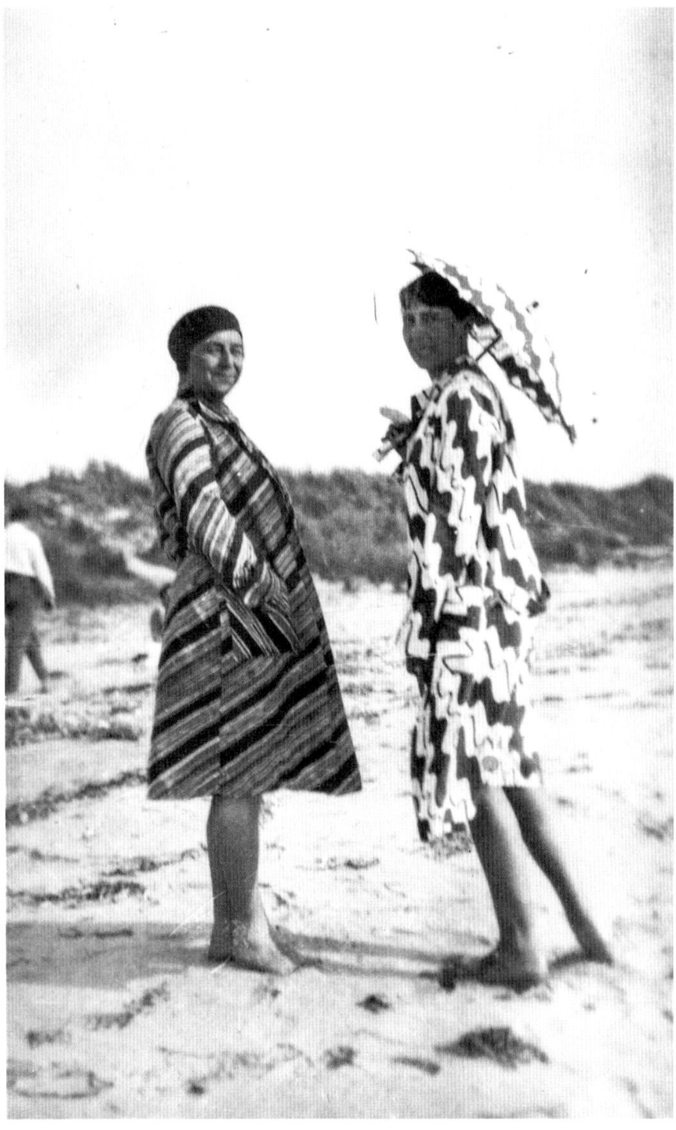

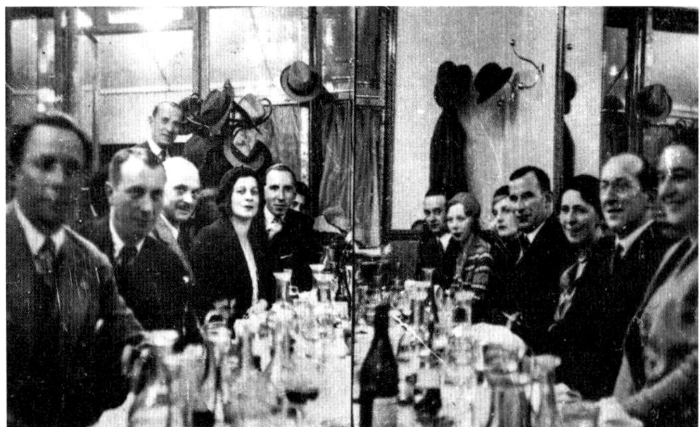

Top: Sonia Delaunay and Sophie Taeuber-Arp wearing simultaneous swimwear designed by Sonia Delaunay, c. 1929
Bottom: The Delaunay couple with friends: From left to middle: Robert Delaunay, Hans (Jean) Arp, Arturo Ciacelli (standing), Henryk Stażewski, Florence Henri, Michel Seuphor, Fernand Léger (in the back). From right to middle: Sonia Delaunay, Piet Mondrian, Sophie Taeuber-Arp, Theodor Werner, Woty Werner, Puma (Tineke) Vantongerloo, Jan Brzękowski

and the home once again becomes a gathering point. She combines fashion and poetry in dresses with poems by Tristan Tzara, the key figure in Dadaism, among others.

1923
She creates costumes for the dancer Lizica Codreano, who is performing at La Licorne gallery in Paris, and for Tzara's absurd theatrical play *Le Cœur à Gaz* at Théâtre Michel. She creates a series of textile designs on commission from a textile manufacturer in Lyon.

1924
At her Atélier Simultané, she sharpens her focus on textile and clothing design. She employs Russian seamstresses and produces embroidered garments. She creates textile designs, both making them in the atelier and selling them on to larger textile producers.

1925
She launches Maison Sonia, a couturier and showroom featuring textiles, clothes and decorative objects. The company is run from the couple's apartment and customers are received in the living room. She makes her international breakthrough at the World's Exposition in Paris. She decorates a Citroën B12 and begins a long-standing collaboration with the luxury department store Metz & Co in Amsterdam, for whom she designs textiles.

1926-1929
Parallel to her design business, Sonia Delaunay continues to create costumes and scenography for projects large and small, including René Le Somptier's avant-garde silent film *Le P'tit Parigot*. She lectures on the influence of painting on fashion at the Sorbonne University in Paris.

1930
In the aftermath of the Wall Street Crash the year before, she shuts down her business but continues to create textile designs for Metz & Co and others.

1932-1934
The couple moves to 16 Rue Saint-Simon in Paris, where Sonia Delaunay lives for the rest of her life.

1937
The Delaunays design major projects for the Aviation and Railway Pavilions at the Paris World's Fair, with the motifs reflecting their fascination with modern technology. Sonia Delaunay is awarded the World Fair's gold medal for her mural *Portugal*.

1939-1940
Sonia Delaunay exhibits carpets, embroidered clothing and textiles at an exhibition at the Grand Palais in Paris. The couple flees to the south of France at the outbreak of Second World War.

1941-1943
Robert Delaunay dies of cancer on 25 October 1941. Sonia Delaunay travels to Château Folie in Grasse, where artist friends Hans (Jean) Arp and Sophie Taeuber-Arp as well as Alberto Magnelli and his wife Susi Gerson live.

1944-1945
Delaunay travels to Toulouse, where she meets friends Tristan Tzara and Wilhelm Uhde, who is now living with the author and art critic Jean Cassou. She stays with them for three months and decorates the Red Cross International Centre. Following the liberation, she returns to Paris.

1946
She arranges the first Robert Delaunay retrospective exhibition at Galerie Louis Carré.

1947-1953
Delaunay participates in a number of abstract art group exhibitions and presents works in Europe, South America, Jerusalem and New York. Sonia Delaunay's first solo exhibition in Paris since 1908 takes place at Galerie Bing.

1954
As a member of the association Groupe Espace, Delaunay participates in the interior design and decoration of the new Maison de la Tunisie residential building at the Cité internationale universitaire de Paris. She designs curtains, carpets and other furnishings, and selects colours for bookshelves designed by Charlotte Perriand.

1955-1957
Her first solo exhibition in the USA opens at the Rose Fried Gallery in New York. She also shows solo exhibitions in Venice, Milan, Rome and Liège. She illustrates Tzara's poetry collection *Le fruit permis.*

1958
Sonia Delaunay's first major retrospective exhibition goes on display at the Städtisches Kunsthaus Bielefeld in Germany. The French state awards her the Ordre des Arts et des Lettres.

1959-1961
The Musée des Beaux-Arts in Lyon presents *Robert et Sonia Delaunay*, the first retrospective exhibition of the couple's work at a French museum. The exhibition is later shown in Turin. Sonia Delaunay works on a glass mosaic for the monastery in Moissac in the south of France, and designs playing cards for the Deutsche Spielkartenmuseum in Bielefeld. She creates graphic works for the publication of Tzara's poetry collection *Juste présent*.

1962
She presents 43 gouaches at the important Galerie Denise René in Paris. *Poésie de mots, Poésie de couleurs*, with screen prints by Sonia Delaunay and poems by Rimbaud, Mallarmé, Cendrars, Delteil, Soupault and Tzara, is published alongside the exhibition.

1964
The French state bestows the Légion d'honneur on Sonia Delaunay. She and her son Charles donate 114 works by Robert and Sonia Delaunay to the Musée National d'Art Moderne in Paris. The donation goes on display at the Musée du Louvre, and the exhibition travels on to Canada.

1967
She decorates a Matra 530 sports car as part of a project to raise money for medical research. Her first major retrospective solo exhibition takes place at the Musée National d'Art Moderne in Paris.

1968
She creates costumes and scenography for a performance of Igor Stravinsky's *Dances concertantes* at the Ballet-Théâtre d'Amiens.

1970
French President Georges Pompidou presents a Sonia Delaunay painting to American President Richard Nixon during an official visit to the USA.

1971-1972
The first major exhibition of her early textile designs takes place at the Musée de l'Impression sur Étoffes in Mulhouse, and works from the Delaunays' years in Portugal are displayed at the Fundação Calouste Gulbenkian in Lisbon. She exhibits 16 new tapestries at the Musée d'Art Moderne de la Ville de Paris.

1973
She is awarded the Grand Prix des Arts for her life's work. The book *Illuminations*, featuring poems by Arthur Rimbaud and prints by Sonia Delaunay, is published.

1975
Sonia Delaunay turns 90 and is honoured with the exhibition *Hommage à Sonia Delaunay* at the Musée National d'Art Moderne in Paris. *Sonia Delaunay*, an English-language monograph by art critic Arthur Allen Cohen, is published. She designs a poster for the UNESCO International Women's Year.

1977
She donates a large collection of books, diaries, letters, photographs and works on paper by the Delaunays to the National Library of Paris.

1978
In collaboration with the artist Patrick Raynaud, Sonia Delaunay designs costumes for *Sei personaggi in cerca d'autore* by Luigi Pirandello. The autobiography *Nous irons jusq'au soleil* is published.

1979
An exhibition of the Delaunay couple's works takes place at the National Museum of Modern Art in Tokyo. Sonia Delaunay dies on 5 December in Paris, aged 94.

The biography has been compiled by Maja Sofie Rasmussen

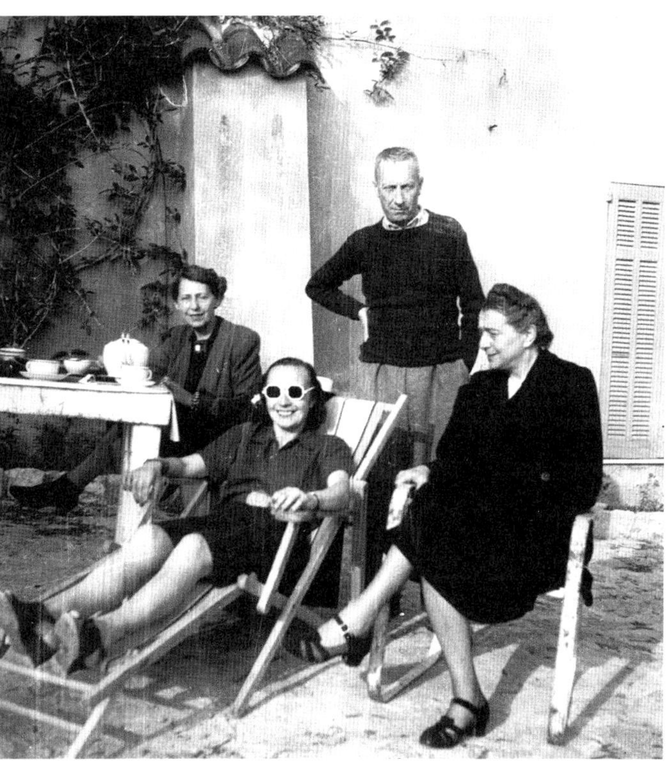

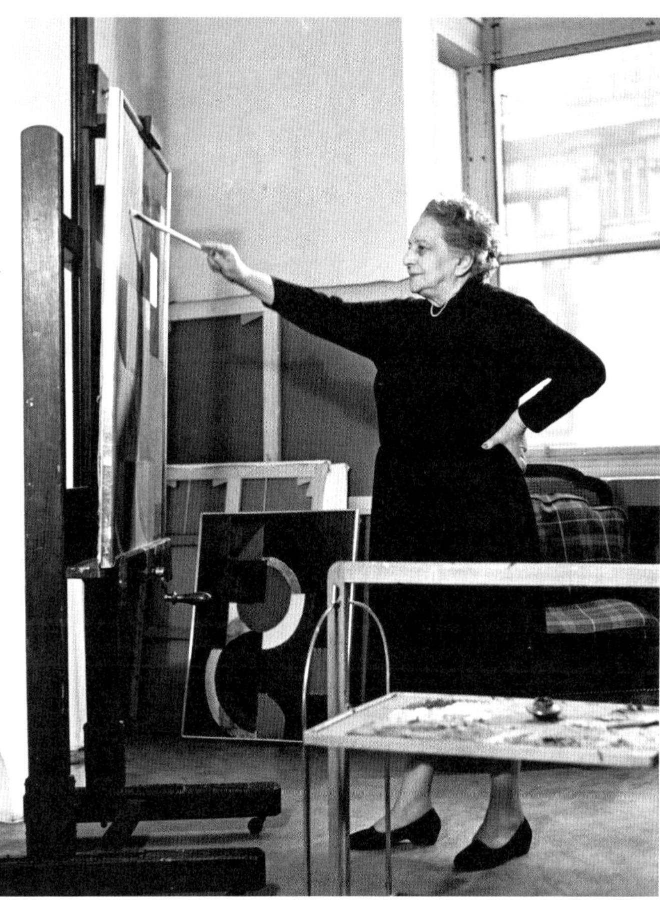

Top: Sophie Taeuber-Arp, Nelly van Doesburg, Hans (Jean) Arp and Sonia Delaunay in Grasse, 1941
Bottom: Robert Danis: Sonia Delaunay in her studio, late 1960s

NOTES

TINE COLSTRUP

1 Sonia Delaunay, *Nous irons jusqu'au soleil*, Éditions Robert Laffont, Paris, 1978, p. 36.
2 Ibid.
3 His theories had previously inspired the Pointillists Georges Seurat and Paul Signac, as well as the Expressionist van Gogh.
4 The poet Guilliaume Apollinaire coined the term Orphism for (especially) Robert Delaunay's colourful style of Cubism. The term is commonly used, but the Delaunays, particularly Sonia, preferred and promoted the term Simultanism.
5 The British designer Phoebe Philo mentioned Sonia Delaunay as an important source of inspiration for a collection she designed for the Céline fashion house in 2014. In 2019, the Dior fashion house recreated one of Sonia Delaunay's dress designs for its autumn collection.
6 Arthur A. Cohen, "Interview with Sonia Delaunay, 22 July 1970," in *The New Art of Color: The Writings of Robert and Sonia Delaunay*, Arthur A. Cohen (ed.), New York, The Viking Press, 1978, p. 216.
7 Juliet Bellow discusses Delaunay's dematerialisation of the body in "Fashioning Cléopâtre: Sonia Delaunay's New Woman" in *Art Journal*, Vol. 68, No. 2, Taylor & Francis, Ltd., College Art Association, 2009, p. 6-25.
8 Sonia Delaunay would probably not have called it that. In interviews, she clearly stated that she did not think in terms of feminism. She was just making art. See Pollock's article in this catalogue and David Seidner, "Sonia Delaunay" in *BOMB*, January 1982, published at bombmagazine.org.
9 See, e.g. Pascal Rousseau, "'Voyelles': Sonia Delaunay and the universal language of colour hearing" in *Sonia Delaunay*, Anne Montfort and Cécile Godefroy (eds.), London, Tate Modern, 2015, p. 70-76.
10 Poésie de mots/ poésie de couleurs/ le rythme des vers/ est construction/ et rapport de valeurs/ La poésie circule/ à travers toutes/ les creations de l'art. English translation by Arthur A. Cohen.
11 From Tristans Tzara's 1918 manifesto, in *Seven Dada Manifestos.*
12 The dresses were reportedly made, but have not survived – in general, very few of Sonia Delaunay's garments have. As utilitarian objects, most have been lost. The existing examples in various museum collections are fragile and are rarely loaned out.
13 In 1979, the musician David Bowie reinterpreted these costumes for an appearance on the American television show Saturday Night Live. A clip of Bowie's appearance is available on YouTube. Bowie recreated the costume of The Eye, a character played by the poet René Crevel in the original production.
14 Sonia Delaunay's friendship with Tzara was a lasting one. After Robert's death during Second World War, she stayed for a period with close friends, the artist couple Hans Arp and Sophie Taeuber-Arp, in the South of France. When the Arps returned to Paris, she sought refuge with Tzara and Jean Cassou in Toulouse, where her ex-husband, Wilhelm Uhde, was also staying. She later illustrated two books of Tzara's poems, *Le fruit permis* and *Juste présent*.
15 As far as I know, nowhere in the literature on Sonia Delaunay is it mentioned that the hat band is her design. However, it is noted in the following article on Duchamp's alter ego: Deborah Johnson, "R(r)Ose Sélavy as Man Ray: Reconsidering the Alter Ego of Marcel Duchamp" in *Art Journal*, Vol. 72, No. 1, Taylor & Francis, Ltd., CAA, 2013, p. 92.
16 I am grateful to Matteo de Leeuw-de Monti for discussing this issue and sharing his extensive knowledge about the dates of Delaunay's various fabric designs.
17 The artists decorated cars of various makes: Carlos Cruz-Diez decorated a Daf, Agam a Simca 1000, Victor Vasarely an Opel Kadett and Arman a Renault 4.
18 Thanks, not least, to the American art historian Clement Greenberg, whose theories of painting evolving towards its own media-specificity were dominant.
19 This quote by Sonia Delaunay appears on the title page of *Sonia Delaunay, 27 tableaux vivants*, Edizioni del Naviglio, Milan, 1969.

GRISELDA POLLOCK

20 Michel Seuphor, "Robert Delaunay," *L'Art abstrait, ses origines, ses premiers maîtres,* Maeght, Paris 1950, pp. 41-7 (p. 42).
21 Ibid. p. 46.
22 L. Degand, "Sonia Delaunay, galerie Bing," *Art d'aujourd'hui,* no. 5, July 1953, pp. 59-61 (p. 60)
23 H. Wescher, "Eaux vives et sources taries," *Cimaise,* 5th series, no. 3, January-February 1958, pp. 23-31 (p. 25).
24 R.V. Gindertaël, "Sonia Delaunay et la poésie pure des couleurs," *xxe siècle,* no. 21, May 1963, pp. 43- 6 (p. 45).
25 Ibid.
26 Guy Weelen, *Robert e Sonia Delaunay,* exhibition catalogue, Galleria Civica d'Arte Moderna, Turin 1960, pp. 9-16 (p. 11).
27 Cindy Nemser, *Art Talk: Conversations with 12 Women Artists,* Charles Scribner's Sons, New York 1975, pp. 35-52.
28 Rozsika Parker and Griselda Pollock, *Old Mistresses: Women, Art & Ideology,* Routledge, London 1981; third edition I B Tauris, London 2013.
29 For a full demonstration of this, see Catherine Gonnard and Élisabeth Lebovici, *Femmes Artistes/ Artistes Femmes: Paris de 1880 à nos jours,* Éditions Hazan, Paris 2007.

ANNE MONTFORT-TANGUY

30 Jean Cassou, introduction, *Donation Delaunay*, exhibition catalogue, Paris, Musée du Louvre, Galerie Mollien, February–April 1964, n.p.
31 S. Delaunay, *Nous irons jusqu'au soleil* (with the collaboration of Jacques Damase and Patrick Raynaud), Paris: Robert Laffont, 1978, p. 196.
32 Examples are the portraits photographed by Leon Hershtritt in 1971 and in 1965 during a report by the Keystone agency.
33 Nicolas Poussin's self-portrait, in the Louvre, is a textbook case. The artist appears in court costume surrounded by his creations, some of which, facing the wall, can only be guessed at from their stretchers.
34 S. Delaunay-Terk, note dated 24 July 1946, in S. Delaunay, *Nous irons jusqu'au soleil*, op. cit., p. 151.
35 S. Delaunay-Terk interview with Arthur Allen Cohen (1970), *The New Art of Color: the Writings of Robert and Sonia Delaunay,* New York: Viking Press, 1978, p. 217.
36 S. Delaunay, *Nous irons jusqu'au soleil*, op. cit, p. 96.
37 Ibid.
38 Ibid, p. 57.
39 Ibid, p. 97. The French term, "tableaux vivants" has been translated literally here, as the term is used in its literal sense of "living paintings."
40 "Sur la robe elle a un corps" is one of the *Dix-neuf poèmes élastiques* written between 1913 and 1914 and published by Blaise Cendrars.
41 Quoted by A. Sidoti Genèse and report on a controversy*: La Prose du Transsibérien et de la Petite Jehanne de France*, Archives no. 4, Paris: Lettres Modernes, 1987, p. 50
42 Hence her strong disagreement with Vasarely on the question of the multiples produced by the Denise Renée gallery.

MATTEO DE LEEUW-DE MONTI

43 See also previous publications by the same author: "Sonia Delaunay: The Force of Colour," in *Sonia Delaunay. Art, Design, Fashion*, ed. by Marta Ruiz de Árbol, exhib. cat. Museo Thyssen-Bornemisza, Madrid 2017 (Madrid, 2017), pp. 152-203; "Sonia Delaunay – the designs for Metz & Co," in *Sonia Delaunay*, exhib. cat. Tate Modern, London 2015 (London, 2014), pp. 174-81; "Metz & Co, de Stijl und Sonia Delaunay," in *To open eyes. Kunst und Textil vom Bauhaus bis heute*, ed. by Friedrich Meschede and Jutta Hülsewig-Johnen, exhib. cat. Kunsthalle Bielefeld 2013/14 (Bielefeld, 2013), pp. 36-57; Matteo de Leeuw-de Monti and Petra Timmer, *Colour Moves: Art and Fashion by Sonia Delaunay*, exhib. cat. Cooper-Hewitt, National Design Museum, New York 2011 (London, 2011).
44 According to entry no. 1173 of female births in the Israelite birth register of 1885 in Odessa on 1 November / Kislev 5. This corresponds

to 14 November in our Gregorian calendar.

45 Israel Sack (1831-1904) author of *Die Religion Altisraels*, 1885, and *Die Altjüdische Religion*, 1889.

46 Abraham Sack (1828-1893) had made a fortune building the first Russian railways and became director of the St. Petersburg Discount and Credit Bank. Highly respected, he was allowed to settle and live in the centre of St. Petersburg, which was forbidden to ordinary Jews. He advised the Russian government on the accumulation of gold reserves and was given the noble title of "Real State Councillor" by the Tsar. On the career of the Sack brothers, see also Pauline Wengeroff, *Memoiren einer Großmutter*, Verlag M. Poppelauer, Berlin 1910. Wengeroff was the sister-in-law of Abraham Sack.

47 Dr. Arnold Sack (1863-1940) was born in Odessa, studied medicine in Heidelberg and Strasbourg. He died in the French internment camp Gurs.

48 The Malerinnenschule was an art school for women painters and existed from 1885 to 1923.

49 Madame Minsky – Isabella (later Lyudmila) Nikolaevna Vilkina (1873-1920) – was a Russian poet, writer, translator, publicist, and literary critic. She was the second wife of the author Nikolai Maksimovich Minsky (1855-1937). Sonia Delaunay created covers for some of his books. Minsky was befriended by the Sack family; Vilkina was related to Pauline Wengeroff, see footnote 46. A good example of Delaunay's widespread connections.

50 Rudolf Großmann (1882-1941), German painter and graphic artist, member of the Berliner Sezession, whose work was later considered 'Entartete Kunst' and confiscated.

51 Wilhelm Uhde (1874-1947); See also Uhde, *Von Bismarck bis Picasso: Erinnerungen und Bekenntnisse*. Römerhof Verlag, Zürich 2010.

52 Michel Eugène Chevreul, *De la loi du contraste simultané des couleurs et de l'assortiment des objets colorés* (Paris, 1839). Chevreul was a Member of the Royal Society of Science of Copenhagen, of the Royal Academy of Science of Stockholm, and Officer of the Legion of Honour and Knight of the Danish Order of Dannebrog.

53 The original Bakst designs had been destroyed by fire. The opening of *Cleopatra* took place at the London Coliseum 21 Oct., 1918.

54 Jacques Heim (1899-1967) ran his parents' fur fashion house in the 1920s. In 1930 he opened his own fashion house 'Heim' with branches in Biarritz and Cannes. Maison Heim closed in 1969. Over the years, he used numerous designs by Sonia Delaunay, especially for swimwear and scarves. Girau-Gilbert was a Fine Leather Factory, 26 Rue du Faubourg du Temple, Paris.

55 Olga Samarow, Vera de Bosset-Soudeikin, Ise Frank, Martha Erps, Louise Maas respectively.

56 For the complete history of Metz & Co, see: Petra Timmer, *Metz & Co, de creatieve jaren*, 010 Publishers, Rotterdam 1995.

57 Joseph de Leeuw was a self-made man from a modest Jewish background. At the age of 13, he had started as an apprentice at Metz & Co, initially a wholesaler of French silks. He proved to be a clever businessman with a keen interest in music, literature, art, and design. The aesthetics of William Morris and the Arts and Crafts movement influenced him. In 1902 he acquired the sole agency of the London firm Liberty & Co, moved Metz & Co to the centre of Amsterdam in 1908, transformed it into a department store and became the owner.

58 Worth mentioning are Bart van der Leck, Gerrit Rietveld, Vilmos Huszár, Georges Vantongerloo, Friedrich Vordemberge-Gildewart, Marie Laurencin, Pavel Mansouroff, Léopold Survage, Cassandre, Josef Hoffmann, Alvar Aalto, Marcel Breuer, Le Corbusier, Franco Albini, Gio Ponti, and Poul Kjærholm.

59 In 1973 Hendrik de Leeuw withdrew from business life and sold Metz & Co to Liberty. There have been several owners since. Metz & Co finally closed as a retail store in 2013.

60 Sonia Delaunay's journals from 1933 to 1969 are in the Bibliothèque National de France (BNF). The diaries from 1970 to 1977 are in the Bibliotheque Kandinsky at the Musée National d'Art Moderne – Centre Pompidou.

61 Journal, 25 May 1933.

62 Sergei Chekhonin (1878-1936), a Russian artist, former head of the State Porcelain Factory in Petrograd, had invented a machine with a new printing technique, but conned the investors. By 1935 De Leeuw had spent over 200,000 francs in patents alone. Late 1935 the project was finally abandoned but a long drawn legal battle continued even after Chekonin's death.

63 Félix Aublet (1903-1978) was an architect, interior decorator and designer.

64 *l'Hélice*, *Le Moteur* and the *Tableau de Bord* for the Palais de l'Air (Skissernas Museum, Lund), *Voyages lointains* and *Portugal* for the Palais de chemin de fer.

65 These designs are numbered 100-135, some with addition G. or S.G.; Robert Perrier (1898-1987) produced luxurious fabrics for the haute couture. Sonia Delaunay had not designed fabrics for him before. In 1946 Perrier acquired her old leftover stock of 1300 designs and sketches, only a few of which he reedited 1946-1949. Perrier closed down in 1967.

66 Journal 9 August 1943.

67 Journal 8 August 1944.

68 Journal 14 January 1947.

69 Journal 1 February 1953. The designs in question are: A53, B53, C53, Cbis 53. They were incorrectly dated 1924 in earlier publications.

CÉCILE GODEFROY

70 On all these questions, I refer readers to the catalogue of the *Sonia Delaunay* exhibition Anne Montfort and I co-curated at the MAMVP and Tate Modern in 2014-15, and to my book *Sonia Delaunay. Sa mode, ses tableaux, ses tissus*, published by Flammarion in 2014.

71 Camilla Gray, *The Russian Experiment in Art: 1863-1922*, London: Thames & Hudson, (1962) 1986, p. 54.

72 Guillaume Apollinaire, "Les réformateurs du costume," *Le Mercure de France*, Paris, 1 January 1914, no. 397, p. 219-220.

73 See the exhibition catalogue *Sonia Delaunay. Arte diseño moda*, (Marta Ruiz del Árbol, ed.), Museo Thyssen-Bornemisza, Madrid, 2017.

74 In 1929, Maison Sonia became Tissus Delaunay. This closed in 1930 but the artist continued with her textile activities until just after the war, as in the case of her special collaboration with the Metz & Co stores in the Netherlands.

75 Nicolas Beauduin, Vladimir Mayakovsky, Joseph Delteil, Guillaume de Torre, Soupault and Iliazd.

76 Apart from a few private collections, most of Delaunay's garments and textiles are kept at the Musée Galliera – Paris, the Musée des Arts Décoratifs, Paris, and the Musée de l'Impression sur Étoffes in Mulhouse.

77 The photographs are kept by the Bibliothèque Nationale de France (Department of Prints, Delaunay collection, donated 1977, Oa-887-(1-7) Pet. Fol.), the Musée National d'Art Moderne – Centre Pompidou (Bibliothèque Kandinsky, Fonds Delaunay, donation Charles Delaunay 1985, box 13) and the Delaunay Estate. See my study, "La photographie au service du Simultanisme. L'utilisation de l'image de mode par Sonia Delaunay," *Etudes Photographiques*, Paris, November 2002, no. 12, p. 148-159.

78 For the list of photographers, see my article, "Images Simultanées. Les photographies de mode de Germaine Krull commandées par Sonia Delaunay," *Histoire de l'Art*, Paris, June 2001, no. 48, p. 99-113 [p. 110].

79 The term "garçonne" owed its popularity to the eponymous novel by Victor Margueritte, published in 1922. See Christine Bard, *Les Garçonnes : modes et fantasmes des années folles*, Paris: Flammarion, 1998, p. 57.

80 See Deborah Fausch et al., *Architecture: in Fashion*, New York: Princeton Architectural Press, 1994.

81 Krull and the fashion photographer Luigi Diaz set up the Photos Presse Paris agency in 1926 and worked for the houses Heim, Worth, Lanvin, Poiret, Lelong and Sonia.

LIST OF WORKS

Philomène, 1907
Oil on canvas, 55 × 46.5 cm
Centre Pompidou, Paris
Musée national d'art moderne–Centre de création industrielle
Donation de Sonia Delaunay et Charles Delaunay en 1964

Portrait de Mme Minskaya (L. N. Vilkina), 1907
Portrait of Mme Minskaya (L. N. Vilkina)
Oil on canvas, 55 × 46.1 cm
Museum of Avant-Garde Mastery of Europe (MAGMA of Europe)

Nature morte, 1909
Still Life
Watercolour and graphite on paper mounted on cardboard
50 × 40 cm
Centre Pompidou, Paris
Musée national d'art moderne–Centre de création industrielle
Donation de Sonia Delaunay et Charles Delaunay en 1964

Bookbinding: Herwarth Walden: *Zehn Dafnislieder* Op. 11, Berlin, Morgen Verlag, 1912-1913. Oil on primed leather, 31.5 × 25.8 × 1.5 cm
Centre Pompidou, Paris
Musée national d'art moderne–Centre de création industrielle
Donation de Sonia Delaunay et Charles Delaunay en 1964

Bal Bullier, 1913
Oil on canvas, 97 × 132 cm
Kunsthalle Bielefeld

Book cover for *La Prose du Transsibérien et de la Petite Jehanne de France*, 1913
Oil on leather, 22.5 × 19.5 cm
Courtesy Galerie Le Minotaure

Étude de lumière (Prismes électriques), 1913
Study of Light (Electric Prisms)
Gouache and Conté crayon on cardboard prepared with white paint, 31.4 × 21.3 cm
Victoria and Albert Museum, London

Sonia Delaunay in collaboration with Blaise Cendrars: *La Prose du Transsibérien et de la Petite Jehanne de France*, 1913
Prose on the Trans-Siberian Railway and of the Little Jehanne of France
Printed, multi-coloured text and gouache colouring with stencil, 198.7 × 35.7 cm
SMK – National Gallery of Art

Les prismes électriques, 1913
The Electric Prisms
Pastel on silk paper mounted on cardboard, 29.5 × 21 cm
Centre Pompidou, Paris
Musée national d'art moderne–Centre de création industrielle
Donation de Sonia Delaunay et Charles Delaunay en 1964

Prismes électriques, no 41, 1913-1914
Electric Prisms, No. 41
Oil on canvas, 54 × 46 cm
FNAC 28998. Centre national des arts plastiques (France)

Zénith Étude, 1914
Study for Zénith
Encaustic on paper
29 × 45 cm
Courtesy Galerie Le Minotaure

Zénith (Poster design), 1914
Crayon and watercolour on paper, 19.7 × 25.4 cm
Bibliothèque nationale de France
Estampes et photographie

Zénith (Poster design), 1914
Watercolour and pencil on paper, 19.9 × 25.3 cm
Bibliothèque nationale de France
Estampes et photographie

Chanteurs de flamenco, 1915
Flamenco Singers
Encaustic on laid paper
45.8 × 33 cm
Centre Pompidou, Paris
Musée national d'art moderne-Centre de création industrielle
Donation de Sonia Delaunay et Charles Delaunay en 1964

Chanteurs Flamenco (dit *Grand Flamenco*), 1915-1916
Flamenco Singers (known as Large Flamenco)
Wax and oil on canvas
174.5 × 143 cm
CAM – Fundação Calouste Gulbenkian, Lisbon

La marchande d'oranges, 1915
The Orange Seller
Gouache on coloured paper
45.8 × 51 cm
Paris Musées / Musée d'Art moderne

Marché au Minho, 1915
Market in Minho
Crayons on canvas
98 × 122 cm
Museum of Avant-Garde Mastery of Europe (MAGMA of Europe)

Album No. 1, 1916
Album No. 1
Encaustic on paper
21.6 × 22.2 cm
Courtesy Galerie Le Minotaure

Auto-Portrait, 1916
Self-Portrait
Gouache and wax on paper
32 × 30 cm
CAM – Fundação Calouste Gulbenkian, Lisbon

Chanteur Flamenco (dit *Petit Flamenco*), 1916
Flamenco Singer (known as Little Flamenco)
Gouache, oil and encaustic on paper, 36.1 × 42.1 cm
CAM – Fundação Calouste Gulbenkian, Lisbon

Chocolat, 1916
Chocolate
Encaustic, graphite and crayon on paper, 35.5 × 44.5 cm
Centre Pompidou, Paris
Musée national d'art moderne–Centre de création industrielle
Donation de Sonia Delaunay et Charles Delaunay en 1964

Danseuse, 1916
The Dancer
Watercolour, wax and gouache on paper mounted on cardboard, 38.2 × 33 cm
Skissernas Museum – Museum of Artistic Process and Public Art, Sweden

Draft for catalogue book cover for the Stockholm exhibition, 1916
Encaustic and stencil with metallic paint on two sheets of paper mounted on a supporting sheet, 33.8 × 45.2 cm
Centre Pompidou, Paris
Musée national d'art moderne–Centre de création industrielle
Donation de Sonia Delaunay et Charles Delaunay en 1964

Cover designs for *Vogue*, 1916
Gouache, crayons and pencil on two pieces joint paper
34.5 × 46.7 cm
Centre Pompidou, Paris
Musée national d'art moderne–Centre de création industrielle
Donation de Sonia Delaunay et Charles Delaunay en 1964

Poster design for Liqueur, 1916
Watercolour on paper
21.8 × 24.3 cm
Bibliothèque nationale de France
Estampes et photographie

Poster design for Liqueur, 1916
Watercolour on paper
31.9 × 24.1 cm
Bibliothèque nationale de France
Estampes et photographie

Costume design for Cleopatra for the ballet *Cleopatra*, 1918
Watercolour on paper,
57 × 36.5 cm
Courtesy Galerie Le Minotaure

Costume design for (Léonid) Massine for the ballet *Cleopatra*, 1918
Gouache on paper
38.5 × 24 cm
Bibliothèque nationale de France. Arts du spectacle

Costume design for three Egyptians for the ballet *Cleopatra*, 1918
Pencil and gouache on paper
20.5 × 26.2 cm
Bibliothèque nationale de France. Arts du spectacle

Three costume designs for the ballet *Cleopatra*, 1918
Watercolour on paper
23.7 × 30.7 cm
Courtesy Galerie Le Minotaure

Danse de la robe, 1922
Dance of the Dress
Ink and pencil on paper mounted on cardboard, 24 × 16.8 cm
Centre Pompidou, Paris
Musée national d'art moderne–Centre de création industrielle
Donation de Sonia Delaunay et Charles Delaunay en 1964

Design for Jacques Doucet (Man's vest), 1922
Crayon and watercolour on paper, 19 × 41.7 cm
Bibliothèque nationale de France
Estampes et photographie

Poster design for Chocolat Bensdorf, 1922
Crayon and watercolour on paper, 32.3 × 24.9 cm
Bibliothèque nationale de France
Estampes et photographie

Poster design for Chocolat Bensdorf, 1922
Crayon and watercolour on paper, 13.8 × 25.5 cm
Bibliothèque nationale de France
Estampes et photographie

Poster design for Chocolat Bensdorf, 1922
Crayon and watercolour on paper, 10.3 × 24.9 cm
Bibliothèque nationale de France
Estampes et photographie

Poster design for Chocolat Bensdorf, 1922
Crayon and watercolour on paper, 9.9 × 19 cm
Bibliothèque nationale de France
Estampes et photographie

Robe poème no. 688, 1922
Poem Dress No. 688
Watercolour, gouache and pencil on paper, 31.2 × 23.8 cm
The Museum of Modern Art, New York. Purchase, 1980
Accession Number: 303.1980

Costume design for Dancer with Discs, 1923
Pencil and gouache on paper
54 × 41.5 cm
Bibliothèque nationale de France. Arts du spectacle

Miss Mouth and Mr. Eye. Costume design for the play *Le Cœur à Gaz*, 1923
Ink and pencil on paper
31 × 22.8 cm
The Museum of Modern Art, The Joan and Lester Avnet Collection, 1978
Accession Number: 29.1978

Yellow Dancer. Costume design for the play *Le Cœur à Gaz*, 1923
Watercolour, ink and pencil on paper, 36 × 28.9 cm
The Museum of Modern Art, New York. Gift of Mr. and Mrs. Lewis Cullman, 1980
Accession Number: 306.1980

Pajamas for Tristan Tzara, 1923
Watercolour and pencil on paper, 31 × 22.8 cm
The Museum of Modern Art, New York. The Joan and Lester Avnet Collection, 1978
Accession Number: 301.1980

Pyjama, 1923
Pajamas
Crayon, gouache and watercolour on paper, 21 × 14 cm
Bibliothèque nationale de France
Estampes et photographie

Robe poème no. 1328, 1923
Poem Dress No. 1328
Watercolour and pencil on paper, 36.9 × 30.7 cm
The Museum of Modern Art, New York. Purchase 1980
Accession Number: 304.1980

Robe poème no. 1329, 1923
Poem Dress No. 1329
Watercolour, gouache and pencil on paper, 36.9 × 23.7 cm
The Museum of Modern Art, New York. Purchase, 1980.
Accession Number: 301.1980

(Robe-poème) Le Ventilateur tourne dans le cœur de la tête ..., 1923
(Poem Dress) The Ventilator Rotates in the Head's Heart ...
Chinese ink on paper
30.4 × 20.4 cm
Bibliothèque nationale de France
Estampes et photographie

Robe, 1923-1925
Dress
Crayon, gouache and watercolour on paper, 20.9 × 13.3 cm
Bibliothèque nationale de France
Estampes et photographie

Bookbinding: Tristan Tzara: *De nos oiseaux*, Paris, Edition de la Sirène, 1923
Paint on leather, sewn onto book cover, 15.6 × 12.8 × 1.7 cm
Centre Pompidou, Paris
Musée national d'art moderne–Centre de création industrielle
Donation de Sonia Delaunay et Charles Delaunay en 1964

Bookbinding: Iliazd: *Ledentu le Phare*, dramatic poem in Zaoum, 1923
Paint on leather, sewn onto book cover, 20 × 14.5 × 1.8 cm
Centre Pompidou, Paris
Musée national d'art moderne–Centre de création industrielle
Donation de Sonia Delaunay et Charles Delaunay en 1964

Scène d'intérieur, 1923
Indoor Scene
Gouache on cardboard,
25 × 26 cm
Couretsy Galerie Le Minotaure

Three studies for vests, 1923
Drawing, 29 × 16.3 cm, 28.4 × 12.3 cm, 28.7 × 15.8 cm
Bibliothèque nationale de France
Estampes et photographie

Design for Simultané fabric, No. 30, 1924
Drawing/Gouache, 48 × 32 cm
Paris, Musée des Arts Décoratifs

Design for Simultané fabric, No. 33, 1924
Drawing/Gouache, 47 × 33.8 cm
Paris, Musée des Arts Décoratifs

Design for Simultané fabric, No. 34, 1924
Drawing/Gouache, 52 × 33.5 cm
Paris, Musée des Arts Décoratifs

Design for Simultané fabric, No. 50, 1924
Drawing/Gouache, 27 × 21 cm
Paris, Musée des Arts Décoratifs

Study for fabric design, 1924
Gouache on paper, 23.5 × 31 cm
Louisiana Museum of Modern Art, Humlebæk. Donation: The Joseph and Celia Ascher Collection, New York

Design for three dresses, c. 1924
Crayon, gouache and watercolour on paper, 25.1 × 16.1 cm
Bibliothèque nationale de France
Estampes et photographie

Four studies for dresses, 1925
Watercolour on paper,
20.3 × 10.8 cm, 21.1 × 9.8 cm
21.8 × 12.2 cm, 20.1 × 8.8 cm
Bibliothèque nationale de France
Estampes et photographie

Four studies for fabric for the Sonia Delaunay Store, undated
Crayon and gouache on paper
19 × 41.7 cm
Bibliothèque nationale de France
Estampes et photographie

Coat for Gloria Swanson, c. 1925
Woolen embroidery
120 × 60 cm
Private Collection

Robe, 1925
Dress
Ink on paper on cardboard
27.1 × 20.9 cm
Centre Pompidou, Paris
Musée national d'art moderne–Centre de création industrielle
Donation de Sonia Delaunay et Charles Delaunay en 1964

Robes simultanées (Trois femmes, formes, couleurs), 1925
Simultaneous Dresses (Three Women, Forms, Colours)
Oil on canvas, 146 × 114 cm
Museo Nacional Thyssen-Bornemisza, Madrid

Shawl, design by Sonia Delaunay, probably bought at Metz & Co, Amsterdam, 1925
Silk, 210 × 125 cm
Kunstmuseum Den Haag, The Hague, The Netherlands

Sonia Delaunay, ses peintures, ses objets, ses tissus simultanés, ses modes, 1925
Sonia Delaunay, Her Paintings, Her Objects, Her Simultané Fabrics, Her Designs
5 sheets, lithography à 56 × 38 cm
Skissernas Museum – Museum of Artistic Process and Public Art, Sweden

Three designs for women's clothing, 1925
Drawing, 22.1 × 13.4 cm, 31.4 × 23.5 cm, 21.9 × 12.8 cm
Bibliothèque nationale de France
Estampes et photographie

Design for Simultané fabric, No. 156, 1926
Drawing/Gouache, 26 × 35 cm
Paris, Musée des Arts Décoratifs

Design for Simultané fabric, No. 170, 1926
Drawing/Gouache, 22.5 × 23 cm
Paris, Musée des Arts Décoratifs

Design for Simultané fabric, No. 186, 1926
Drawing/Gouache, 31 × 47 cm
Paris, Musée des Arts Décoratifs

Dress, c. 1926
Pleated blind, green, white, black
Private Collection, Germany

Design for dress for the film *Le P'tit Parigot* (The Small Parisian One), 1926
Pencil and gouache on paper
54 × 41.5 cm
Bibliothèque nationale de France. Arts du spectacle

Design for dress for the film *Le P'tit Parigot* (The Small Parisian One), 1926
Pencil and gouache on paper
54 × 41.5 cm
Bibliothèque nationale de France. Arts du spectacle

Dress, c. 1926
Silk, red, yellow, green
Private Collection, Germany

Pierrot Éclair, 1926
Flash Pierrot
Watercolour and pencil on paper, 22.8 × 19.4 cm
Centre Pompidou, Paris
Musée national d'art moderne–Centre de création industrielle
Donation de Sonia Delaunay et Charles Delaunay en 1964

Dessin 198, 1927
Design 198
Gouache on paper, 31 × 51 cm
Private Collection

Dessin 205, 1927/1934
Design 205, Pancarte
Gouache, ink and pencil on paper, 21.4 × 24.2 cm
Private Collection

Design for Simultané fabric, No. 764, 1928
Drawing/Gouache
27.6 × 21.6 cm
Paris, Musée des Arts Décoratifs

Costume design for Carnival in Rio. Coat for Whipping-top dress, 1928
Pencil and gouache on paper
27.5 × 20.3 cm
Bibliothèque nationale de France. Arts du spectacle

Costume design for Carnival in Rio. Dress with spherical and semi-spherical motives in red, yellow, green and orange, 1928
Gouache on paper
30.5 × 24.3 cm
Bibliothèque nationale de France. Arts du spectacle

Costume design for Carnival in Rio. Soap Bubble dress, 1928
Gouache on paper
27.5 × 20.5 cm
Bibliothèque nationale de France. Arts du spectacle

Costume design for Carnival in Rio. Tricolore Dress, 1928
Gouache on paper
54 × 41.5 cm
Bibliothèque nationale de France. Arts du spectacle

Set design for the ballet *The Four Seasons*. Autumn, 1928-1929. Pencil and gouache on paper, 30 × 40 cm
Bibliothèque nationale de France. Arts du spectacle

Costume design for the ballet *The Four Seasons*. Connected triangles, 1928-1929
Pencil and gouache on paper
21.5 × 27.2 cm
Bibliothèque nationale de France. Arts du spectacle

Set design for the ballet *The Four Seasons*. Spring, 1928-1929. Pencil and gouache on paper, 18.5 × 23.5 cm
Bibliothèque nationale de France. Arts du spectacle

Set design for the ballet *The Four Seasons*. Red, black, white parasols. Sea with waves, 1928-1929
Gouache and Indian ink on paper, 21.5 × 27.2 cm
Bibliothèque nationale de France. Arts du spectacle

Set design for the ballet *The Four Seasons*. Spirals on a background of herringbones and circles, 1928-1929
Gouache and Indian ink on paper, 21.5 × 27 cm
Bibliothèque nationale de France. Arts du spectacle

Set design for the ballet *The Four Seasons*. Winter, 1928-1929
Pencil and gouache on paper
19.5 × 21.5 cm
Bibliothèque nationale de France. Arts du spectacle

Dessin 903, 1929/1937
Design 903
Gouache and pencil on transparent paper, 51.5 × 37 cm
Private Collection

Dessin 945, 1929
Design 945
Gouache on paper
26.9 × 20.9 cm
Private Collection

Dessin 951bis, 1929/1930
Design 951bis
Gouache on transparent paper
21 × 16 cm
Private Collection

Dessin 953bis, 1929/1930
Design 953bis
Gouache and pencil on paper
31 × 24 cm
Private Collection

Dessin 1189, 1929/1933
Design 1189, Working drawing
Gouache and pencil on paper
26.5 × 37.5 cm
Private Collection

Dessin A 989, 1930
Design A 989
Gouache on paper
64.7 × 50.2 cm
Private Collection

Dessin 253, 1930/1931
Design 253, Pancarte
Gouache, ink and pencil on paper, 21.6 × 24.1 cm
Private Collection

Dessin 253, 1930/1931
Design 253
Gouache on millimetre tracing paper, c. 44 × 35 cm
Private Collection

Dessin 253, 1930/1931
Gouache on transparent paper, mounted to paper
56.2 × 34.2 cm
Private Collection

Dessin 253, 1930/1931
Design 253, Metz & Co fabric sample. Cotton Mousseline
68 × 92 cm
Private Collection

Dessin 253, 1930/1931
Design 253, Metz & Co fabric sample. Cotton Mousseline
15.5 × 21 cm
Private Collection

Dessin 253, 1930/1931
Design 253, Metz & Co fabric sample. Cotton Mousseline
19.4 × 13 cm
Private Collection

Dessin 253, 1930/1931
Design 253, Metz & Co fabric sample. Cotton Mousseline
21 × 12 cm
Private Collection

Dessin 951bis, 1930
Design 951bis, Set of 7 Metz & Co fabric samples
Silk, 16.5 × 60 cm
Private Collection

Dessin 965, 1930
Design 965
Gouache on transparent paper, mounted to paper
50 × 32.5 cm
Private Collection

Dessin 965, 1930
Design 965, Pancarte
Gouache and pencil on paper
21.6 × 24.2 cm
Private Collection

Dessin 965, 1930
Design 965, Metz & Co fabric sample. Cotton Mousseline
14.5 × 15 cm
Private Collection

Dessin 965, 1930
Design 965, Metz & Co fabric sample. Cotton Mousseline
12.5 × 13.5 cm
Private Collection

Dessin 965, 1930
Design 965, Metz & Co fabric sample. Cotton Mousseline
13 × 12 cm
Private Collection

Dessin 965, 1930
Design 965, Metz & Co fabric sample. Cotton Mousseline
11 × 11 cm
Private collection

Dessin 965, 1930
Design 965, Metz & Co fabric sample. Cotton Mousseline
13.5 × 12 cm
Private Collection

Dessin 965, 1930
Design 965, Metz & Co fabric sample
Cotton voile, 94 × 89 cm
Private Collection

Dessin 989, 1930
Design 989, Set of 5 Metz & Co fabric samples
Silke, 13 × 12 cm
Private Collection

Dessin 989A, 1930
Design 989A, Pancarte
Gouache, ink and pencil on paper, 21.4 × 24 cm
Private Collection

Dessin 945, 1930
Design 945, Set of 5 Metz & Co fabric samples
Silk, crêpe de chine
25 × 33 cm
Private Collection

Shawl, c. 1930
Silk, 195 × 92 cm
Private Collection

Dessin 1044, 1930/1931
Design 1044
Gouache on transparent paper, 23 × 22.2 cm
Private Collection

Dessin 1044, 1931
Design 1044, Metz & Co fabric sample
Cotton Georgette
51 × 86 cm
Private Collection

Dessin 1044, 1931
Design 1044, Metz & Co fabric sample
Cotton Georgette
17 × 12 cm
Private Collection

Dessin 1044, 1931
Design 1044, Metz & Co fabric sample
Cotton Georgette
15 × 17.5 cm
Private Collection

Dessin 1044, 1931
Design 1044, Metz & Co fabric sample. Cotton Georgette
13 × 20 cm
Private Collection

Dessin 1044, 1931
Design 1044, Metz & Co fabric sample. Cotton Georgette
17.5 × 20 cm
Private Collection

Dessin 1152, Dessin de travail
Design 1152, Working drawing
Gouache and pencil on paper
49.8 × 32.9 cm
Private Collection

Dessin 1152, 1933
Design 1152, Metz & Co fabric sample. Silk, 14 × 15.5 cm
Private Collection

Dessin 1152, 1933
Design 1152, Metz & Co fabric sample. Silk, 12 × 11.5 cm
Private Collection

Dessin 1152, 1933
Design 1152, Metz & Co fabric sample. Silk, 16.5 × 8 cm
Private Collection

Dessin 1152, 1933
Design 1152, Metz & Co fabric sample. Silk, 10 × 15 cm
Private Collection

Dessin 1152, 1933
Design 1152, Metz & Co fabric sample. Silk, 15.5 × 13 cm
Private Collection

Dessin 1152, 1933
Design 1152, Metz & Co fabric sample. Silk, 20.5 × 9 cm
Private Collection

Dessin 1153, 1932/33
Design 1153
Gouache, ink and pencil on paper, 14.7 × 20 cm
Private Collection

Dessin 1153, 1933
Design 1153, Metz & Co fabric sample. Silk, 14.5 × 13 cm
Private Collection

Dessin 1153, 1933
Design 1153, Metz & Co fabric sample. Silk Albène, 18 × 15 cm
Private Collection

Dessin 1153, 1933
Design 1153, Metz & Co fabric sample. Silk, 14 × 13.5 cm
Private Collection

Dessin 1153, 1933
Design 1153, Metz & Co fabric sample. Silk, 15 × 14 cm
Private Collection

Dessin 1153, 1933
Design 1153, Metz & Co fabric sample
Silk, 16 × 12 cm
Private Collection

Dessin 1153, 1933
Design 1153, Metz & Co fabric sample
Silk, 14.5 × 14.5 cm
Private Collection

Dessin 1176, 1933/1934
Design 1176
Gouache on paper
27.4 × 22.5 cm
Private Collection

Dessin 1177, 1933/1934
Design 1177
Gouache on paper
22.5 × 20.8 cm
Private Collection

Dessin 1177, 1933/1934
Design 1177
Gouache on paper
23.2 × 19.5 cm
Private Collection

Dessin 1177, 1933/1934
Design 1177
Gouache on paper
22.7 × 21 cm
Private Collection

Dessin 1177, 1933/1934
Design 1177
Gouache on paper
22.5 × 20.8 cm
Private Collection

Dessin 1177, 1933/1934
Design 1177
Gouache on paper
22.5 × 20.8 cm
Private Collection

Dessin 1177, 1933/1934
Design 1177
Gouache on paper
22.8 × 21 cm
Private Collection

Dessin 1177, 1933/1934
Design 1177
Gouache on paper
48.2 × 19.8 cm
Private Collection

Dessin 1177, 1933/1934
Design 1177
Gouache on paper
48 × 18.5 cm
Private Collection

Dessin 1189, 1933
Design 1189, Metz & Co fabric sample. Silk, 35.5 × 10 cm
Private Collection

Dessin 1189, 1933
Design 1189, Metz & Co fabric sample. Silk, 27 × 10 cm
Private Collection

Dessin 1189, 1933
Design 1189, Metz & Co fabric sample. Silk, 35 × 8.5 cm
Private Collection

Dessin 1189, 1933
Design 1189, Metz & Co fabric sample. Silk, 30 × 11.5 cm
Private Collection

Dessin 1189, 1933
Design 1189, Metz & Co fabric sample. Silk, 16.5 × 11.5 cm
Private Collection

Dessin 1189, 1933
Dessin 1189, Metz & Co fabric sample. Silk, 16 × 13 cm
Private Collection

Dessin 1189, 1933
Design 1189, Metz & Co fabric sample. Silk, 30 × 10 cm
Private Collection

Dessin 1189, 1933
Design 1189, Metz & Co tie
Silk, 140 × 7.5 cm
Private Collection

Dessin 1189, 1933
Design 1189, Metz & Co tie
Silk, 143 × 9 cm
Private Collection

Dessin 1189, 1933
Dessin 1189, Metz & Co bow tie
Silk
84.5 × 5 cm
Private Collection

Dessin 1219, 1933
Design 1219
Gouache on transparent paper, 20.5 × 22.8 cm
Private Collection

Dessin 1219, 1933
Design 1219
Gouache on transparent paper, 21 × 20.5 cm
Private Collection

Dessin 1219, 1933
Design 1219
Gouache on transparent paper, 21 × 21.5 cm
Private Collection

Dessin 1219, 1933
Design 1219
Gouache on transparent paper, 19.5 × 19 cm
Private Collection

Dessin 1219, 1933
Design 1219, Metz & Co fabric sample
Silk Mousseline, 34 × 18 cm
Private Collection

Dessin 1219, 1933
Design 1219, Metz & Co fabric sample
Silk Mousseline, 45 × 18 cm
Private Collection

Dessin 1219, 1933
Design 1219, Metz & Co fabric sample
Silk Mousseline, 41 × 18 cm
Private Collection

Dessin 1219, 1933
Design 1219, Metz & Co fabric sample. Silk Mousseline
49 × 11 cm
Private Collection

Dessin 1219, 1933
Design 1219, Metz & Co fabric sample
Silk Mousseline, 50 × 18 cm
Private Collection

Dessin 1219, 1933
Design 1219, Metz & Co fabric sample
Silk Mousseline, 98 × 45 cm
Private Collection

Dessin 1257, 1933
Design 1257
Gouache on paper, black background, 19 × 32.2 cm
Private Collection

Dessin 1257, 1933
Design 1257, Metz & Co fabric sample. Silk, crêpe de chine, 37 × 27 cm
Private Collection

Dessin 205, 1934
Design 205, Set of 2 Metz & Co fabric samples
Artificial silk, 50 × 54.5 cm
Private Collection

Dessin 1293, 1934
Design 1293
Gouache on paper
32.5 × 32.2 cm
Private Collection

Dessin 1303, 1934
Design 1303
Gouache on paper, 27 × 20.9 cm
Private Collection

Dessin pour soie 1317, 1934
Design for silk 1317
Gouache, ink and pencil on paper, 21.4 × 24.2 cm
Private Collection

Dessin 1317, 1934
Design 1317
Gouache and pencil on paper
26.9 × 20.9 cm
Private Collection

Dessin 1317, 1934
Design 1317, Set of 5 Metz & Co fabric samples
Tussar silk, 89.5 × 48 cm
Private Collection

Dessin 1318, 1934
Design 1318, Pancarte
Gouache, ink and pencil on paper, 21 × 23.8 cm
Private Collection

Dessin 1318, 1934
Design 1318, Pancarte
Gouache, ink and pencil on paper, 21.2 × 23.9 cm
Private Collection

Dessin 1318, 1934
Design 1318
Gouache on paper
27.3 × 20.8 cm in Metz & Co fabric book, 1931-1935
Designs 175-195,
45 × 35 × 8 cm (Closed)
Private Collection

Dessin 1324, 1934
Design 1324, Pancarte
Gouache, ink and pencil on paper, 21.4 × 24.2 cm
Private Collection

Dessin 1324, 1934
Design 1324
Gouache and pencil on paper
32.5 × 32.4 cm
Private Collection

Dessin 1303, 1935
Design 1303, Metz & Co scarf
Silk, 90 × 19 cm
Private Collection

Dessin 1324, 1935
Design 1324, Metz & Co fabric sample
Silk, 90 × 50 cm
Private Collection

Dessin 1324, 1935
Design 1324, Metz & Co fabric sample
Silk, 16 × 10.5 cm
Private Collection

Dessin 1324, 1935
Design 1324, Metz & Co fabric sample
Silk, 13 × 9.5 cm
Private Collection

Dessin 1324, 1935
Design 1324, Metz & Co fabric sample
Silk, 17 × 12 cm
Private Collection

Dessin 1324, 1935
Design 1324, Metz & Co fabric sample
Silk, 11 × 9 cm
Private Collection

Dessin 1324, 1935
Design 1324, Metz & Co fabric sample
Silk, 11 × 9 cm
Private Collection

Dessin 1324, 1935
Design 1324, Metz & Co fabric sample
Silk, 11 × 11 cm
Private Collection

Dessin 1324, 1935
Design 1324, Metz & Co fabric sample
Silk, 14.5 × 10 cm
Private Collection

Dessin 1355, 1935
Design 1355, Variation
Gouache and ink on paper
50 × 32.4 cm
Private Collection

Mica-tube, 1935
Gouache on paper
23.5 × 13.7 cm
Museo Nacional Centro de Arte Reina Sofía, Madrid
Depósito temporal de Pedro y Ary Altamiranda, Panamá, 2010

Dessin 1386, 1936
Design 1386
Gouache on paper
30.3 × 24.7 cm
Private Collection

Dessin 1386, 1936
Design 1386
Gouache on paper
32.6 × 25.2 cm
Private Collection

Dessin 1386, 1936
Design 1386, Set of 4 Metz & Co fabric samples. Silk, crêpe de chine, 77.5 × 50 cm
Private Collection

Dessin 1389ter, 1936
Design 1389ter
Gouache on paper
30.3 × 24.7 cm
Private Collection

Dessin 1398, 1936
Design 1398
Gouache and pencil on paper
30 × 24.5 cm
Private Collection

Dessin 1398, 1936
Design 1398, Metz & Co fabric sample. Silk, crêpe de chine
49 × 76.5 cm
Private Collection

Dessin 1398, 1936
Design 1398, Metz & Co fabric sample. Silk, crêpe de chine
50 × 77 cm
Private Collection

Poster design for Couleur Linel, 1936
51 × 34.8 cm
Bibliothèque nationale de France
Estampes et photographie

Poster design for Mica-tube lamps, 1936
Gouache on paper, 21 × 31 cm
Bibliothèque nationale de France
Estampes et photographie

Poster design for Mica-tube lamps, 1936
Gouache on paper
29.2 × 39 cm
Bibliothèque nationale de France
Estampes et photographie

Poster design for Zig-Zag cigarette rolling paper, 1936
Gouache on paper
26.9 × 21 cm
Bibliothèque nationale de France
Estampes et photographie

Poster design for Zig-Zag cigarette rolling paper, 1936
Gouache on paper
26.9 × 20.9 cm
Bibliothèque nationale de France
Estampes et photographie

Design for Simultané fabric, 1937
Drawing / Gouache, 65 × 50 cm
Paris, Musée des Arts Décoratifs

Dessin 198, 1937
Design 198, Metz & Co fabric sample. Silk, crêpe de chine
7.5 × 13.5 cm
Private Collection

Dessin 198, 1937
Design 198, Metz & Co fabric sample. Silk, crêpe de chine
7.5 × 13.5 cm
Private Collection

Dessin 198, 1937
Design 198, Metz & Co fabric sample. Silk, crêpe de chine
7.5 × 13.5 cm
Private Collection

Dessin 198, 1937
Design 198, Metz & Co fabric sample. Silk, crêpe de chine
37 × 9 cm
Private Collection

Dessin 198, 1937
Design 198, Metz & Co fabric sample. Silk, crêpe de chine
17 × 12 cm
Private Collection

Dessin 198, 1937
Design 198, Metz & Co bow tie
Silk, crêpe de chine, 76 × 4.5 cm
Private Collection

Dessin 890f, 1937
Design 890f, Set of 3 Metz & Co fabric samples. Silk, crêpe de chine, 45.5 × 13.3 cm
Private Collection

Dessin 890f, 1937
Design 890f, Peignoir / Chamber cloak of Hendrik de Leeuw, Director of Metz & Co. Silk
Kunstmuseum Den Haag, The Hague, The Netherlands

Poster design: Delaunay at any Occasion (Un Delaunay est bon à toute heure), 1937
Gouache on paper
49 × 32 cm
Bibliothèque nationale de France
Estampes et photographie

Poster design for Pernot Fils, 1937
Gouache on paper
50 × 32.5 cm
Bibliothèque nationale de France
Estampes et photographie

Portugal, 1937
Gouache and pencil on paper
53.4 × 97.4 cm
Skissernas Museum – Museum of Artistic Process and Public Art, Sweden

Voyages lointains, 1937
Distant Journeys
Gouache, watercolour and pencil on cardboard
34 × 95 cm
Centre Pompidou, Paris
Musée national d'art moderne–Centre de création industrielle
Donation de Sonia Delaunay et Charles Delaunay en 1964
Attribution au Musée national d'art modern / Centre de création industrielle le 27/07/1964

Dessin 903, 1938
Design 903, Metz & Co fabric sample. Silk, crêpe de chine
90.5 × 31.5 cm
Private Collection

Dessin 1451, 1938
Design 1451
Gouache on paper mounted to paper, 50 × 33 cm
Private Collection

Dessin 1455, 1938
Design 1455
Gouache on paper mounted to paper, 29.5 × 24 cm
Private Collection

Dessin 1456, 1938
Design 1456
2 gouaches on paper mounted to paper, 29.5 × 24 cm
Private Collection

Dessin 1460, 1938
Design 1460
Gouache on paper mounted to paper, 29.5 × 24 cm
Private Collection

Dessin 1470, 1938
Design 1470
Gouache on paper
29.5 × 24 cm
Private Collection

Dessin 1475, 1938
Design 1475
Gouache on paper, 27 × 18 cm
Private Collection

Gouache 1938 no. 1, 1938
Gouache 1938 No. 1
Gouache and pencil on paper
59 × 44.5 cm
Private Collection

Rythme, 1938
Rhythm
Oil on canvas
182 × 149 cm
Centre Pompidou, Paris
Musée national d'art moderne–Centre de création industrielle
Donation de Sonia Delaunay et Charles Delaunay en 1964

Dessin 1486, 1939
Design 1486
Gouache on paper
30.8 × 23.8 cm
Private Collection

Dessin 1487, 1939
Design 1487
Gouache on paper
31 × 23.5 cm
Private Collection

Dessin 1488, 1939
Design 1488
Gouache on paper
30.8 × 23.8 cm
Private Collection

Dessin 1489, 1939
Design 1489
Gouache on paper
30.8 × 23.7 cm
Private Collection

Dessin 1492, 1939
Design 1492
Gouache on paper, 48 × 31 cm
Private Collection

Dessin 1493, 1939
Design 1493
Gouache on paper, 48 × 31 cm
Private Collection

Dessin 1494, 1939
Design 1494
Gouache on paper, 48 × 31 cm
Private Collection

Study for decoration of Red Cross' international reception centre, 1944
Gouache on paper
56 × 38 cm
Bibliothèque nationale de France
Estampes et photographie

Dessin 485, 1947/1948
Design 485
Gouache and ink on transparent paper, 85 × 85 cm
Private Collection

Dessin 485, 1947/1948
Design 485, Pancarte
Gouache and ink on paper
21.5 × 24.2 cm
Private Collection

Design for fabric F 1425, 1948/1949
Drawing/Gouache
31.5 × 23.5 cm
Paris, Musée des Arts Décoratifs

Design for fabric, No. 4943, 1948
Drawing/Gouache
37 × 30 cm
Paris, Musée des Arts Décoratifs

Dessin 4901, 1949
Design 4901
Gouache and pencil on paper
45 × 73.3 cm
Private Collection

Sonia Delaunay colour samples (16 pcs.), c. 1950
Gouache on paper
à c. 7 × 13 cm
Private Collection

Sonia Delaunay Blocks, 1951
Metz & Co fabric roll
Printed linen, 840 × 125 cm
Private Collection

Dessin Rayures, 1951
Design, stripes
Set of 5 Metz & Co fabric samples. Woven cotton
58 × 25.5 cm
Private Collection

Dessin Écossais Losange, 1952
Tartan design, Metz & Co fabric sample
Cotton, 40 × 61.5 cm
Private Collection

Dessin Écossais Losange, 1952
Tartan design, Metz & Co fabric sample
Cotton, 32 × 63 cm
Private Collection

Dessin Écossais Losange, 1952
Tartan design, Metz & Co fabric sample
Cotton, 31 × 62 cm
Private Collection

Metz & Co Spring Catalogue, 1952
Printed matter, 21 × 15.8 cm
Private Collection

Rythme coloré, 1952
Coloured Rhythm
Gouache on paper
56 × 76 cm
Centre Pompidou, Paris
Musée national d'art moderne–Centre de création industrielle
Donation de Sonia Delaunay et Charles Delaunay en 1964

Sonia Delaunay skirt, Metz & Co, for Miss H. de Leeuw, 1952
Woven cotton, 68 × 98 cm
Private Collection

Dessin A53, 1953
Design A53
Gouache on paper
36.5 × 28.8 cm
Private Collection

Dessin B53, 1953
Design B53
Gouache and pencil on paper
36.5 × 28.8 cm
Private Collection

Dessin B53, 1953
Design B53. Large version 1
Gouache on paper
100 × 75 cm
Private Collection

Dessin B53, 1953
Design B53. Large version
Gouache on paper
100 × 75 cm
Private Collection

Dessin C53, 1953
Design C53
Gouache on paper
36.5 × 28.8 cm
Private Collection

Dessin C53bis, 1953
Design C53bis
Gouache on paper
36.5 × 28.8 cm
Private Collection

Coloured Rhythm, 1953
Gouache and pencil on paper
53.6 × 68.5 cm
The Museum of Modern Art, New York. The Riklis Collection of McCrory Corporation, 1985
Accession Number: 869.1983

Meilleurs Voeux pour 1954, 1954
Best Wishes for 1954
Gouache on paper
14.5 × 10.5 cm (folded)
Private Collection

Rythme coloré, Paris, 1954
Coloured Rhythm
Gouache on paper, 57 × 76 cm
Würth Collection, Germany

Rythme coloré (no. 614), 1954-1957
Coloured Rhythm (No. 614)
Oil on canvas, 130 × 95.3 cm
Courtesy Galerie Le Minotaure

Rythme coloré (694), 1958
Coloured Rhythm (694)
Oil on canvas, 112.5 × 192.5 cm
Private Collection

Rythme couleur no. 889, 1959
Rhythm Colour No. 889
Gouache on paper, 75 × 54 cm
Würth Collection, Germany

Rythme profondeur, 1960
Deep Rhythm
Oil on canvas
130 × 161.5 cm
Centre Pompidou, Paris
Musée national d'art moderne–Centre de création industrielle
Donation de Sonia Delaunay et Charles Delaunay en 1964

Sonia Delaunay & Tristan Tzara
Juste présent. Eaux-fortes de Sonia Delaunay, 1961
Just Present. Etchings by Sonia Delaunay
Etching on Japanese paper
40 × 30 × 5 cm
Bibliothèque nationale de France. Réserve des livres rares

Poésie de mots, poésie de couleurs, 1961/1962
Word Poetry, Colour Poetry
Silkscreen print on Rives paper, Album with 6 sheets
65 × 50 cm
Würth Collection, Germany

Rythme couleur, 1961
Rhyhtm Colour
Gouache and pencil on paper
76 × 56 cm
Centre Pompidou, Paris
Musée national d'art moderne–Centre de création industrielle
Donation de Sonia Delaunay et Charles Delaunay en 1964

Rythme couleur, 1961
Rhyhtm Colour
Gouache and pencil on paper
76 × 56 cm
Centre Pompidou, Paris
Musée national d'art moderne–Centre de création industrielle
Donation de Sonia Delaunay et Charles Delaunay en 1964

Tzara, 1961
Gouache on paper
66 × 50.5 cm
Würth Collection, Germany

Triptyque, 1963
Triptych
Oil on canvas, 99.7 × 200 cm
Tate: Purchased 1966

Maquette d'affiche, 1964
Poster design
Gouache on paper
72 × 50 cm
Centre Pompidou, Paris
Musée national d'art moderne–Centre de création industrielle
Don de l'artiste en 1968

Rythme couleur, 1964
Rhythm Colour, Oil on canvas
97.5 × 195.5 cm
Paris Musées / Musée d'Art moderne

Design on fabric, 1967
Painting on silk, 49 × 45.5 cm
Bibliothèque nationale de France
Estampes et photographie

Rythme couleur, 1967
Rhythm Colour
Oil on canvas, 199.5 × 150 cm
Private Collection

Rythme syncopé (dit *Le serpent noir*), 1967
Syncopated Rhythm (known as The Black Snake)
Oil on canvas
125 × 250 × 3.8 cm
Musée d'arts de Nantes

Matra 530 A, 1967
420 × 120 × 162 cm, 900 kg
Musée Matra, Espace Automobiles. Ville de Romorantin-Lanthenay

Disques, 1968
Discs
Wollen carpet
230 × 163.5 cm
Paris Musées / Musée d'Art moderne

27 tableaux vivants, 1969
Leporello, 435 / 650, sign.
Print on vellum
285 × 200 cm
Private Collection

Syncopé, 1970's
Syncopated
Hand-woven tapestry
188 × 170 cm
ATELIERS PINTON, Felletin

Avec moi-même (Portfolio de seize éléments dont dix planches), November 1970
With Myself (Portfolio: sixteen elements, containing ten etchings)
Etching on Arches paper
66 × 50 cm
Centre Pompidou, Paris
Musée national d'art moderne–Centre de création industrielle
Don de l'artiste en 1976

Colour Rhythm No. 1921-1973, 1973
Gouache and pencil on paper
69.2 × 55.9 cm
The Museum of Modern Art, New York. The Riklis Collection of McCrory Corporation, 1985
Accession Number: 870.1983

Rythme Couleur no. 1916, 1973
Rhythm Colour No. 1916
Gouache and pencil on paper
37.8 × 49.3 cm
Louisiana Museum of Modern Art, Humlebæk
Donation: The Riklis Collection of McCrory Corporation

Rythme Couleur no. 1919, 1973
Rhythm Colour No. 1919
Gouache and pencil on paper
36.8 × 55.5 cm
Louisiana Museum of Modern Art, Humlebæk
Donation: The Joseph and Celia Ascher Collection, New York

Sonia Delaunay & Arthur Rimbaud
Les Illuminations (extraits), 1973
The Illuminations (extracts); gouaches by Sonia Delaunay
Gouache on paper
55 × 41.5 × 3.7 cm
Bibliothèque nationale de France
Réserve des livres rares

Robert Delaunay
Portrait de Tristan Tzara, 1923
Portrait of Tristan Tzara
Oil on paperboard
104.5 × 75 cm
Museo Nacional Centro de Arte Reina Sofía, Madrid

SONIA DELAUNAY

Edited by Lærke Rydal Jørgensen and Tine Colstrup
Graphic Design: Louisiana Design Studio
Font/Digitalisation of Sonia Delaunay's typography: Signe Marie Ohrt
Photo Editors: Sidse Buck and Kim Hansen
Translations: Glen Garner (Tine Colstrup), Adam King (foreword, biography), Charles Penwarden (Anne Montfort-Tanguy, Cécile Godefroy)
Proofreading: James Manley

Cover, front: Detail of *Prismes électriques no 41* (Electric Prisms, No. 41), 1913-1914
Oil on canvas, 54 × 46 cm. FNAC 28998. Centre national des arts plastiques (France)
Cover, back: Germaine Krull: Sonia Delaunay in her studio, Boulevard Malesherbes, Paris, c. 1925
Inside of cover and endpapers, front: Detail of Dessin 4901 (Design 4901), 1949
Inside of cover and endpapers, back: Detail of *Bal Bullier*, 1913
Endpapers, front: Detail of Dessin B53 (Design B53), 1953
Endpapers, back: Dessin 253 (Design 253), 1930/1931
Page 1: Detail of Design for fabric, No. 4943, 1948
Page 2: Detail of Dessin 1486 (Design 1486), 1939
Page 3: Dessin C53bis (Design C53bis), 1953
Page 4: Book cover for *La Prose du Transsibérien et de la Petite Jehanne de France* (Prose on the Trans-Siberian Railway and of the Little Jehanne of France), 1913

Litho/Print: Narayana Press
ISBN: 978-87-93659-53-7
Printed in Denmark 2022
www.louisiana.dk

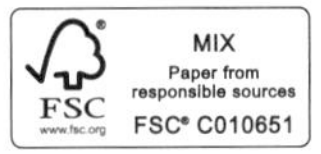

The catalogue is published on the occasion of the exhibition
Sonia Delaunay
Louisiana Museum of Modern Art, Humlebæk
12 February 2022 – 12 June 2022

Curator: Tine Colstrup
Curatorial Assistant: Maja Sofie Rasmussen
Curatorial Coordinator/Registrar: Arne Schmidt-Petersen
Exhibition Architect: Jens Kamp
Graphic Design: Marie Lübecker
Conservator/Exhibition Producer: Jesper Lund Madsen

The exhibition at the Louisiana Museum of Modern Art is supported by:

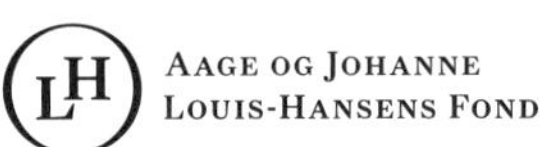

The exhibition has been realised with exceptional participation from Bibliothèque nationale de France

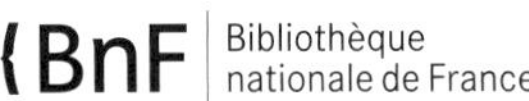

Louisiana's Main Corporate Partner
FRITZ HANSEN

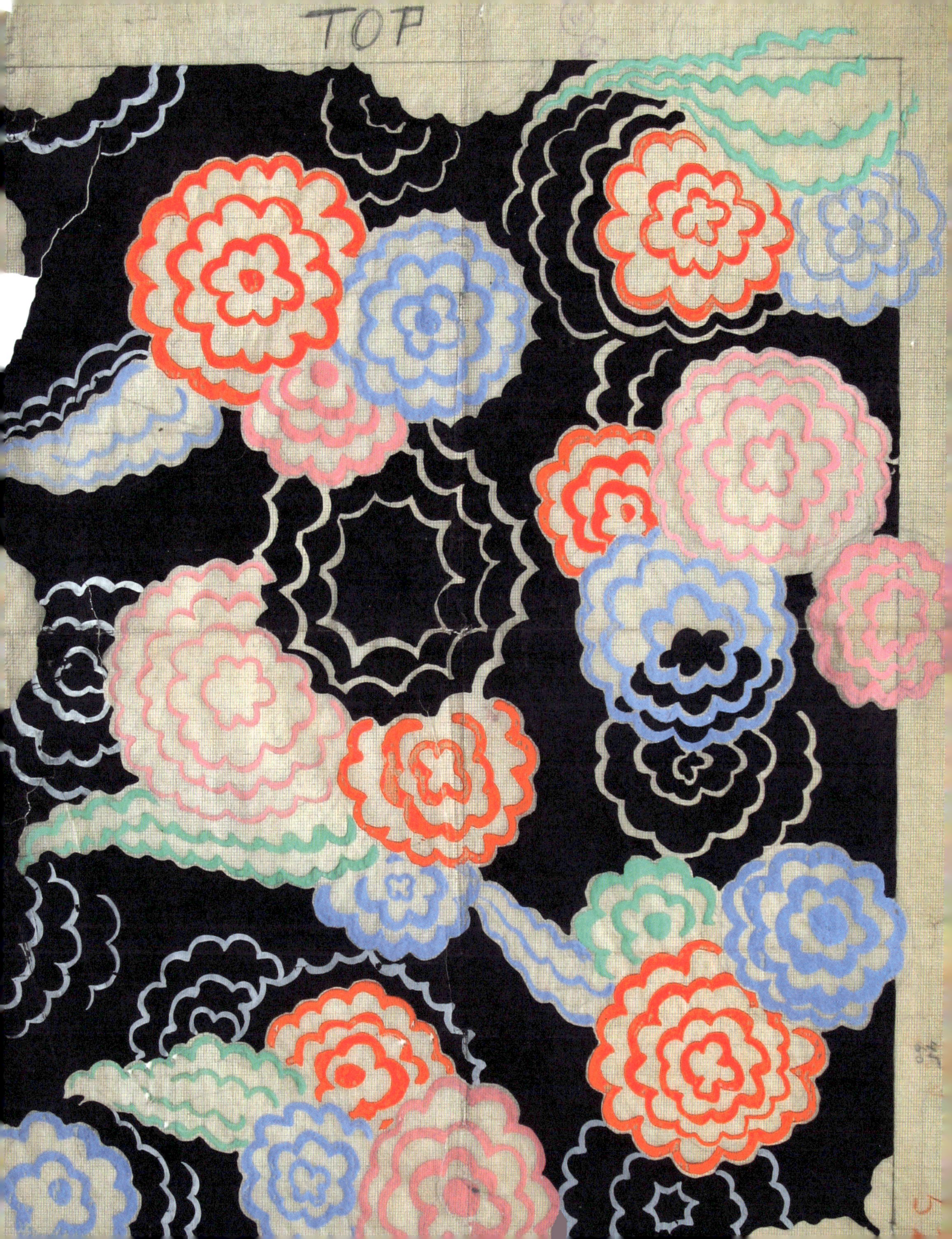
TOP

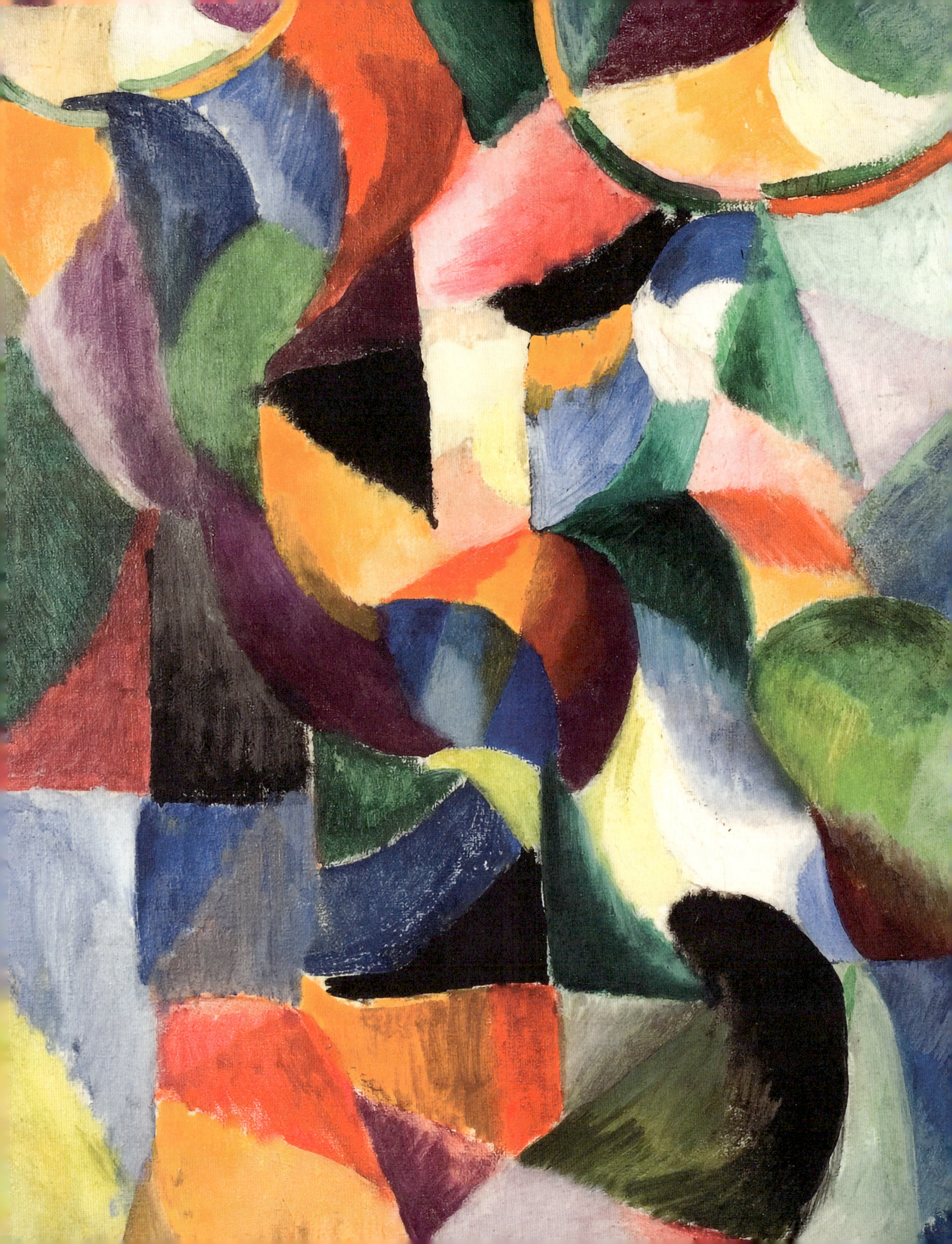